BURTON AND TAYLOR

A week before, Alan Jay Lerner had been vacationing on nearby Capri. Richard and Elizabeth paid him a visit. "They told me an extraordinary story," he said, years later. "I've never forgotten it, and I think it says something about their relationship. Richard said that the night before they came to see me he had dreamed he was in a boat with Elizabeth, rowing, and the boat capsized. He was in a terrible panic because he couldn't swim, but he knew he had to, in order to save her. But he couldn't find her in the water. He kept calling to her. Elizabeth suddenly woke up. She had been dreaming too, and was awakened by hearing Richard call her name. She had been dreaming that she had been in a boat that capsized and that she was looking for him.

"I can't believe they made it up," Lerner said, "and it indicated to me that there was more closeness between them, a merging far beyond what most people assumed. I very much doubted after that day that they would leave each other."

THE LOVERS

BURTON

BURTON

HOLLIS ALPERT

PaperJacks LTD.

TORONTO   NEW YORK

PaperJacks

BURTON

PaperJacks LTD.

330 STEELCASE RD. E., MARKHAM, ONT. L3R 2M1
210 FIFTH AVE., NEW YORK, N.Y. 10010

G. P. Putnam's Sons edition published 1986

PaperJacks edition published January 1987

ISBN 0-7701-0545-9
Printed in Canada

Acknowledgments

Few figures in the entertainment world, now or in the past, have led so public a life as Richard Burton. For this biography a problem was less the lack of information than the extraordinary amount of it. To cut through it in search of chronology, place, and relevant statements made by the subject, I was able to call on help from several institutions: in New York, the Theatre Collection of the New York Public Library at Lincoln Center; in Los Angeles, the Library of the Motion Picture Academy of Arts and Sciences and the Library of the American Film Institute; in London, the British Film Institute; in Rome, the Time-Life Bureau. For staff assistance, for facilities, for noblesse oblige, my grateful thanks.

Burton, through the years, was remarkably generous about giving interviews. In doing so he recorded a great deal of his own life, often repeating himself with different interviewers. (Statements made to me by him, for example, I have found in articles and news reports by others.) Wherever possible, I have indicated the source of a particular quotation. And I have naturally depended on my own recollections and material when I was in the vicinity, so to speak. As a film journalist and critic during many of the years, I did a considerable amount of coverage.

In the main, though, for close-up views of the career and person-

ACKNOWLEDGMENTS

ality of Burton, I have made use of the recollections of many who were involved with him and knew him well. Without their generous help, this particular account of a life would not have been possible. Ernest Lehman was a friend in great need. We spent many hours together as we pored over his voluminous record of the time he spent with Richard and Elizabeth. Mike Nichols was kind enough to fill out the record even more, and to provide details of his friendship with Richard.

The names of several others who, with the author, attempted to solve the "mystery" of Burton are mentioned in the text. To them I express gratitude, and notably to Alan Jay Lerner, Daniel Petry, Peter Glenville, Philip Dunne, Martin Ritt, Elaine Dundy, Emlyn Williams, John Hurt, Jack Brodsky, John Springer, Mike Merrick, Noel Behn, Dennis Browne, and Kate Burton. I owe a special debt to my London colleague, David Lewin, who followed Burton through much of his career and shared with me his wealth of information and his insights. In Port Talbot, South Wales, I have good memories of several citizens, especially a delightful afternoon spent with Dilwyn Dummer, a boyhood chum and relative of Burton's.

Kitty Kelley provided me with much essential information, as well as leads to more. Janet Roach provided more leads and put me in touch with Joan Chase in Puerto Vallarta. I received aid of various kinds from Jack Fields, Arthur Knight, and Milton Goldman. Most helpful was Colin Campbell, director of the Long Island Council on Alcoholism. For assistance on research, typing, and transcribing I am grateful to Judith Lutz, Betty McIvor, Joan Carlson, Pamela Pedlow, and my good friend Susan Rosenstreich. For aid in photo research: Mary Corliss of the film stills archive of The Museum of Modern Art, and Lynne Crowley of The Bettmann Archive. My agent, Mitch Douglas, my editor, Ellis Amburn, and Dan Silverman were always there with help, advice, and counsel. This to preserve an accurate image of Burton before he fades into time's distance.

For Jack X Fields

BURTON

Prologue

For most of his life, Richard Burton had made a habit of wearing at least one article of clothing that was red—the color of the dragon on the Welsh national flag. Burton, a star of truly international magnitude, who had resided in Switzerland for nearly thirty years, never failed to insist on his native Welshness, and so, when it came time to bury him, one of his last wishes was honored: that he wear something red in his coffin.

On that Thursday, August 9, 1984, the day of his burial in the tiny Swiss village of Céligny, near Geneva, Sally Hay Burton, his fourth wife, had had him outfitted in red trousers, red polo-necked sweater, and a red jacket. On the top of his coffin, in the little Protestant church, the Welsh dragon was outlined with red roses and white lilies. This service was for the benefit of family members and a very few close friends. There would be other services in other places and on other days for the host of those who had known and cared about him.

Even so, the twenty-two pews of the church in the town's center were filled. Friends from nearby Geneva had come, and townspeople, too. Outside, other townspeople for whom Burton had been a familiar figure gathered to hear the services over a loudspeaker that had been provided.

BURTON

He had died four days before, very suddenly, in his fifty-ninth year, a man so famous that his name was rocketed at once into headlines around the world. He had suffered a massive stroke that ended his life in a Geneva hospital within hours of its onset. Soon enough, his life would be reviewed in all of its sensational complexity, but this day in Céligny was one of dignity, yet lightened now and then—as befitted the nature of the deceased—with touches of irreverence.

The sad and shocking calls had gone out from his villa in Céligny, to London, to South Wales, to California, to those places where those closest to him through the years resided. They included seven surviving brothers and sisters; his actress daughter Kate; the Welsh playwright and actor Emlyn Williams and his son and longtime helpful companion of Burton's, Brook Williams; his manager and agent in California, Valerie Douglas; his mentor and adopted father, Philip Burton; and the woman he had married twice, and divorced twice, Elizabeth Taylor.

She, however, was asked not to attend the Céligny funeral, not only out of respect to his thirty-six-year-old widow, Sally, who had been married to him for only a short thirteen months, but because if Elizabeth came the outsiders would scamper in with cameras and microphones and make havoc out of the day. The ceremony was to be simple, in line with Richard's wishes.

Inside the church, Kate Burton, who, as it happened, had only just finished acting with her father in a television film, recited a favorite poem of her father's, Dylan Thomas's *Do Not Go Gentle into That Good Night*. Richard had known Dylan, had loved and felt a deep affinity for his words, and with little encouragement could recite virtually his complete works. Those who tuned into the BBC over the years had heard his renditions, including a quite marvelous performance of the verse play *Under Milk Wood*, which he had also narrated as a film.

Kate's voice hardly faltered as she read:

> *And you, my father, there on the sad height,*
> *Curse, bless me now with your fierce tears, I pray.*
> *Do not go gentle into that good night.*
> *Rage, rage against the dying of the light.*

BURTON

Few were able to hold back their tears, and least of all Cecilia James, Richard's eldest sister, now a frail seventy-nine, whom he had always adored. She was the one who had raised him, the mother he had missed having. He had declared, in an autobiographical story he had written, that for him she was the epitome of beauty, and once he achieved fame and fortune she never again ever lacked for anything. Nor did the other members of his family.

Sally, his wife, tried not to cry at all. She was dressed appropriately, and smartly, in a black silk suit, and she wanted to maintain her composure and to look and be as Richard would have wanted her to look and be. But she faltered once, and rested her head on the shoulder of Graham Jenkins, Richard's younger brother. Then she raised her head and became brave.

She had known Richard for not much more than two years and, in a sense, had been plucked by him out of obscurity. But she had learned quickly how to deal with the pleasures and perils of celebrity. It was going to be a difficult time for her, she already knew, and she was girding herself to handle it. John Hurt, the English actor, stood near her. He had spent Richard's last weekend with him and Sally; he had acted with Richard in a film yet to be released, and they had become companionable and close. He was the one who answered calls from the press and assisted her with arrangements. Brook Williams, too, had rallied round Sally.

Graham Jenkins stepped to the pulpit to read from I Corinthians, Chapter 13. "Though I speak with the tongues of men and of angels, and have not charity . . ." Graham looked toward Cecilia James. Richard, he said, as a child, had learned the verse from her. But beyond that, there was little pomp, and only a simple prayer, because Richard had wanted no priests to intercede for him in the dark kingdom.

He had chosen his own burial place, a plot in a small old cemetery, shaded by trees, bordered by farmland, just outside the village. His coffin was taken there and placed on trestles, surrounded by floral displays. Among them was a single red rose. No one mentioned who had sent it, out of respect for Sally. Brook Williams read from another Dylan Thomas poem, *And Death Shall Have No Dominion*. Then Sally walked to the coffin beside the grave and placed an envelope on it—a last letter she had written to Richard. Whatever sentiments and messages it contained would be forever sealed with him.

Richard, all felt, would have appreciated the music at his funeral. Three of his brothers, two sisters, and Brook Williams formed an impromptu choir and sang something not exactly fit for a funeral. It was a family favorite, the Welsh rugby anthem, "Sospan Fach." They sang it so loudly, it seemed as though they were attempting to wake Richard from the dead. Even Sally could not suppress a giggle.

And Richard, if he had known, certainly would have smiled.

The family had left Céligny by the time Elizabeth Taylor flew from Beverly Hills to Geneva. She wanted a moment with Richard by herself, but the photographers were out in force, waiting for her in Céligny, and so she fretted through a day, then visited the grave site at six the next morning, surrounded by four bodyguards. It had been that way for her and Richard when together in life, and it was still that way at his death. As early as it was, the photographers were there. Elizabeth knelt at Richard's grave for several minutes. In the half-dark, under the trees, the photographers, kept away by her guards, heard her sobbing.

For many years she had said that she would be buried next to Richard in Pontrhydyfen, Wales, had even picked out her plot, but so many of their plans had changed and now Richard would remain in Switzerland without her. But their life together had been full and vivid—truly, in the words of Dylan Thomas, a roaring life. And no one ever again would think of Richard Burton without thinking of her. She had that much, at least.

Two days after the service in Céligny, a similar one was held in Pontrhydyfen, but on this occasion there were thousands of his countrypeople who crowded the streets outside the Bethel Baptist Chapel to pay him his last tribute. As some five hundred mourners entered the chapel, led by Sally and Kate, a genuine Welsh choir rocked the white walls with "Sospan Fach." The choir followed with a more funereal Welsh hymn, "Who Is Taking the King Home?" If there was anything resembling a eulogy, it was spoken by Brook Williams, who said of Richard that "above all else, he never forgot his roots,

BURTON

the rock he was hewn from," and as a prayer he read one of Richard's favorite passages from *Under Milk Wood*.

The obituaries had appeared, and the summings-up were off the presses by the time Emlyn Williams spoke of Richard at the memorial service held at St. Martin's-in-the-Fields, Trafalgar Square, in London a week later. Elizabeth Taylor had been invited, and Williams acknowledged her presence when he said, "Our dear Richard, here we all are, joining Sally and Kate and all your family—and Elizabeth—in thinking about you, and talking a little about you. Yes, I can see the old twinkle in the eye, as if to say, 'Well, now that the smoke's clearing away . . . what are *you* going to say about me? Not going to be easy, is it?' "

The man had a passion for life, Williams said, "and where there is passion, there has to be—sooner or later—trouble. Side by side with the light, the dark; behind exaltation . . . melancholy."

Richard Burton had his ups and his downs; his notices were mixed. He had a voice that thrilled, shining gifts, and used them well, yet many spoke of flaws and failure. As for his life, Williams said, "We only hope the notices won't be too bad."

He could not help but glance at Elizabeth Taylor as he added, "To be fair to them, Richard, you sure did supply them with copy!"

PART
ONE

Richard Burton stood alone on the stage of the Majestic Theater taking one curtain call after another. For ten months he had triumphantly played and sung the role of King Arthur in Lerner and Loewe's musical *Camelot*, and this September evening in 1961 the audience was fully aware that it had witnessed his final performance. His fellow cast members were discreetly allowing him to have this moment by himself. Then, astonishingly, dozens in the audience left their seats and made their way to the stage, stretching out their hands to him. Burton grasped as many as he could before the curtain descended the last time. "The King of Broadway," as he had been called, was abdicating his throne to journey to Rome to play opposite Elizabeth Taylor in the film *Cleopatra*.

Backstage, a champagne party was waiting for him. It went on far into the early-morning hours, with many toasts to his departure and his future career. Moss Hart, who had directed *Camelot*, gave a farewell speech.

"Actors like Burton are born once in fifty years," he told the company. "Most stars are not really people—their magnetism disappears away from the footlights. But this man Burton stays full size."

The Welsh-born Burton was in his thirty-sixth year. He had run a gamut of roles that on the stage included Hamlet and the Henrys of Shakespeare, plays by Anouilh and Fry, and the silver-shining Arthur of *Camelot*. For these alone he had gained a large measure of distinction, enough for him to be compared to such illustrious elders as Gielgud and Olivier. Physically resembling the latter, he was regarded as his heir apparent as the leading actor of the English stage.

However, he had not gained similar luster in films. He was a middling star at best, his striking stage presence seldom carrying over to the screen. He often derided his work in that medium, and blamed the studio system for forcing him into unsuitable films. His remarkable voice, so powerful and often thrilling on the stage, was less effective in films. Even so, he had been nominated twice for Academy Awards. Because he and his wife, Sybil, had been cautious with his earnings, he now and again spoke of retiring to their comfortable villa in Switzerland, from which he would emerge for stage forays in classic roles. Colleagues and critics thought his logical future lay in that direction.

"You're rich now," Moss Hart counseled him that night at the Majestic Theater. "The next five years may decide whether or not you'll become the leading actor of the English stage."

Hart was perceptive enough to be aware that Burton was at a crucial turning point in his career. *Cleopatra* had been a problem-plagued project for several years. First envisioned as a low-budget epic starring the likes of Joan Collins and Stephen Boyd, it had turned into a fearfully extravagant vehicle for Elizabeth Taylor, who herself had barely survived an ordeal of illnesses. Directors had changed, screenplays been thrown out, and sets jettisoned. The new script required an Antony and a Caesar who could speak the literate lines being fashioned by the new director, Joseph L. Mankiewicz. That is what led to the approach to Richard Burton. Handsome, husky, and barrel-chested, he was physically appropriate for the role of Antony, and as an actor with a noble way with words, he was unsurpassed. He would be able easily to hold his own with Rex Harrison, who would play Julius Caesar. Elizabeth Taylor was getting choice companions.

To obtain him, Twentieth Century-Fox was willing to pay him substantially more than his previous price for a film, but only a quarter of the amount being paid Taylor. She was the first star to demand and get a million dollars for one motion-picture role.

Moss Hart must have realized the certain perils for Burton in becoming involved in an undertaking as huge and problematic as *Cleopatra*, already overpublicized—from the vicissitudes of its star to the vast expenses incurred by the studio before a single foot of film was shot. Fortunes and reputations, even the fate of the studio, were riding on the outcome. For Burton to play opposite the screen's leading and most glamorous star could lift him to a new plane of film stardom, but he could also go down with what appeared to some to be a sinking ship. Burton, with his energies and his lust for living, was always in danger of overreaching himself. He was restless. The talk about retiring was a fantasy. Richard could be bored easily.

Alan Jay Lerner had mentioned to Moss Hart a little anecdote about Richard. He had been walking with him along Broadway during the run of *Camelot* when Richard remarked: "Someday, luv, I'm going to be the richest, the most famous, and the best actor in the world."

"You can't be all three, Richard," Lerner said. "You can be the best, and you might even be the most famous, but you'll never be the richest and the best, or if you're the most famous and the richest, you won't be the best. You can't be all three."

"Luv," said Richard, "I intend to be all three."

"Good luck," Lerner said.

When an actor or an artist of any kind puts fame and money on an equal footing with accomplishment, his image tends to tarnish. There have been actors with God-given gifts of talent who lacked respect for those gifts and squandered them. John Barrymore made a drunken, woman-chasing buffoon out of himself. Marlon Brando, after a brilliant stage beginning, went into movies and stayed there, and eventually only stayed home. Several of the finest actors of stage and screen have gone on extended alcoholic binges, others on drugs. Why the self-destructive urge in these people who appear to have so much? There are some who would put Richard Burton, dead of a massive cerebral hemorrhage at age fifty-eight, in the same company—but his case (if we are to regard him as a case) is vastly more complicated. He was an actor of—at times—brilliance, but his mind

BURTON

was brilliant, too. Those who knew him well felt he could have been successful at anything he chose to do.

Burton, as though acknowledging this, often said he became an actor by accident. He said he saw it as a way of making enough money to lift himself out of his impoverished origin in Wales. Yet, when he had more than enough money, he continued to act.

He had gargantuan appetites, for women, for drink. Perhaps, then, his vitality was such that it could not be satisfied with money alone, or fame alone, or greatness alone. So he wanted all three.

There are differing views of Burton in his home country, England, and in America. In England, the way it was supposed to go for him was that he would play all the important Shakespeare roles—Hamlet, Macbeth, Lear, et al.—then, like Gielgud and Olivier, he would direct plays, devote himself to a company such as the Old Vic, and eventually, just as with Sir John and Sir Laurence, would become Sir Richard. That's what should have happened, according to a surprisingly large number of British obituary writers.

In America, there is no Shakespearean tradition to speak of. No one faults Robert De Niro or Dustin Hoffman for not doing *Hamlet* on Broadway. Actors (and actresses) who are successful are expected to earn large amounts of money. There may be something of a caste gap between those who are stars of television and those who are film stars—and while stage actors are respected, the farther away from Broadway they get, the less they shine. In America, too, there is another category—celebrity. Above all else, that is what Burton became.

So, in England, while there were many who saw him as a sellout, even a failure, almost everywhere else he was regarded as a more-than-life-size celebrated personality on whom was bestowed just about all that anyone could want. Leaving *Camelot* for *Cleopatra* turned out to be a decisive moment of the kind Shakespeare warned about in *Julius Caesar.* Moss Hart was more perceptive than he was ever to know. (He died three months later.) When Richard Burton left for Rome, he could hardly have known the extraordinary turn his already crowded life would take. Soon enough, the whole world would take notice of him.

With a certain self-mockery, Burton told the friends who habitually congregated in his dressing room at the theater, "Well, I guess

BURTON

I've got to don my breastplate once more to play opposite Miss Tits." The disrespectful reference was to the rather full-bosomed Elizabeth Taylor. Another time he called the same woman "that fat little tart." Burton's tongue could be wicked at times.

His costar in *Camelot*, Julie Andrews, gave him due warning. Miss Taylor, then Mrs. Eddie Fisher, was made of powerful stuff. He told her he was only off to Rome for the money—which was too good to ignore—and for a matter of a few months' work. It was a fine arrangement. He would get a house in Rome for himself and his family, with servants, all expenses paid, and extra expenses for incidentals. He would have a car and a chauffeur. He didn't like planes, but at least he and his would be traveling in the comfort of first class.

The day following his final curtain calls in *Camelot*, he was with his family waiting for his flight in the appropriately named Celebrity Lounge. The news that he would be starring opposite Elizabeth Taylor was already having its effect, for the room was crowded with reporters and photographers. What, he was asked, were his feelings about appearing with Miss Taylor in what already looked to be the most expensive film ever made?

He weighed his words carefully. "Let's say that we know and respect one another. And we will, I am sure, find it very interesting to play together."

True enough.

2

Throughout his life Richard Burton was an endless and remarkable raconteur. He liked most of all to delve into the past and tell of his origins in South Wales. He was nostalgic about his birthplace, Pontrhydyfen, a small village that looks across the Afan Valley and a river that flows in the valley's crease. In fact, the name of the village, Richard explained, means "the bridge across the valley." The Afan River coursed just below the garden patch in back of the house in which he was born—Number 2 Dan-y-bont.

Before adopting the name Burton, he was Richard Walter Jenkins Jr., named after his father, a miner. Jenkins Senior, though only five feet four inches tall, was powerfully built and, according to Richard, wielded a mean pickax. There is in that part of Wales, said Burton, a great coal seam, world-famous and part of what he believed was called the Great Atlantic Fault.

"It starts in the Basque country of northern Spain, goes under the Bay of Biscay, and comes up in South Wales. It then goes under the Atlantic and surfaces again in Pennsylvania. If you took a Basque, or Welsh, or Pennsylvania miner, blindfolded and transported them, they would know the coal face the minute they saw it."

His father, he went on, would talk about this coal face the way some men would talk about the beauty of women. "He would look at the seam of coal, would almost surgically make a mark on it, and then he would ask his boy helper to give him a number-two mandrel. That's a half-headed pick. Then, having stared at this gorgeous black-shining ribbon of coal, he would hit it with an enormous blow. If he hit it just right, something like twenty tons of coal would fall out of the coal face. It was thrilling and exciting."

He would extol the virtues of miners. They regarded themselves as the aristocrats of the working class, superior to all other kinds of manual laborers. "In my valley everyone's dream was to become a miner." This was an exaggeration. The dream of many families was to keep their sons out of the mines. There was, however, a phase in his youth when Richard did, indeed, consider going into the mines. His father was known familiarly as Dic, and in the immediate family as Daddy Ni. Though meagerly educated, "he was," said Richard, "a remarkable fellow in many ways. He spoke perfect English [in addition to his native Welsh] and, to put it mildly, had a predilection for strong liquor." He had a passion for beer, too, and a love of words—the longer the better. These he passed on to Richard.

Dic met Edith Maude Thomas, Richard's mother, at a pub in a nearby village, where she was employed as a barmaid. He was twenty-four, she seventeen. He was a handsome fellow with a mustache and black hair worn low on his brow. "He looked very much like me," said Richard. "That is, he was pockmarked and devious, and smiled a great deal when he was in trouble. He was, also, a man of extraordinary eloquence, tremendous passion, great violence." Edith was taller than Dic by several inches, a fair-haired attractive girl of sweet disposition. Children came along in rapid progression. Richard was the twelfth, born on November 10, 1925. Two earlier girls had died in infancy. Left were four sisters and five brothers. Edith's last child, the thirteenth, a boy, was born two years after Richard; a week after the birth, aged forty-four, she died. Richard would later blame the medical care of the time for her death. "She was a very strong woman who died of puerperal fever, which is hygienic neglect."

Times were hard, then, in Pontrhydyfen and made worse by a general strike in 1926. The older boys worked in the mines along with their father. Richard was sent to live with his sister Cecilia, five miles away in Taibach, a section of Port Talbot, while his younger brother, Graham, went to an older married brother. Richard, relatives told him, was so attached to his mother that he had followed her around like a puppy, but he had no memory of her at all. He was put on a bus to Taibach, where, unlike Pontrhydyfen, English was spoken. Richard had learned to speak only Welsh. It was much like growing up in a foreign land. No wonder, then, that his happiest times were spent on weekends, when he went to visit his father and other members of the family in Pontrhydyfen. But living in the house of his English-speaking brother-in-law, Elfed James, soon enough made him bilingual.

Elfed was a miner, like almost everyone else in Richard's family, and became in effect an adoptive father. His sister Cecilia, who was nineteen years his senior, gave him his early rearing. He adored her. In later years he grew sentimental about her, never more so than when he wrote in a memoir called *Christmas Eve in Aberavon*:

"She was more mother to me than any mother could ever have been. I was immensely proud of her, I shone in the reflection of her green-eyed black-haired gypsy beauty. She had a throat that should have been colored with down like a small bird. . . . She was innocent and guileless and infinitely protectable. She was naive to the point of saintliness and wept a lot at the tragedies of others. I had read of the Knights of Chivalry and I knew that I had a bounden duty to protect her from all others. It wasn't until thirty years later, when I saw her in another woman, that I realized I had been searching for her all my life."

Richard would insist that in spite of hard times and what appeared to others as poverty and deprivation, he had a happy childhood. Cecilia doted on him as much as he on her. It was better, he said, to have older brothers and sisters, and aunts and uncles spoil him and compete with each other for his affection and love. "I would wander about from family to family, and be slipped sixpence by one, and threepence by another. I would hint at the fact that one family gave me more than another." He came early, he said, by the knack of acquiring money.

His favorite of his older brothers was Ifor, who worked in the mines but was also a star forward on the local rugby team. Daddy Ni was a rugby enthusiast too, but both he and Ifor regarded education as of paramount importance, the only route away from the mines, and they decided early on, family members said, that Richard

BURTON

would be the one among them to go to Oxford. Just how this was to be accomplished was left unclear. "The idea of a Welsh miner's son going to Oxford," said Richard, "was ridiculous beyond the realm of possibility."

The school system in the South Wales of that time was hardly favorable to the possibility. One went first to the infants' school, then to the elementary school until the age of twelve or thirteen; beyond that a competitive examination determined the minority that would continue on into the secondary or "grammar" school. Those who didn't make it were expected to be part of the laboring or clerking class. If Richard had not passed his "scholarship," as it was called, the world at large might never have heard of him. And it was also fortunate that his schooling took place in Taibach and Port Talbot, because it was in these adjoining towns that he encountered the men who were to determine his future course.

At elementary school he was remembered as intelligent and an avid reader, and by the age of ten his memory for what he read was extraordinary. He could provide Bible quotations word for word. His sister Cecilia recalled him reading through an entire night, or falling asleep with a book in front of the fire. In his *Christmas* memoir he mentioned his habit of reading in bed by candlelight or under the covers with the aid of a cheap flashlight.

As a boy he had a knack for earning money. Miners got up between four-thirty and five in the morning; so did Richard. Taking a sack and a shovel, he would head up to the hills, fill the sack with horse and cow manure, and take it back home. A bath was necessary—cold, because there was no hot water—before he could face the world again. By this time the express train from London would be due in with the morning newspapers. Richard and his cousin Dilly (Dilwyn Dummer), a boy the same age who lived in the adjoining house, would deliver newspapers to their customers for a shilling each a week. The dung Richard collected he sold to people with gardens for sixpence a bucket. At a fish-and-chips shop he dug the eyes out of the potatoes. There was a potato-peeling contraption, but it didn't remove the eyes.

On a good week, with tips, he might clear as much as ten shillings a week, almost as much as a miner's minimum wage. He could go to the local cinema with his own money, and he had both a bicycle and roller skates, which he shared with Dilly. "We each used a skate," Dilly recalled.

From age eight until he was nearly twelve he attended what was known as Eastern Boys' School, where he took the examination for the "scholarship." Enter the first of the important influences in his life, one Meredith Jones, who conducted the scholarship class. The subjects were English and arithmetic. Few were able to pass the demanding test, and Jones inspired and bullied and coached the few from Taibach who did. About one in twelve made it to secondary school, where opportunity existed to go further.

Jones was a ginger-haired, formidable teacher who coached the rugby team, too, exhorting his young charges into near-superhuman efforts. Richard fell under his spell, both at rugby and learning, and later gave him credit for changing his life. Jones liked to think of himself as saving boys from the mines, and from hard labor in Port Talbot's steel mills, or from the menial work slated for those who lacked an education beyond age thirteen or fourteen.

Richard took the scholarship exam in March 1937 and learned in June that he had passed, along with nine others, and would be going on to the Port Talbot Secondary School, a squat red-brick building with a concrete schoolyard, not far from the looming steel mills. He was the first member of his family to reach that exalted level.

3

Richard and Graham, while growing up, took singing lessons on weekends from a tin miner. Graham's clear soprano was judged the better, but it was Richard who took first prize in an Eisteddfod, a traditional singing-and-reciting festival held yearly. Richard was anxious to win again the following year. He chose a difficult composition, Sir Arthur Sullivan's *Orpheus with His Lute*, and went for help to the secondary school's new English master, Philip Burton, a large and imposing gentleman who strode briskly through the corridors of the school with his academic gown billowing behind him. Burton told Richard to see him in the assembly hall after the finish of the day's classes.

With Burton at the piano, Richard stood on the stage and began to sing. To his chagrin, his voice suddenly cracked, and the teacher broke into a whoop of laughter. Not aware of what was causing his voice to behave so waywardly, Richard turned red with humiliation. He growled at Burton as he left the stage, "I'll show you someday."

Philip Burton thought no more of the incident then. Richard at age fourteen was just another of the miners' sons, most of whom would end up in the traditional occupations of the area. Philip Burton's father had been a miner too, but Philip had made his way through the University of Wales; brilliantly educated as he was, he had come to Port Talbot Secondary School to teach mathematics and English. His passion, though, was theater. He wrote plays and put on the school's dramatic productions; he kept a vigilant eye out for promising boys who might go on to acting careers or work on radio for the BBC. One of his students had gone on to the Old Vic, until the war cut short his career. Richard, at first encounter, in no way struck him as promising.

But at rugby, Richard excelled. He was competitive and combative, and won the approval of the feisty Meredith Jones. In spite of bad cases of boils and acne, the girls looked on him with approval, and Richard looked back. Jones around that time had a pet project, the Taibach Youth Center. He made of it a recreational gathering place for the local boys and girls. There were Ping-Pong tables, a canteen, and equipment for the sports teams. Jones enlisted part-time instructors in music, arts and crafts, and dramatics. With his outgoing personality and enthusiasm, he dominated the center.

In later years, Richard wrote, "All day long he taught eleven-plus boys the rudiments of arithmetic and English to prepare them for entrance into the local grammar schools. At night he presided in the same school over a youth club.

"When the club was closed for the night he would invariably say, 'Walk home with me, boys,' and delightedly we would; for we all knew that some lecture to be delivered would be only half-completed by the time of our arrival at his house, which would mean a further half-hour of talk while he offered to walk us back home. A further walk might even be necessary while he talked and talked. His subjects were legion.

"His impact on me was decisive but not immediate. It was cumulative, not a blinding moment of revelation. I felt with him that my mind broadened with every step I took. He taught me to love the English language without actually talking about the English language. He taught me to be a reader without actually being much of a reader himself."

Not everyone remembered Meredith Jones so lyrically; there were those who regarded him as a slave-driver. Not all the boys were favored with his encouragement. It was said he was clever at picking out the boys who could succeed. He could use his fists on a boy, too, or wield an ever-present cane. For Richard, he opened the doors of his mind and revealed to him the possibilities that lay in self-improvement.

When the war came, Richard volunteered for fire-watching duty several nights a week. From a perch on the side of a mountain he could see incendiaries being dropped on Swansea, across the estuary, ten miles westward. Port Talbot was not a primary target, but he heard the drone of the German bombers as they headed farther west. When a spray of incendiaries landed on Port Talbot's outskirts, it was regarded as a mistake.

Richard made his first stage appearance in a school production of Shaw's *The Apple Cart*. The role was small and made little impression on the director, Philip Burton, or anyone else. Toward the end of 1941, he decided to leave school. There were problems at home. Elfed James wasn't able to work because of illness; his meager finances were drained, and there was little pocket money left for Richard. He was sixteen, with a full chest and strong legs. He and Dilly Dummer talked about going into the mines.

"He wanted his independence," Dilwyn recalled. "He wanted to be able to take a girl to the movies, to join older boys in the pubs. We were always close, so I wanted to go with him into the mines, but our families put a stop to that idea. If Richard wanted to work, it had to be above ground. They found him a job selling men's underwear—woolies, you know—in the clothes department of the Taibach Cooperative Wholesale Society. He hated the job, but he liked having a little extra cash left over after contributing to the family."

In Elfed's view, Richard already had enough education, having gone beyond the obligatory fourteen-year-old mark. In this difficult moment old sores were revealed. Elfed's side of the family had never looked with favor on his taking in the boy and becoming responsible for raising him. On the other hand, Richard wasn't overly admiring of the stolid, hardworking Elfed. ("But a fine, decent man," said Dilwyn.)

Richard was not an ideal employee at the co-op. He ignored wartime rationing rules and sold items without the requisite coupons. One of his sisters claimed he was too kindhearted to turn people down. If he ran errands he took too long getting back. The co-op managers complained he was never around. He began regretting leaving school and giving up a chance at a university scholarship. Once left, it was all but impossible to get back into the school. He thought of becoming a preacher, because he was supposed to be able to talk well, but he couldn't discover much religious feeling in himself. He tried boxing, fought twice, won the first time, and was clobbered the second. His earnings amounted to only a couple of pounds.

He still sang and went to festivals and recitals with his sister and brother-in-law, wearing his best suit. But now there was another side to his life. As a wage earner, he felt he had the right to do as he pleased, and began hanging around with the boys whose schooling had ended early, like his. He took up smoking, and though underage, began downing a pint or two at a local pub. He frequented an ice cream parlor where a pretty girl did the serving. He would wait around to take her home, much to the annoyance of her father, who was suspicious that the boy might try to become a man, as he put it.

He joined the Port Talbot Squadron of the Air Training Corps as a cadet, and, as it happened, Philip Burton was the squadron commander. Burton wrote a radio documentary about the squadron for the Welsh studios of the BBC, and Richard auditioned for a part. He got it, and this gave him the notion that through acting he might find his way out of selling haberdashery. He returned to the Taibach Youth Center, where a young drama group was forming. A new influence entered his life. Leo Lloyd, a worker in a local steel mill, was passionately devoted to the theater. Meredith Jones had asked him to take charge of a play to be performed at a youth Eisteddfod. *The Bishop's Candlesticks*, as it was called, was taken from Hugo's *Les Misérables*, and Lloyd saw enough in sixteen-year-old Richard to give him a major role. Oddly enough, the whole play was done in silence, and Richard, as an escaped convict, mimed his role.

Richard usually tended to be generous in his assessments of those who helped him along, and he gave credit to Lloyd for developing in him a fascination with acting. "He taught me the fundamentals of the job; to stand and move and talk on the stage with confidence. He taught me the power of the spoken word. He changed my discontent and made me want to be an actor."

BURTON

He took a prize at the Eisteddfod, and many years later, residents of Port Talbot still remembered his performance. There was something about him on the stage, they said, that made you watch him.

Meredith Jones stopped in at the local co-op one day and saw Richard behind a counter. His red mustache bristled. "Whatever are you doing here?" he wanted to know. Richard explained his situation as best he could. Probably Jones already knew it. With the aid of a local politician, Richard was readmitted to the school for the up-coming fall term of 1942. Meanwhile, because Richard's reputation was that of something of a wild boy, Jones asked Philip Burton to keep an eye on him when he returned.

Burton, a confirmed bachelor at age thirty-eight, roomed with a Mrs. Smith, a widow who took in lodgers in her house near the steelworks. Aside from his teaching, he was leading an active life on other levels. On a University of Wales scholarship he had traveled around the United States for five months in 1939. He wrote radio plays for the BBC, and took frequent theater trips to London, two hundred miles away. He wrote plays of his own, produced them in the school and the town, and occasionally acted in them.

In a book he later wrote about his career, he confessed to having a "Pygmalion complex. It's a deep urge to fulfill myself as an actor or writer through another person. Perhaps I should be unkinder to myself and call it a Svengali complex."

Whether as Pygmalion or Svengali, Philip Burton was to have an incalculable effect on the young life of Richard Walter Jenkins Jr.

4

When Richard Jenkins returned to school in October 1942, he was a year older than the others in his form. He was handsome and his looks, his stalwart build, his relative maturity, made him particularly attractive to the girls in his classes. "All the girls were excited," one remembered. He took her to the movies, and quoted poetry to her on the walk home. "He was not a groper," she claimed. "He had more class than that. In a strange way I became one of his birds, but it was all very innocent."

He worked hard at his studies, but also played hard at rugby, and, a natural leader, captained both the rugby and cricket teams. While at the co-op he had earned the nickname of "Wild Jenk," but aside from a few pranks and outbursts, at school he applied himself to the job at hand, which was to learn and to pass the Certificate examination, and, as he put it, "to go on and get an education of any kind." He knew the story of Owen Jones, the boy from Port Talbot who had gone on to a successful career in the theater, and knew that it was Philip Burton who was responsible for working the magic. The idea of making a living in the theater appealed to him. If he was to have a go at it, Philip Burton was the one he had to impress.

When he got his chance in a school production Philip Burton was putting on at the local YMCA, he gave his part all the emotional juice he was capable of at that age. Philip was not so much impressed as angry over what he felt was Richard's distortion of the balance of the play, but at the same time he sensed the boy's fierce determination to excel, and clear, too, was his feeling for language and poetry. If Richard was unconsciously looking for a guide and a father (Daddy Ni had retired from the mines and was living with one of his sons), the bachelor Philip, in much the same way, was unconsciously seeking a son. Like Jones, he was deeply sympathetic to those trying to transcend their mean circumstances. It was not uncommon practice in that part of Wales for benefactors to help worthy boys and girls. By Richard's account, "I was determined to attract his [Philip Burton's] attention." He went directly to him and asked for private coaching. Philip was not encouraging. "I went back two or three days later—I don't know how many times—and persisted, but eventually he took it upon himself to ask me home for tea and began the first lesson."

"If I had doubts at first," Philip Burton recalled later, "I should have known better. I'd never met a person before with such determination."

Richard, at best, was a rough gem greatly in need of polishing. For one thing, if he was to become the kind of actor that Philip aimed for, he would need to rid himself of his thoroughly local Welsh accent and learn to speak a clear and precise English. Nor could his education be neglected. Burton was a feared taskmaster in the school, and he was even harder on Richard as his tutor. "It was the most painful and hardworking period of my entire life," said Richard.

Knowing his love for reading, Burton gave Richard a list of great books. He took him to the summit of a mountain called Mynydd Margam and had him spout Shakespeare into the wind. He moved farther away and called: "Make me hear you. Don't shout, but make me hear you."

At the school, Burton gave him parts in plays, small at first, then larger. In one play, as a bank manager, he was on the stage alone, talking into five telephones. He had to dart from phone to phone. Burton spent days making him repeat the scene over and over. On each phone he had to imagine the person on the other end of the line, keep each one in his mind, and use different tones in speaking to each. Through this exercise and others, Burton taught Richard coordination and precision in speaking.

At home there was trouble for Richard. Meredith Jones had been mainly responsible for convincing the family that Richard should return to school, but Elfed James grumbled about the expense of keeping the boy. The rancor that was generated in the home upset Richard's sister Cecilia. Richard, one evening, simply walked out of the house, saying he wasn't coming back. He went to the street where Philip Burton boarded in one of the row houses and called up to him. "I can't go home. I have no place to stay," Richard told him. Philip explained to his landlady, Mrs. Smith, that he had a student outside who had no place to spend the night because of a problem at home. Richard not only stayed the night, but stayed for the next year in a small upstairs room.

(In later years, when he had the power to do so, Richard specified in his film contracts that he would not work on March 1, a Welsh anniversary known as St. David's Day, which was also the day he came to stay with Philip Burton.)

Just as Philip Burton was like a member of the Smith family through his residence there of seventeen years, Richard became one too. His manners had to be improved; Mrs. Smith helped on that. Stories in Port Talbot had it that he didn't know how to use his knife and fork. He had no money, so Burton bought him clothes and lent him his socks when Mrs. Smith and her daughters complained about Richard's smelly feet. Philip Burton doted on the boy; there was no question of that. Disciplinarian though he was, he also poured genuine affection on him. Their closeness was such that when Richard had shredded wheat for breakfast, Burton sifted sugar on it for him.

The relationship became one, in effect, of guardianship. Because he was already taking care of his room and board, as well as educating and training him, Philip looked into legally adopting Richard. The law specified, though, that he would have to be twenty-one years his senior, and Philip was a year less than that. Instead, he made him his ward. As remembered by Burton, "Richard was my son to all intents and purposes. I was committed to him. He knew I was doing it out of love. I did feel very much his guardian and his father, and

BURTON

was proud of him even in those days. It was a fine relationship." He was stimulated by Richard's restless determination to learn and improve, his continual questioning. Richard was stimulated, in turn, by Burton's brilliant mind and scholarship. But he was also driven remorselessly by Burton to excel. Richard once spoke of it later: "It was hell"—without in the least denying Burton any of the credit due him.

Several years later, a writer, in conversation with the two of them, asked when it was that Philip had adopted Richard. "He didn't," Richard broke in. "I adopted him."

In June 1943, Richard took the School Certificate examination, and learned the results in September. He passed all seven subjects, and received a superior grade in five of them, thus qualifying for entrance into a university. Lacking funds, though, he would need a scholarship. With the approach of his eighteenth birthday, he was due for military service. He was already a cadet in an air training squadron, commanded by Philip, who had an idea. The RAF had a program of "short courses" at leading universities which could be taken by qualified cadets prior to their active service. Philip urged Richard to apply for the program. If accepted, he would get the equivalent of a six-month scholarship.

The better to deal with matters of class distinctions, still prevalent in the services, Burton acted on a suggestion that Richard's name be changed to his own. The name change, signed by Richard's father, albeit reluctantly, took effect in the autumn of 1943. Shortly afterward, Richard was accepted at Exeter College, Oxford, the course to begin in April 1944. But another event intervened.

While waiting for the results of his examination, and not sure of his prospects, Richard had thought of going into the mines for a year. He still had a respect for the work one did with one's hands, the kind all his family had done before him. But he was making progress with his acting, as he demonstrated with a performance as Professor Higgins in the school production of Shaw's *Pygmalion*. The local paper reviewed the play when it was performed at the YMCA, and picked out Richard for special mention. And he collected his first professional fees for acting when Philip, through his contacts and his own work with the Wales BBC, got him some small radio parts.

BURTON

It was while Philip Burton and his squadron were at summer training camp that he came across an advertisement in the Cardiff *Western Mail*: "EMLYN WILLIAMS WANTS WELSH ACTORS."

The ad went on to say that Mr. Williams was looking for several Welsh actors and actresses for his production of a play due to open in the autumn of 1943. A Welsh boy actor was required. Applicants were to write to Williams in London.

Here was a genuine opportunity of the first order. Philip wrote the letter of application to Williams on Richard's behalf. He was advised of a date on which Williams and his casting director would be holding auditions in the city of Cardiff. When they arrived in Cardiff, Philip telephoned Williams and told him about the exceptional talent of the youth he was bringing to the audition.

There was no way he could have been aware of it, but forces were marshaling that would propel Richard into a theatrical career. There was Emlyn Williams, already a distinguished actor, director, and playwright. The play, *The Druid's Rest*, was being presented by England's leading theatrical organization, H. M. Tennent, directed by the powerful Binkie Beaumont. His casting director was a lovely woman in every sense of the word, Daphne Rye. And she was the one who interviewed Richard in Cardiff. There were hundreds of applicants, all Welsh boys, one of whom was the youthful Stanley Baker. Williams had mentioned to her to keep an eye out for a Richard Jenkins. (He had not yet changed his name.) Richard was tense and nervous, but Daphne Rye saw that he was a definite possibility for the smaller part of an older boy and sent him on to see Williams. She said later that he made a remark that she construed as a pass at her.

Williams recalled: "It was an evening in Cardiff at the Sandringham Hotel. After a dismal procession of no-goods, Philip Burton introduced himself as the man who had written and telephoned me about his promising amateur pupil. He beckoned and the boy stepped forward: a boy of seventeen, of startling beauty, and quiet intelligence. He looked . . . imperishable. I asked young Jenkins what was the last part he had played, at school. The answer came, clear as a bell, 'Professor Higgins in *Pygmalion*.' It wasn't a large part, but it was a very effective one. He read a few lines and I knew at once he would be excellent."

5

The larger world loomed. Rehearsals of *The Druid's Rest* were held in London. The play would open in Liverpool, travel to other cities, and wind up in London. Stanley Baker was with the company as Richard's understudy, and the two boys quickly became friends. They had similar backgrounds; both were the sons of miners, but Stanley, young as he was, was professionally ahead of Richard, in that he had already had a part in a movie. He was big for his age, and liked beer as much as Richard. Soon enough they were exploring pubs together.

During rehearsals Richard caught Emlyn Williams' attention early on. "He did something very rare: he drew attention by not claiming it. He played his part with perfect simplicity."

Offstage, Williams found Richard immediately likable. "He was quietly pleasant—not shy, just reserved, except for the sudden smile which—there's no other word for it—glowed."

One evening, as they left the theater together after a late rehearsal, Williams asked him what was the book he was carrying.

"Dylan Thomas," Richard said.

Williams was only just acquainted with the name of the Welsh poet who was to become so famous.

"He is a great poet," Richard said.

BURTON

Then he suddenly stopped and recited: " 'They shall have stars at elbow and foot . . .' "

Williams always remembered the moment—the blackout, the words loud in the street. He thought: Here is a *voice*. "And behind the voice, a mind which, like my own, was in love with the English language."

He broke the spell by asking Richard if his digs were all right. Richard said they were. Was he behaving himself in London? Richard said he was.

"Even then," Williams said, "I doubted it."

Richard made his professional stage debut at the Royal Court Theater in Liverpool on November 22, 1943, using for the first time the name Burton.

The play had to do with the suspicions of a young boy in a Welsh village who imagines that a stranger in their midst is a notorious murderer. Richard played the boy's older brother. He described it later on as "a nothing part. I hardly spoke at all, but I was on the stage the whole time. My one speech had to do with my explaining to my little brother the story of Jekyll and Hyde, very haughtily, with a thick Welsh accent. The local newspapers ignored me completely. I wasn't all that upset, because I wasn't all that keen about acting. But I thought it was quite interesting that people were willing to pay me ten pounds a week for it, which was three times what the miners got."

"At that stage," Baker agreed, "Richard couldn't sit back and say there was a burning ambition to become an actor. One's main ambition was to get out of the valleys and improve yourself. It didn't matter which way."

Ten pounds a week was a fortune. On their own, free of small-town restraints, they could roam at will through the big cities. Their favorite pub in Liverpool was a dimly lit dive filled, said Baker, "with completely worthless characters."

Richard met an usherette at the theater and confided to Baker that she seemed to be willing. Stanley egged him on, saying, "Go on, boyo, it's wonderful." He took her home after a performance, endured an endless tram ride. The girl's parents were in bed upstairs. Richard and the girl sat on the floor and took off their shoes. "We tried to make love," Richard confided to a writer. "It was a painful experience, and I was filled with blind horror and worry. I fell asleep

and dreamed I was in hell, suffering the torments of the damned."
He woke to discover his foot had landed in the fireplace and his sock
was burning. "I did not learn much about sex from that girl," he said.

In January 1944, the play opened in London. Williams took Richard
in for a few weeks until he could find a place of his own. London
swarmed with uniformed men and women of many nations, with a
large quota of Americans. It was an exciting time, with talk of an
invasion of the Continent in the air. The V-1 rockets had stopped
coming over, and the larger V-2's had not yet appeared. Richard's
brother Ifor showed up to keep an eye on him, and Philip Burton
came too. When *The Druid's Rest* had its opening night at St. Martin's
Theater in the West End, a film called *Lassie Come Home* opened at
a cinema in Leicester Square. The film starred, in addition to the
dog, a child actress named Elizabeth Taylor.

Richard looked for reviews the days after his London debut. He
was curious, he told Baker, "because why be an actor if you can't
be the best?"

The play garnered mild reviews for the most part, but one critic,
James Redfern, in *The New Statesman*, put it down on several counts—
writing, directing, and acting. "However," he wrote in the last line
of the review, "in a wretched part Richard Burton showed exceptional ability."

"That's when the bug hit," Richard recalled. All he did was serve
drinks and talk about Jekyll and Hyde. What did the critic mean?
That single sentence, he said, "changed my life. Well, all right then,
I thought, I'll stick to this business."

He stayed in the play until April, when, still an air cadet, he was
due to take the short course at Oxford. Upon arrival in that historic
town he opted for courses in English literature and Italian. With
other cadets he took basic training two days of the week, and attended
classes on the other days. That is, he was supposed to attend lectures,
but by his account, he seldom did, preferring the atmosphere of the
town's pubs. He also acquired further sexual education. "I met a girl
student there who was older than I was, and she showed me what
to do." No further problems.

For an eighteen-year-old air cadet with only six months at Exeter
College, Oxford, Burton made a considerable impression. Some of

BURTON

this may have been due to his own storytelling ability. One of his tales had to do with breaking the Exeter "sconce" record. A "sconce" was a fine for a breach of manners in the dining hall. Whatever his lapse was, the punishment was to down two pints of beer in thirty seconds or less. Richard had the ability to pour the liquid down his throat without swallowing, and emptied the two pints in ten seconds. His proud boast was that in all the years that followed, no one "ever whacked that feat."

Having discovered the joy of sex, Richard went after records in that department, too. He became known for his ability to spot a girl in a pub, cozy up to her, and get her into bed. He admitted he usually selected plain, quiet girls. "For some reason," he told a friend, "I seem to go with the sleepwalkers," and later he noted that his girls grew prettier the more successful he became.

He couldn't play rugby at Oxford because it was the wrong season, and by the time it began he would be off to active service. So he was led to drama. With summer coming on, he learned of a production of *Measure for Measure* being put on by Nevill Coghill, a professor of English literature, as the yearly play of the OUDS (for Oxford University Dramatic Society). When he went to see Coghill he was told the play was already cast. Well, then, asked Burton, could he be part of it in some way, if only to attend rehearsals? As a demonstration, he recited the "To be or not to be" soliloquy from *Hamlet*.

Coghill was impressed. He was struck, particularly, by Richard's ability to switch from his normal Welsh-accented voice to "Shakespearean" English. Coghill told him he could understudy the role of Angelo, being played by an RAF officer while on leave at Oxford. The officer had already mentioned to Coghill that he might not be able to complete the scheduled performances before being called back to duty.

Richard liked to say that he ruthlessly prayed for the other actor to fall sick, but that wasn't necessary. The officer, soon to leave, had Richard take over the part earlier than he had expected. Philip Burton, who was in Cardiff working for the BBC, sent Richard letters of advice on how to play Angelo, and came to Oxford to oversee his last rehearsal.

Professor Coghill was more than pleased with Richard's perfor-

mance, but a student critic—as is often the way with student critics—
cut Richard down to size: "Mr. Burton is pretty," he wrote, "with
a good voice and nothing else."

Richard was supposed to meet Philip Burton (who was sharing
his room) after the performance, but as he was to explain eventually,
he took "ten minutes after the play to drop in at a party given by a
very rich woman." There he was fascinated by a sideboard on which
was displayed "a collection of all kinds of liquor—brandy, cordials,
and whiskey. I tried them all, became suitably ill, and passed out.
When I woke up, I was locked in."

He escaped at dawn, and created another legend while climbing
the spiked railing to get back to his quarters without being discovered: he impaled himself on his hind quarters. Philip Burton was
alarmed by his pale appearance and torn clothing, but Richard refused
to see a doctor.

Professor Coghill invited several noteworthies to see his production, and especially Richard's performance. Among those who came
were John Gielgud, Terence Rattigan, and Binkie Beaumont. Having already seen Richard in *The Druid's Rest*, Beaumont suggested
he look him up after he completed his war service. The suggestion was another important link in the chain that led to an acting
career.

At the end of Richard's six months at Oxford, he headed to Tor-
quay for the Air Force classification examinations, hoping to be
accepted for pilot training. He was disappointed when his vision
turned out to be below par, and he was classified as a navigator
trainee. By this time, with the Luftwaffe all but knocked out of the
skies, and the American Air Force roaming the continental skies in
great force, Britain was overstocked with pilots. More the problem
was what to do with an oversupply of cadets. Richard was shunted
from one RAF training camp to another, his only benefit being able
to get in some rugby matches. He was on the high seas headed for
more training in Canada just as the war in Europe came to an end.

In June, he and a friend, a Welshman like himself, decided to spend
three weeks of accumulated leave on a visit to the United States.
Leaving from Winnipeg, with only a few dollars in their combined
pockets, they hitchhiked their way to New York, where Richard

BURTON

planned to look up a married couple who were friends of Philip Burton's. They were in Vermont, however, and the two young RAF men had to cope on their own. Richard managed to get them permission to sleep in a Columbia University fraternity house—unused at that moment because of the semester's end—and for drinks and food they sang Welsh songs in bars that ranged from uptown Broadway to Greenwich Village.

His advanced training in navigation of little use to the British or anyone else after the surrender of Japan, Richard was ferried back to England to hang about in one Air Force facility or another until his time for demobilization. This took two years. Rugby, drinking, girl-chasing, and an occasional brawl were his principal occupations. A broken nose he received in a fight required resetting by a surgeon. Philip Burton was beside himself when he heard of what might have been critical damage to Richard's fine features; he was still pushing an acting career for him. Now a drama producer for BBC Welsh radio, he got Richard some parts to play. More important to Richard was the opportunity to play rugby with an Air Force team. He played well enough to capture the attention of a famed team member, Bledden Williams, who in Wales was legendary.

Williams later wrote a reminiscent book about his career, page 37 of which was treasured by Richard, for it contained the following paragraph:

"I played with a wing forward who soon caught the eye for his general proficiency and tireless zeal. His name: Richard Burton. But it was in CinemaScope that he caught the eye after the war. A pity, because I think Richard would have made as good a wing forward as any we have produced in Wales."

He also achieved notice when, after consuming several pints of beer, he decided to test a theory that one could break a pane of glass with a fist without sustaining cuts. He and two companions raced through a street breaking windows, a hundred and seventy-nine of them by Richard's count, and not a single cut. The feat cost him seven days in the brig.

In the spring of 1946 there was cricket to take the place of rugby, and in the summer Philip Burton treated him to a week at Stratford-on-Avon, where he was most deeply impressed by a performance of Marlowe's *Dr. Faustus*. Thinking that Richard might perform the role of Faustus someday, Philip coached him in the lines, and with his retentive ability Richard was able to commit them to memory.

Navigational training was beside the point by this time, and the RAF made use of him by assigning him to an RAF hospital in Wiltshire, where as Aircraftsman First Class Burton he clerked, mostly typing out demobilization orders. He regarded the assignment with contempt, but he had learned to behave himself in order to conserve his weekend passes—important because of the small radio parts that came his way in London. He was proud of the money he earned from it, and once showed a friend his postal savings book. It contained nearly thirty-two pounds, an impressive sum to the friend.

At the hospital he found himself a nineteen-year-old girl, an assistant cook in the kitchen. She was pretty, and plump, according to a witness to the affair, but wasn't able to get out more than three or four words in sequence. But she appreciated Richard's way with words; just about everything he said made her burst into a high-pitched giggle. Richard treated her with an almost exaggerated courtesy.

Alan Grainge (later to become a journalist) was with Richard during his assignment at the hospital, and described him then as having a "face with a slightly coarse skin texture. He walked with a springy step that was not quite a swagger. He seemed aware of every movement, as if he were appearing before an imaginary audience. He would assume moods such as flippancy, anger, boredom, in a way that others might choose a book from a shelf." He could also mimic, and brought laughter to his fellows with his rendition of Churchill's famous "We will fight on . . . ah . . . the beaches . . ." The imitation would prove useful later on.

He became more seriously involved when he met an attractive actress, Eleanor Summerfield, while appearing with her in an early BBC television production of Emlyn Williams' *The Corn Is Green*. Eleanor was four years his senior, a busy and rising actress. He began seeing her as steadily as his weekend passes allowed, suffering the long train ride from Wiltshire to London, and writing her letters in between the visits.

Their backgrounds were poles apart. She had been brought up in a quiet London suburb by genteel and well-off parents. Richard regarded himself as engaged to her, but Eleanor was apparently less serious. She did, however, invite him to her home for Christmas, presumably for her parents to have a look at him. Whatever they saw, they didn't particularly like, for when Richard showed a snapshot of his girlfriend at a local pub, he said, "Her family, though, doesn't approve of me." From the other side, Philip Burton was also opposed to a union; he didn't want Richard encumbered with a wife while making his way in the theater. The relationship soon enough melted away, and with his own demobilization approaching, Richard had a decision to make. Should he return to Oxford, which he could now attend because of his nearly three years of RAF service, complete his education and think about a career later, or head for London and see what was available to him in the theater?

Oxford attracted him because of the educational advantages he would obtain, and also because of the chance to represent the university on its rugby team. With these in mind, he wrote to Professor Coghill and asked his advice about when to return. Coghill wrote back, suggesting he wait for two years: "There are two things you want to do, to get a first, and a blue for rugby."

"The pile-up of veterans was so great," Richard later explained, "that Oxford now had one of the greatest rugby teams in the world, and I would have had no chance of making the team. Chances would be better in two years, when those others had gone back to New Zealand, Australia, and South Africa."

So, to London he went, after his discharge from the RAF on December 16, 1947.

Hugh (Binkie) Beaumont, a benevolent czar, made it a practice to place promising young actors under contract to the Tennent organization. For five hundred pounds a year each, or thereabouts, he had a pool to call on for the firm's theatrical productions. Richard Burton was in London only a day or two when he walked out of Beaumont's office with a year's contract at the prevailing rate. Not only had he been remembered by Beaumont, but Daphne Rye, the casting director for Tennent, was on his side. He needed a place to live, and she offered him rooms on the top floor of her house in Pelham Crescent, in Kensington, only a few doors away, as it happened, from where Emlyn Williams and his wife lived.

The propinquity worked to Richard's advantage. Daphne Rye was both casting and directing a play called *Castle Anna*. She gave Richard a small role in it, and also had him understudy the lead.

Three years in the RAF had brought neither discipline nor order to Richard's way of life. He enjoyed filling himself with beer in pubs, keenly followed the rugby matches, and kept an eye out for the handy girl. Coupled with this was his fondness for poetry, which he spouted with the slightest amount of encouragement. Many who knew him at the time regarded him as a kind of highbrow peasant. But he was also ruggedly handsome, although pockmarked from his bouts with acne, and had a voice that could cause shivers in audiences. Almost from the moment he joined the cast of *Castle Anna*, his fellow performers regarded him as destined for greatness. He had it all—looks, talent, and, one actress with him at the time remembered, "this tremendous brain."

He managed to raise eyebrows, even in the complaisant atmosphere of the London theatrical world, with his aggressive heterosexuality. "He acquired that reputation very early," said director Peter Glenville. Richard played the lead in *Castle Anna* only once, and in April 1947 was sent out into the provinces in Shaw's *Captain Brassbound's Conversion*. While touring, he was suddenly called by Emlyn Williams to return to London for a screen test.

Williams had a go-ahead from the film mogul Alexander Korda to make a film from an original idea of his, a comedy about a Welsh village doomed to destruction by a villainous real-estate speculator. Williams wanted Richard for one of the important roles—a villager who accidentally kills the realtor and prevents the village from becoming extinct. Richard hurried to London during the night, tested for the role, and was back to his play by evening. A wire from Williams awaited him: "You have won the scholarship." Richard knew what it meant. It was a line from *The Corn Is Green*.

Filming of *The Last Days of Dolwyn* was done during the summer and early autumn months of 1948. Williams was well aware of Richard's profligate habits. The late nights boozing and the girls he picked up here and there without much discrimination belied, Williams thought, a private and sensitive person.

It was a summer afternoon at a film studio outside London, and the cast was lazing around in the sunshine, waiting for the lighting to be ready. "And what did you do last night?" Williams asked Richard.

"Nothing very special," he answered. "Took some floozy to a nightclub."

"Really?" said Williams. "Isn't it time you settled down a bit, took out some nice sensible girl for a change? One of the nice ones in the picture? That one over there, for instance, sitting by the tree." He pointed out a slim young girl sitting nearby on the grass. "She's a really sweet girl—her name is Williams, too—Sybil Williams."

BURTON

"Perhaps I will," Richard said. "I'll introduce myself."

The girl in question was an eighteen-year-old drama and music student. Williams needed five girls who spoke Welsh for minor parts in the film. Many had applied, among them Sybil, and he had included her in the final group, and had then dropped her because though she had been born in Wales, she was not really good in the language. Sybil was badly disappointed. Her music teacher at the drama academy where she studied telephoned Williams and wondered if he couldn't find a way to make use of Sybil.

"I thought to myself," Williams recalled, "it's only eight pounds a week, and Korda can well afford it." So he used six girls instead of the original five.

Her background had certain parallels with Richard's. She too came from a mining family—though her father was a step up in status from his; he was a mine foreman. Richard would invariably make a point of her more "posh" background, though they were born hardly twenty miles apart. She lost her mother as a child, and at fifteen her father died. Attracted early on to the theater, she was in amateur theatricals by the time she was thirteen. When her father died she took a job in a village dress shop, then went to live with an older sister in Northampton. It was only a few months before the meeting with Richard that she had enrolled in the London Academy of Music and Drama. It was a thrill for her to be involved in a film production; it was less the chance to act than to be around the excitement of a story in the making. And it was a thrill to have handsome Richard come over to her and introduce himself.

This one was different, Richard soon realized. She had wit and intelligence, had spirit, could *talk* intelligently, and she was Welsh. He took her out a few times, and they got along well together. From the film location in Wales it was necessary for her to return briefly to London to take a test at her academy. Richard wanted her phone number in London, so he could ring her in the evening to learn the results. She waited until after midnight for a call which never came. This disillusioned her; just another actor using his charm on the girls. But back on the set she melted when he asked her what was wrong with her telephone. He had called and called. Less naive than willing to believe him, she accepted his invitation to the theater, and for the duration of filming they saw each other constantly.

"We were very positive then about what was good or bad about everything," Sybil said. "I was eighteen and Richard was just reaching twenty-three, and we were at that stage where we knew the last word about everything. I thought him very worldly, experienced, and sophisticated, which he certainly was compared to me."

One evening he confided to a friend, "I love Sybil dearly, and she assumes I will marry her. And I suppose I shall." Her qualities reminded him of his sister Cecilia when he had lived with her. Like Cissie, Sybil was a good housekeeper; she was tolerant of Richard's ways, understood him, literally worshiped him. When the filming was over and each would be going a different way, he was struck by how important she had become to him. She filled his need for stability, and gave him a self-sustaining kind of love that all his bachelor conquests couldn't match. He took her to meet his family, and they approved. She wasn't an obviously pretty girl; at nineteen her hair was already turning silver; but she was warm and cheerful, confident of herself, shrewd and capable. The family thought she was perfect for Richard. He called her "Boot," short for "beautiful." "Boot," he told her, "we're getting married."

There were some work commitments first—radio for the BBC, and another film part. She meanwhile found a job as assistant stage manager and understudy in a London production of *Harvey*. The wedding date was the morning of February 5, 1949, at the registry office in Kensington. Present were only a few friends and relatives. Following the ceremony, Daphne Rye gave them a champagne reception in her house. It was Saturday matinee day and Sybil had to leave early to go onstage in her play. When she returned to the party, most had left, and Richard was deep in gloom. But it wasn't over her absence. Wales had played Scotland that day in rugby, and the Welsh team had lost.

After listening to the game on the radio, Richard was drowning his sorrow with the help of a bottle.

Daphne Rye made more room for the new couple in her house, and they settled into their routine, if it could be called that. Richard's brother Graham and sister Cecilia were amazed at Sybil's tolerance of his ways. He had a habit of getting up the moment he awoke, which could be as early as four in the morning, then prowling the kitchen with his cup of tea. He would say he would be home for lunch, then fail to return until late evening. Sybil seldom complained. He was bad at remembering occasions, such as her birthday or Christmas, but made up for it by buying her gifts at odd moments.

Not long after the marriage, *The Last Days of Dolwyn* opened in theaters and was respectfully treated by the critics. Richard was picked out for his "acting fire, manly bearing, and good looks." He was "destined," one reviewer said, "for the pinnacles of fame."

And his career looked to be well on the rise when Daphne Rye sent Richard up for an important part in *Adventure Story*, a play about Alexander the Great by the distinguished playwright Terence Rattigan.

The director was Peter Glenville. "The part he auditioned for was Hephaestion, stalwart friend of Alexander, a good part, a strong and important part," Glenville said. "He auditioned for me alone on the stage and I saw at once that he was a brilliant young actor. I gave him the part immediately."

Richard was overjoyed. Alexander was being played by Paul Scofield, one of England's finest younger actors; the chance to work with him was important in itself, and moreover, all the leading critics would be in attendance. Richard felt it was his biggest step upward yet, and in his mood of euphoria he helped his young friend Stanley Baker get a walk-on part in the play.

Rehearsals began. Glenville held a reading of the play on the stage with the full cast, and suddenly said, "Richard, I'm terribly sorry, you won't do." Richard stared at him in disbelief. He was crushed. It was a moment of what he took to be failure that he never forgot. Rattigan wrote him a letter of regret, but Richard took it only as rejection, pure and simple.

Glenville explained: "I suddenly realized when I saw him standing next to Scofield, who is well over six feet, that Richard was physically wrong. It was as simple as that. Here Scofield was to clasp his shoulder and say something on the order of 'You are my pillar of strength,' all the while towering over him. Hephaestion was supposed to be this strong, steady, idealized figure, and I saw that they would simply not make a couple. It had nothing to do with talent, regardless of what Richard said afterward. In fact, I replaced him with a less talented actor who looked absolutely right for the part."

As for Richard: "I felt suicidal. Everybody had told me this was my big chance. It made me fighting mad and I vowed it would never happen again."

Daphne Rye, to soften the blow, sent him immediately to John Gielgud, who was casting for Christopher Fry's verse play *The Lady's Not for Burning*, with Gielgud as director and star. It was an early-evening audition. Richard was nervous. On the stage with him were Gielgud, Binkie Beaumont, Fry, and the star, Pamela Brown. A pretty eighteen-year-old actress—like him, under contract to Beaumont—was there to read with him. Her name was Claire Bloom, and she was nervous too. It seemed to her that Richard was more at home with the lines than she was, but she noticed his hands were shaking. Gielgud was uncertain, and asked him to come back the following day. This time he got the part, at a salary of fifteen pounds a week, five pounds more than the Tennent organization was already paying him.

Richard thought he ought to have more for a good part in a prestigious play, with as fine a director as Gielgud. "I went to see Binkie Beaumont," he said, when telling one of his favorite stories, "and told him I thought I should have twenty pounds a week. I made my case, and finally Binkie compromised—seventeen pounds, ten shillings.

"I was so flushed with success, I took a taxi [instead of the bus] back to Pelham Crescent. As the taxi drew up, Emlyn Williams emerged from his house and hailed it. He saw me inside, and asked what I was doing. I told him I had been to see Binkie about the money I was going to get. He asked what the role was and said sharply, 'Get back in the taxi and go back and ask for thirty.' I was caught between the two men I was most terrified of. I went back, and Binkie was not so pleasant. Finally he said, 'Very well.' And as I was going out the door he said in a sharp-edged voice, 'I suppose that old Welsh pit pony put you up to this.' "

Like Emlyn Williams, John Gielgud was also struck by Burton's feeling for the theater, and in the very first rehearsal by his immediate understanding of the part. He spoke it beautifully, said Gielgud, and was perfect-looking. And to Claire Bloom he pointed out the difference between her way of working and Richard's. She was studied, he natural and relaxed. "He just was," said Claire. There are those who saw Richard's performance in the play who still speak of a scene in which Richard hardly did overtly more than scrub a floor. He was mostly silent in the scene, only at intervals interjecting a word or two into the action being carried on by Gielgud and Pamela Brown. "Somehow," Emlyn Williams said, "he had this peculiar power, an intensity, an ability to make the audience aware of his presence." Another actor in the play said, "You couldn't take your eyes off him."

The year 1949 turned out to be a very good one for Burton. The play was a huge success and ran on and on. His second film, *Now Barabbas Was a Robber*, came out while he was in the run and won him the praise of the important film critic C. A. Lejeune: "Mr. Burton is an actor whose progress I shall watch with great curiosity. To my mind he has all the qualifications of a leading man that the British film industry so badly needs at this juncture: youth, good looks, a photogenic face, obviously alert intelligence, and a trick of getting the maximum of attention with the minimum of fuss." Philip Burton's drilling had not been in vain.

To Sybil's other sterling qualities was added a caution about money and its uses, shared in common with her husband. Richard was not only working in the play, he was doing a slew of radio work for the BBC, enough for him to acquire an agent to deal on his behalf. Sybil, too, continued to work, mostly bit parts in plays. Their income was enough for them to buy a house in Hampstead, but they prudently rented out the downstairs rooms and lived upstairs.

"We weren't taking chances," Sybil said about that period in their lives. "I performed most of the household tasks, like cooking and cleaning. Richard was trying to do so much." One night, in bed alone, she heard voices in her parlor, Richard's and John Gielgud's. She heard Gielgud loudly say, "My dear boy, this place is a bit of a mess. I see buckets and buckets of dust all around. Doesn't Sybil clean your digs?" Outraged, she stormed into the parlor. But there was no Gielgud, only Richard, who was laughing.

"Gielgud's influence on me was so profound," Richard remarked later in his career, "that I had a devil of a job getting rid of his particular way of speaking. I wanted so to be like him."

If there were similarities in their speech patterns, no one seemed to notice. What was becoming ever more apparent was Richard's greater self-discipline. He still liked to say that the acting profession had chosen him, but now his desire was to be the best at it. "He was already recognizably a star," Claire Bloom remembered from that time working in the play with him, "a fact he didn't question."

During an eleven-week tour of the play before it came to London, a friendship developed between the two. Richard, she said, let her hang around with him and other young actors in the pubs. But while they all drank beer, she drank lemonade, after which they would see her safely on the bus homeward. While on tour in such places as Oxford, Brighton, and Newcastle, she and Richard entertained each other by reading poetry in their rooms. Other than that, their relationship at that time was innocent, she being, she wrote in an autobiography, a girl of ideals so high that no one could hope to satisfy them.

In London, *The Lady's Not for Burning* was a major hit, and so was another Christopher Fry play, *Venus Observed*. Interest in Fry was so strong that John Gielgud decided to revive an old play of his called *The Boy with a Cart* and gave Richard the starring role. This play was in a long single act and dealt with a legend about a boy who hears a mysterious call to build a church, and carts his aged mother over most of England in search of the right place to build. Gielgud, who directed Richard in this, too, said about him that "It was one of the most beautiful performances I have ever seen."

Although it was well reviewed, and Richard was noted for his "tremendous simplicity," the play had more impact on Richard than it did on audiences.

He once described his own reaction to that performance: "At the end of the play I had to explain to the audience—as I build the church all in mime—that I'd been told by God to wheel my mother in a barrow all over England . . . and I'd been wheeling this fragile old lady all over the stage . . . until God told me to stop at this mound (on the stage) and build a church. Finally we stop, and I build the church—I and the audience have to imagine it. As I tell the villagers in the play how it happened, I could feel the absolute stillness of the audience. The atavistic hairs on the back of my neck rose and I thought: what an extraordinary feeling. That was the first time I felt a sense of the power of acting, of being the medium through which

BURTON

the emotions in the words could be felt. That's when I thought: I'll go on with it."

The play lasted only a month, but during the run a visit to the play was made by Anthony Quayle, not only an actor of distinction, but planner of the 1951 Shakespeare season at Stratford, to be held in conjunction with the Festival of Britain, a series of events that would signify Britain's emergence from its postwar economic gloom. Quayle was looking for actors to appear in the Shakespeare historical cycle, and in particular needed a Prince Hal for *Henry IV, Parts One and Two*. The moment he saw Richard, he knew he was the solution, and got his agreement to play the parts, even though this meant that Richard would likely have to give up an extended sojourn in New York. *The Lady's Not for Burning* was scheduled to open there in November, and Richard was to be part of the troupe.

Meanwhile he kept on with his movie work, and signed a contract with Alexander Korda at a stipend of a hundred pounds a week ($400); the money was easily recouped by Korda, who lent him out to other film companies. None of those films he made were of any great distinction, but they kept him before the public and even created some attention for him in British fan magazines. He was tabbed as one of the young British film stars of the future.

But he was already on his way to New York, with Sybil, a pleasant five-day sea voyage during which the liquor flowed and thick un-English steaks sizzled. The American production of *The Lady's Not for Burning* boosted his salary considerably, and the play was a smash hit there, too. The movie studios sniffed him out, but they would have to deal with Korda, who held his contract. And in any case, he had given his word that he would return to England for the Stratford season.

Olivia de Havilland was planning a stage appearance in *Romeo and Juliet*, and Richard was approached to play opposite her. His ground for refusal was that he was not cut out to be a romantic actor. And something else: he had an aversion, he said more than once, to intimacy on a stage. "When I have to kiss a woman on stage—horrors start up." He couldn't even bear to be touched. Thus he had to be very selective about whom he played opposite. Perhaps coincidentally, Claire Bloom was one of those he was not touchy about on stage or screen.

7

Kenneth Tynan, who was then the young drama critic for the London *Observer*, was looking through the papers one morning when he said to his wife: "Richard Burton is doing Prince Hal at Stratford. He was at Oxford for a time when I was there." He and his wife, Elaine Dundy, then a young actress and later a novelist, went up to Stratford for Richard's opening in *Henry IV, Part One*, and witnessed the birth of a major star of the British theater. For if there was a moment when Richard Burton could be said to have achieved stardom, it was the evening of April 3, 1951.

"His playing of Prince Hal," Tynan wrote in his review, "turned interested speculation to awe almost as soon as he started to speak; in the first intermission the local critics stood agape in the lobbies."

"He was not only magnificent," Elaine Dundy remembered, "he was beautiful to look at. I all but swooned." After the performance she and Tynan made their way to his dressing room, "where we were greeted with great hellos and bear hugs all around, and where Burton in his euphoria said, 'One of these days I'll take on Larry,' meaning, of course, Laurence Olivier."

The Tynans saw a good deal of the Burtons while at Stratford, and, said Elaine, "we did perhaps a little too much drinking, but in those days it was almost customary to drink until one got smashed or the others were under the table. We weren't aware of the potential danger in it. So we weren't alarmed by Richard's drinking. It was part of his prowess, his huge gusto."

Tynan in his review went on: "His Prince Hal is never a roaring boy; he sits hunched or sprawled, with dark, unwinking eyes. . . . 'He brings his cathedral on with him,' said one dazed member of the company. If he can sustain and vary this performance through to the end of *Henry V*, we can safely send him along to swell the thin company of living actors who have shown us the mystery and power of which heroes are capable."

The critics were more reserved when he moved on to the mature Henry V, and he was even harder on himself. "I didn't do it," he told the Tynans. "I have no middle range. I can do soft or loud, but no middle range."

Much later on he liked to say that his Henry V was "butchered by the critics." (An overstatement.) "Then a wonderful thing happened. John Gielgud's mother, who'd taken a bit of a shine to me, wrote to say she was coming to see me. We had tea together and then she pulled out of her bag a whole bundle of terrible notices that John had had. I thought: That's it, I'll never read notices again. And I didn't for a long while."

Meanwhile, New York beckoned again. During the summer of what Sybil called "that wonderful year, that great year," he agreed to return to Broadway at the conclusion of the Stratford season in an adaptation of the Jean Anouilh play *Eurydice*, with Dorothy McGuire as his costar. As Orpheus in what would be retitled *Legend of Lovers* he would have his first starring role in America. He was determined to prove that he could indeed be the best; and Anouilh was proving himself to be France's most important and interesting postwar playwright.

There were good times that summer, and Sybil was having the time of her life, too. Her own acting career had advanced very little, no more than playing small parts in the plays given during the season. Her favored companion was young and pretty Rachel Roberts. "Two less ambitious girls would have been hard to find," Sybil told Elaine Dundy. "The way we came on stage—nail polish, wristwatches, hair tucked under our wimples at the last minute—we were simply hopeless." She'd discovered that she loved everything about the theater except performing: "the tea breaks, the backstage gossip, the fun and games." So it was decided between her and Richard that she would cease acting at the end of the season and help handle the details of her husband's rising career. Richard jokingly claimed that it was necessary for him to remove her from competition; she was upstaging him. She said she much more enjoyed being behind the scenes.

They moved in a fancy theatrical crowd now: Michael Redgrave, Hugh Griffith, Anthony Quayle—all performing in the Shakespeare cycle—and with visitors such as the Humphrey Bogarts, who came to see the plays. A friendship quickly sprang up between the two devotees of potent beverages, and when Humphrey and Lauren returned to Los Angeles they sang the praises of the next Olivier, Richard Burton.

In October of "that wonderful year" Richard and Sybil sailed again to New York on a note of triumph; they were to return a few months later on a more sour note. The play, after its tryouts, lasted only two weeks in New York, a clear-cut flop. The producers, attempting to make the play clearer to American audiences, only made it more confusing. The cuts and changes warped the delicate Anouilh material. McGuire was viewed as miscast; Burton came off better.

Early in the new year, in London, Richard took on another French play, *Montserrat*, adapted by the American playwright Lillian Hellman. It was presented at the Lyric, in Hammersmith, the equivalent of a prestigious Off Broadway production. Richard threw himself into the role of an idealistic officer, badgered to reveal the hiding place of the fabled rebel Simón Bolívar, and those audiences that saw it responded with fervor. He had hoped its appeal would be commercial enough for it to be relocated in a West End theater, but *Montserrat* shut down after a month of performances.

After two such trying and disappointing theater experiences there is not much wonder he would listen to the blandishments of Twentieth Century-Fox, now intent on getting him to sign a contract. George Cukor, who was slated to direct *My Cousin Rachel*, from the Daphne du Maurier novel, wanted him for that; Darryl Zanuck, the studio head, had him penciled in for *The Desert Rats*, in which Burton would be a British captain instrumental in stopping Rommel from capturing North Africa.

An arrangement had to be worked out with Korda. Fox would get Richard for three films, the fees split with Korda, who would meanwhile continue paying Richard his annual fee of around fifteen thousand dollars. Sybil remembered Richard totting up the figures of what his total pay would come to—about a hundred and fifty thousand dollars. "He kept thinking of the times he had gone hungry as a boy. He would take that piece of paper out of his pocket and look at it again and again. He just couldn't believe there was that much money in the world and it was coming to him."

Richard would later say that he had no intention of deserting the stage for Hollywood gold and stardom. "All I wanted to do was to live, to pick up a new Jag, and act at the Old Vic." And certainly he was pulled in the two directions; if he had bet on it at the time, it would have been that the Old Vic would eventually win out.

Korda threw a congratulatory party for him the night before he was to leave for Hollywood. The plan was for him to fly there alone, get acclimated, find a place to live, and have Sybil follow in two weeks. Richard celebrated hugely, singing, telling stories, and imbibing all the night through. Sybil and their friends had to virtually pour him on the plane the next day.

He didn't like flying, and this trip was endless—thirteen hours across the Atlantic, another eleven across the country after a stop in New York. When he got off the plane on a sunny early morning at what was called LAX on his baggage tickets, a car was waiting, sent by Charles Feldman, his West Coast representative. With not a word to the driver, unshaven, unpressed, and irritable, he sank into the back seat and allowed himself to be driven to the Beverly Hills Hotel. An invitation awaited him there, for dinner at the home of the writer-producer of *My Cousin Rachel*, Nunnally Johnson. In his room, there was the customary greeting from the hotel manager, a huge basket of fruit, and from the studio, bottles of Scotch and vodka.

A nap, plus some nips from the Scotch bottle, restored his energy and good humor, and he was ready for the evening. He was not fully aware of it yet, but Nunnally Johnson was premium Hollywood quality, a blueblood member of what came to be known as the "A list." A respected writer before he came to Hollywood, he was now one of its most notable writers and producers. Those invited to meet Richard were equally notable. He recognized many famous faces, some quite gorgeous. A few more samples of the liquids being passed around on the trays improved his mood even more.

Pamela and James Mason arrived; they, too, were now high in the Hollywood hierarchy. Richard felt more at home with them here. The party struck him as a trifle dull. The evening needed livening up. He broke into a Welsh song; he recited Dylan Thomas—a name all but unknown to most of the guests; he moved on to Shakespeare, then into some ribald verses. There were those who thought he overdid it, but Pamela Mason said: "Richard was quite noisy, riotous, and full of fun. We all had the impression of an extremely lively and joyous person."

Richard was dinner-jacketed that night, but his more familiar form of dress was a green tweed jacket and unpressed green corduroy pants. There were other parties. Word got out that he was an entertaining guest. David Lewin, a young English journalist, came to Hollywood and was taken by Burton to a party at the home of Charles Feldman.

"It will be worthwhile your going," Burton told him, "because you'll meet everyone worth knowing in Hollywood."

"Oh," said Lewin, "marvelous."

It was a party, he said, where there were indeed famous people. "Cole Porter played the piano, and Judy Garland sang. They turned to Richard and said, 'It's your turn; you do something.' I said to Richard, 'How are you going to top that?' "

"You watch me," Richard said.

"Then," said Lewin, "he proceeded to recite 'To be or not to be' in Welsh. They hadn't the faintest idea of what he was saying, but the expressiveness of the performance knocked them cold. Later I asked him why he had done it. He told me a few could speak Spanish, some knew some French, maybe a word or two of Italian. 'But Welsh . . . in that I can get away with anything.' "

Sybil arrived, and she joined him at the parties. At once, Richard was struck by the beauty of a woman many years older than he was. She sat rather aloof from the other guests.

"I found her absolutely fascinating," he related several times afterward. "I told her some of what I thought were funny stories, and she thought they were funny too. She told me some. To my surprise, they were slightly blue. In fact, I was familiar enough with her to put my hand on her knee. After leaving her, I rejoined Sybil and told her that I'd just met the most fascinating woman. 'Who happens,' Sybil said, 'to be Greta Garbo.' I had never seen her movies." He wrote his sister Cissie in Port Talbot that though she might not believe it, he had put his hand on Greta Garbo's knee. It was a story that entered the ever-expanding book of Burton anecdotes.

James and Pamela Mason met Richard and Sybil at so many parties that they became quite companionable, so much so that after five or six weeks, on an impulse, Pamela suggested the Burtons leave the little apartment they had taken and stay at their large house. Richard and James were, in any case, soon to perform together in *The Desert Rats*, and while they were on location (near Palm Springs) Sybil wouldn't have to be alone.

Hollywood gossip already had it that Richard was tight with money—his manner of dress, for one thing, his way of cadging his lunches at the Fox commissary, of borrowing cars from friends instead of renting or buying his own.

Once on the set filming *My Cousin Rachel* (where Henry Koster had replaced Cukor), Richard went to work with his typical energy. But rumors soon surfaced that sparks were flying between him and the thirty-six-year-old Academy Award-winning star, Olivia de Havilland. It might have been because he had refused to play Romeo to her Juliet. She was quoted as saying: "Burton goes berserk when he is frustrated. He has these violent departures from control. He's a coarse-grained man with a coarse-grained charm and a talent not completely developed, and a coarse-grained behavior which makes him not like anyone else."

About this a friend of Richard's commented: "None of us knew why Olivia hated him, but I always heard that she did. It may have been that Richard made a few sporty remarks to her which she thought were in bad taste."

But Olivia was not always quoted so waspishly. She had nice things to say about him, too. She mentioned his "manliness combined with a little-boy quality."

It was a time when Hollywood was heading for a dizzying downward slide, and not all the golden people were aware of it yet. But studio heads were being chopped; most notably at MGM, where the former czar, L. B. Mayer, was ousted; while at Fox, Darryl F. Zanuck was looking to a new lens system to rescue that company from a large loss statement.

But through the summer and autumn of 1952, Richard and Sybil could only marvel at the lush life enjoyed by the stars. Stewart Granger and his young wife, Jean Simmons, were at the peak of their careers and lived accordingly. On Sundays the stellar members of the British colony often gathered at their spectacular house in Bel Air, with its enormous swimming pool.

"It looked," Richard wrote in a 1965 article for *Vogue*, "as if it had been flung by a giant hand against the side of a hill and stuck." Deborah Kerr was there with her former flying-ace husband; the Masons came; so did the Michael Wildings, who lived in an equally imposing house nearby.

"It was my first visit to a swank house," Richard went on. "There were quite a lot of people in and around the pool, all drinking the Sunday-morning liveners—Bloody Marys, highballs, iced beer. The people were all friendly and they called me Dick immediately. I asked if they would please call me Richard. Dick, I said, made me feel like a symbol of some kind. They laughed, some of them. It was, of course, Sunday morning, and I was nervous."

It was then, in his account, that a girl sitting on the other side of the pool lowered her book, took off her sunglasses, and looked at him. He smiled at her; after a moment she gave him a chilly smile back. The extraordinarily beautiful (his words) Mrs. Michael Wilding—Elizabeth Taylor—was pregnant and considering deserting her film career for one of motherhood. She, too, recorded the moment when she and Richard Burton first became aware of each other. "My first impression was that he was rather full of himself. I seem to remember that he never stopped talking, and I had given him the cold fish eye."

Richard left us a record of the conversation. "I worked my way over to her. She was describing—in words not normally written—what she thought of a producer at MGM. I was profoundly shocked. It was ripe stuff."

Brashly, in his best Oxford-acquired accent, Richard remarked: "You have a remarkable command of Olde English."

To which the violet-eyed beauty replied, "Don't you use words like that at Stratford?"

BURTON

The Bel Air repartee degenerated even further after that, and when he mentioned the meeting to a friend later, he observed sourly, "She probably shaves."

He soon learned to tolerate the free-spoken ways of some of the stars. Humphrey Bogart became a good friend, and the two matched each other drink for drink. They were at a party for a foreign diplomat who spoke English very well. Bogart complimented him, and the diplomat explained that he had had an English governess.

"Oh," Bogart said, "did you fuck her?"

Burton quickly chimed in with, "Unless you did you can't possibly lay claim to being a member of the ruling class."

At another party they noticed a lawyer who had a reputation as Hollywood's leading lady's man. He was working his charms on the beauties present by dancing with them and in Richard's words, "chatting them up." Bogart said, "Let's just stare at him, the two of us." From that moment on they never took their eyes off the poor fellow, who finally became so flustered he stopped his attentions to the women and sat alone in a corner with a drink for comfort.

The two would occasionally get into quarrels—more mock than real—about acting. Bogart would later claim that English actors were merely elocutionists; Burton told him that actors like himself were behaviorists—all they did was play themselves. "Hang on a minute," Bogart said. He went into the next room and came back with an Oscar, which he placed on a table in front of Burton. "Argue with that, kid," he said.

Emlyn Williams arrived in Los Angeles with his Dickens program, and the Burtons made sure he met all their new friends of the film colony. They took him along to a party Lauren Bacall gave while her husband was off on location for a film. Richard imbibed to the point of immobility, and since it seemed impossible to move him, they placed him on a couch to sleep it off. Williams, not exactly a stranger to the situation, took Sybil home. When Richard awoke the next morning, he found one of Hollywood's more notorious gossips staring at him.

By this time, no matter the innocent circumstance of his morning presence in the Bogart household, word about his off-screen behavior was spreading in veiled references in the gossip columns, and also by word of mouth. Details are scanty on how much was true and how much wasn't. Nevertheless, according to Pamela Mason, "Certainly all Hollywood was observing his behavior. People made wisecracks like 'for this guy, the women bring their own mattresses.' Sybil may have decided boys will be boys, and what is the point of making a fuss? If that is the kind of man you are married to, you have to make the best of it."

One of the most often asked questions, in fact, among those who knew Richard and his proclivities, was: "How much did Sybil know about it?"

"I'm sure," Pamela Mason told Ruth Waterbury, a Hollywood columnist and fan-magazine editor, "Burton was not trying to hide his behavior. He is a philanderer, first of all because he is an actor [!]. He wants to be the center of attention. He wants to be a personal hit."

Waterbury claimed Richard had reverted to "the beau-about-town" he had been prior to his meeting Sybil. Nor was he always the aggressor. One prevalent piece of gossip had it that a star at the Fox studio came to his dressing room one day wearing only a coat, which she dropped the moment his door closed behind her. What is a red-blooded, eager-to-please man to do?

And according to Pamela Mason, Richard referred to many women in Hollywood as "sitting ducks."

A reporter for the *Saturday Evening Post*, in an article about Burton, told of Sybil's formula for dealing with "his little escapades: The first week she tells him, 'She's a nice girl. Don't do anything to hurt her.' The second week, 'Richard, don't do anything to hurt us.' "

And Richard told more than one friend: "I'll never divorce Sybil, and she will never divorce me, because she loves me, she understands me, and thinks I am a genius." There are those who assume that geniuses can be forgiven for what ordinary persons can't.

In later life, Richard revealed to a writer his own formula for seduction: "You have to be very careful in approaching a woman in a clichéd way. The response varies according to the woman. Usually I think clichéd words are probably best to use with any woman, unless she is excessively intelligent or brusque or slightly lesbian. So the first thing you do with most women is to say how beautiful they are. Nine times out of ten it works. 'Did anyone ever tell you you were a lovely girl?' 'Did anybody ever tell you your eyes were di-

BURTON

vine?' You can recognize attraction in a woman's eyes because a woman's pupils dilate when she is attracted to a man—so that you can be fairly sure in advance whether you are going to be rebuffed or not." A simple enough formula—the only known simpler one being that of a young actor at another studio who was reputed to have gone to bed with almost all of its contract female stars. "How do you do it?" he was asked. "I just ask them," he replied.

But intimates of Burton's say he was not as ruttish as legend made him out to be. And Burton, too, said, "I was never the kind of chap who went to a party or dance, picked up a girl, took her home, made love to her in the back of his car or in his apartment, then rolled over and went to sleep, or took the woman home." No, rather: ". . . you must first love, or *think* you love the woman. When you are with the *only* woman—the only one you *think* there is for that moment—you must love her and know her body as if you were blind and your hands were reading braille. You must learn her body as you would think a great musician would orchestrate a divine theme. You must use everything you possess—your hands, your fingers, your speech; seductively, poetically, sometimes brutally, but always with a demoniacal passion." This, remember, was before *The Joy of Sex*.

Stewart Granger went off to England to make a film and Jean Simmons, alone in the big house on the side of a Bel Air hill, asked the Burtons to share the place. Richard was impressed by the sweeping view that took in Los Angeles all the way to the ocean. He was even more fascinated by the gadgets in the ultramodern kitchen. For two hours the first night he was there he experimented with the dishwasher and peeled vegetables so he could flush them down the disposal unit.

But Hollywood, with all its luxuries and sunny skies, didn't distract him from his intention of doing *Hamlet* at the Old Vic the following year. He was still on that course: to assume his place as one of the best actors of his time. That was the reason, as Pamela Mason said, Richard and Sybil lived in their gypsy manner.

However, Hollywood had a challenge for him too. Fox was readying its revolutionary CinemaScope system as a challenge to another system, Cinerama, that had been introduced the year before. Both widened and changed the aspect of the screen. But Cinerama, with its interlocked three projectors, was cumbersome when compared to CinemaScope, which needed only one projector, with less alteration in the projection booth. The first CinemaScope picture would be *The Robe*, from an old warhorse of a novel by Lloyd C. Douglas.

First Tyrone Power had been scheduled for the main role of Marcellus, a Roman tribune who, after participating in the crucifixion of Christ, converts and is himself martyred. Laurence Olivier was next in line, but said no thanks. Richard went after the role, declaring himself to be "the poor man's Olivier," and Zanuck decided to anoint him with it while Richard was turning in a workmanlike performance in *The Desert Rats* in the vicinity of the sandlands of Palm Springs.

The publicity drums began banging for him. Jean Simmons and Victor Mature were cast as his costars. And with *My Cousin Rachel* now in release (Richard was reviewed pleasantly), Fox went after an Academy Award for him in the best-supporting-actor category, the competition in that one being less. Eventually he failed to win, but the publicity was helpful to him.

In promoting his own cause he spoke to interviewers of "the terrible, awesome responsibility" he felt in portraying Marcellus, a character of such overwhelming spiritual significance. He had all the sincerity of a snake-oil salesman. In a remarkable tribute to the hacks who had labored to shape a screenplay from the cliché-ridden novel, he told a reporter that "playing Marcellus is like playing Hamlet." It is not known if he threw up afterward. Privately he called it "a prissy role." What he told interviewers often depended on how far in his cups he was. "I'm the kind of ham who wants to rush into every scene and chew the scenery," he said once, but denied it when it was quoted back to him. He also denied his statement that "half the satisfaction of being an actor is getting away from your own disgusting self," blaming it on a publicity man's invention. Publicity men are not known to invent such things. He did seem to be giving the appearance of a man in something of a muddle, beguiled by the power, money, and glitter of Hollywood stardom, and at the same time attempting to maintain his self-image of a poor boy from Wales who had made his way through hard work and integrity. For the most part, though, he managed to keep his sense of humor, and

BURTON

sometimes at his own expense. When a columnist accused him of having gotten a swelled head, he measured its circumference and declared the man absolutely right; his head had expanded an eighth of an inch since he'd left Wales.

While *The Robe* was in production, it was claimed that the most meticulous care possible was being taken to make certain that all sets, props, and costumes were "authentic." This extended to the metal lamps being filled with real olive oil. "Imported or domestic?" Richard asked. When told that the oil was home-grown, he said, "Not really authentic, is it?"

Nor could he always maintain a mood of solemnity while acting. In one scene, he and Mature, who was supposed to be mortally wounded, were in a chariot together, with Mature's head cradled in Richard's arms. The director wanted Mature to indicate that he was still alive by moving his head; to get his face full into the frame, he attempted to raise his head. Sensing a bit of ham, Burton pushed the head down. A mighty struggle ensued and Mature eventually lost the battle. But a few days later he got revenge. He was supposed to massage Burton's back with oil. He substituted ice water.

Mature advised Burton to play along with the studio's publicity efforts. Sooner or later the studios tended to believe their own publicity, which could result in contract bonuses. This proved to be the case for Richard. Zanuck went ahead and negotiated with Korda for the release of Richard's contract with him, then offered Richard a ten-year, ten-picture arrangement which would bring him a million dollars. His agents having negotiated the contract for him, Zanuck was surprised when Richard calmly turned the offer down, saying he would be heading home for *Hamlet*. A suit was threatened, but was resolved when Richard agreed to a less binding contract.

Meanwhile, rumors mounted about a romance between Richard and his costar Jean Simmons, even before the film went before the cameras. If this was the case, it was a clear-cut case of Richard biting the hand that fed him, for he and Sybil were still staying at the Granger house. A New Year's Eve party was given by the Charles Lederers, attended by Sybil, Jean, and Richard. When the chimes of midnight came, Richard and Jean were locked in each other's arms dancing. Most wives and husbands left whomever they were with to join and kiss their mates. But not Richard and Jean. They paused long enough to exchange a fervent kiss, then continued dancing. They were interrupted by Sybil, who, having been left alone with no one to kiss, ran across the room and landed a stinging slap on Richard's face. She then left the party and flounced off.

After the talk about the incident percolated through Bel Air and Beverly Hills, Richard and Sybil left the Grangers' house for a small one they rented from the James Masons, who had acquired some residential properties. It was in the hills off one of the canyons and was hardly more than an apartment with a garden. Sybil cooked and cleaned, and Emlyn Williams, who was a houseguest at the time, remembered seeing little of Richard but his clothes, an enormous pile of which, muddied with makeup, was left in the bathroom every day for Sybil to wash.

It was noticed during the making of *The Robe* that Stewart Granger was driving his wife to the studio each day. However, the marriage was doomed, and gossip had it, of course, that Burton was somewhat responsible. Richard had his own lofty way of countering that and other similar stories. "I was honored by one article accusing me of breaking up nine happy homes. I haven't even met one-third of the couples concerned. Do you know what Sybil did with that article? She papered the smallest room with it."

Nevertheless, as the old joke has it . . . And if Richard was adept at slipping into affairs, he was equally adept at slipping out of them, something of a talent in itself.

When he finished his work in *The Robe*, the studio had him slated for another film, *The Prince of Players*, to be made when he returned from his stints on the English stage. Richard allowed it to be known that he was walking out on a million-dollar contract for a stipend of a hundred and fifty dollars a week at the Old Vic. It was a grander gesture even than it looked on the surface. Was he ready for the challenge of *Hamlet*? He would be following in the august footsteps of Gielgud, Olivier, and others.

In June 1953, he was at one of his last parties before leaving for England. Olivia de Havilland was there. "He was sitting on the floor quite frightened and tormented," she said. "He told me how anxious he was, how agonized with the fear of failure."

BURTON

Humphrey Bogart didn't make it any easier for him by saying, "I never knew a man who played *Hamlet* who didn't die broke." Richard's laughter was hollow; Bogart had touched a nerve. Nevertheless, he returned to London something of a conqueror. A full-fledged movie star, he was yet ready to give his all to the hallowed English stage.

Richard and Sybil came back to his Welsh valley that June of 1953, a greener valley now that some of the mine pits were being closed down. Only one of his brothers, Tom, still worked in the mines. His oldest brother, Ifor, was a bricklayer, Verdun a machinist, David a police sergeant, and his younger brother, Graham, had become a financial clerk for the town council.

His sister Cecilia prettied up a bedroom for them in the house he had grown up in at 73 Caradoc Street, in Taibach. They visited his father, now seventy-seven and still a patron of every pub in the vicinity. Daddy Ni had seen *My Cousin Rachel* and had not liked the fervent love scenes between his son and Olivia de Havilland; he couldn't understand how Sybil could have allowed such goings-on. It was hard for him to grasp just where this Hollywood was, and even harder for him to understand why the place paid Richard the outlandish sums of money he talked about.

Richard said, "I think my father believed Hollywood was a small place on the other side of the Welsh mountains. He just greeted me with, 'Well, Rich, how are you getting on?' as though I'd been down to Swansea for the weekend."

To the others in his family, and friends, he told tales about a city where no one walked, where you never saw poor people—an unreal place, and not a place to stay in very long. He was in Hollywood pictures for the fame it could bring, and yes, the money, for there was a lot of money to be made there. Other than that, he didn't take movies very seriously, so he said.

He didn't stay long in Port Talbot, just long enough to see and meet with all the relatives and down a good many pints of beer with friends at a string of pubs. After two days they returned to London. The visit evoked waves of nostalgia in him, but he had outgrown Port Talbot, Taibach, and Pontrhydyfen, and there was no going home again, not then.

He rehearsed his *Hamlet* with the Old Vic company in July, and had a reunion with Claire Bloom, who was to be Ophelia. Philip Burton hovered helpfully about. The play was done first at the Edinburgh Festival in August, and then came to London. Richard had committed himself to the Old Vic for thirty-nine weeks, a rigorous schedule that involved some touring in the English provinces, performances of *Hamlet* at Kronborg Castle in Elsinore, Denmark, and then in Zurich. He took on a role in *King John*, played Caliban in *The Tempest*, and struck his highest and most triumphant note in *Coriolanus*, his rich voice supremely well suited to the heroic quality of the speeches.

When the press came to see him, he complained loudly about the pittance remaining after British taxes had whittled away his Hollywood earnings. By his own account, his first three films there had earned him more than $225,000. After taxes, he said, he had been able to keep only about $17,000. True enough, British taxes were easy on the poor at that time and hard on those of high earning power, but if he had so little left, his main need was a better accountant. His hunger for money and the security it would bring kept him working overtime in radio for the BBC.

It was his presence at the Old Vic that made the Shakespeare season a commercial success. Young people were predominant in the *Hamlet* audiences. They liked the aggressive way he played the role, although some wondered if the style was appropriate for so indecisive a character. Of elders in the audience, one was no less a personage than Winston Churchill. Richard became aware of his presence in the stalls when he heard someone muttering his lines along with him. During the intermission, Churchill came to Richard's dressing room. "My Lord Hamlet," he said, "may I use your lavatory?"

Richard was now one of the elite and the elect; and he and Sybil moved in select company: the Alec Guinnesses, the Oliviers, John Gielgud—the latter not too happy with his Hamlet. While waiting to go out to dinner with him after a performance one evening— Richard was expansively greeting friends and well-wishers in his dressing room—Gielgud asked: "Shall I go ahead and wait until you're better? . . . ah, I mean ready?" Richard was well aware of the hint, and tried putting a touch of the Gielgud interpretation into his own. But there were those at high and remote levels who were aware of the young man's rise to prominence. He and Sybil were invited to attend the annual garden party at Buckingham Palace. They, and seven thousand others.

At the high levels at Twentieth Century-Fox, Burton was undergoing reevaluation, even though *The Robe* was a smash. What was being noticed about Richard was a lackluster quality on the screen. His acting ability was not faulted. It was something else, and Darryl Zanuck may have put his finger on it when he said, "I put him among the three finest actors in the world, but this doesn't automatically make him a star. He has acted his parts so far, but as for his personality, he hasn't had the opportunity to show it yet." On the other hand, Zanuck had high praise for Jean Simmons. Burton, he said, would creep up on audiences slowly.

Richard had a commitment with Fox for three films, but it was well over a year before he was in Hollywood again as Edwin Booth in *The Prince of Players*, from a novel about the actor brother of the infamous John Wilkes Booth. The film was regarded as an ideal vehicle for Richard, calling as it did for an actor who would lead a company in scenes from Shakespeare. Back in California in the late summer of 1954, Richard was lively on the set and seductive in his dressing room. Those who took note of the female traffic in and out said it was even heavier than before.

Sybil arrived, and Richard found a place for them—nothing fancy, just a small two-bedroom house they sublet from Roland Petit and Jeanmaire, who were off on a tour. Their party-going resumed and Richard was as entertaining as ever, now with a new stack of stories based on his Old Vic experiences. On Sundays there were lots of swimming pools available for lounging, drinking, and conversing.

Philip Dunne, the director and producer of *The Prince of Players*, had taken notice of Richard as far back as 1949 when he had seen him in *The Lady's Not for Burning* in London. "He played his smallish part," Dunne said, "with an intensity, a smoldering fire, and a sense of the poetry in Fry's play." When he returned to New York, he sent word to Darryl Zanuck about the talented young actor he had seen, but Zanuck told him the studio was already interested in him. Now given the opportunity to direct his first film, Dunne asked for Richard. He would have liked Paul Scofield for the role of John Wilkes Booth, but had to settle instead for young John Derek. There was a scene with Richard and Derek, at the end of which Richard raised his eyes heavenward, as if to say: "What more can I do?"

Another scene had Edwin Booth carousing in a New Orleans house of pleasure, as such places were known in the restrictive days of the Production Code. He is to play Romeo, and his determined Juliet (Maggie McNamara) is searching for him. When she finds him, he is on a drunken spree.

"Before I do this, how would it be if I had a couple of belts?" Richard asked Dunne.

"What a marvelous idea," Dunne agreed, knowing Richard's fabled capacity. So, at ten in the morning, they left the set, went to a nearby bar, and Dunne treated Richard to two stiff drinks of Scotch, which Richard tossed down as if it were his morning orange juice. When he returned to play the scene, it was with a perfect touch of unsteadiness, just what Dunne wanted.

So taken was director Philip Dunne with Richard's performing in *The Prince of Players* that he began to have visions of a great success and numerous Academy Awards. But in a projection room, viewing rushes, he began having dark second thoughts. What Zanuck had noticed, now Dunne saw. "The fire and the intensity were there, but that was all. He hadn't mastered yet the tricks of the great movie stars, such as Gary Cooper, who knew them all. The personal magnetism Richard had on the sound stage didn't come through the camera." It was to be a complaint that would dog Richard for several years. In this case, *The Prince of Players* became the first CinemaScope flop.

In Hollywood, a studio could build a star through publicity and suitable vehicles, but at a certain point the would-be star had to learn the intricacies of his trade. Lighting could enhance or destroy. It was wise to have friends among the assistant directors and the soundmen, to entrust oneself to the director for guidance through the intricacies of a shooting schedule. Richard, one of the finest actors ever to come to Hollywood, had not yet learned enough about starring.

Toward the tail end of 1954 Richard and Sybil were back in London, where he met with Robert Rossen, the writer, producer, and director of *Alexander the Great*. This film, of epic proportions, looked right to Richard. He respected Rossen, an Academy Award winner for his *All the King's Men*, and Rossen assured him that he had been researching the subject for years to guarantee historical accuracy. It would be a literate spectacle, with human motivations behind the sweep of historical events. Richard believed it; he wanted to believe it—and it would be made away from Hollywood, in Spain, where the six-million-dollar budget would look like at least twice that.

With nothing in mind for him at that moment, Fox loaned him to United Artists, with a fee for Richard of $100,000 plus a percentage of the profits—the latter something new in the business to intrigue stars from their studio moorings.

Richard still had his phobia about flying, so in February he and Sybil sailed for Lisbon. There they hired a car and drove across Portugal and into Spain, stopping at small inns and hotels, and celebrating their sixth wedding anniversary along the way. Evenings were spent quietly; Richard was now in the habit of bringing a bagful of books with him when he traveled; he consumed them often at the rate of one a day. After a time, the bag of books became a trunkful.

In Madrid they put up at the luxurious Castellana Hilton hotel—a fine older hotel taken over by the Hilton chain and run with the best and latest of amenities. It was also taken over more and more by American film people who were attracted to Spain by the favorable exchange rate, the studio facilities, and the Spanish Army, which could be rented from Generalissimo Franco.

In the cast as Richard's mother was Danielle Darrieux, who complained prettily to reporters that she hardly looked older than her supposed son. Claire Bloom arrived at the hotel and had a reunion with Richard that was warm enough to draw a comment from a reporter that "He was enthusiastic about his leading lady and she about him." Discretion prevailed, however, though it was noted that Sybil went back to London for a time.

Richard got along well with Rossen, too. The Spaniards were delighted to have their American and British guests, and gave parties. Richard attended the bullfights and was presented with bulls' ears. He even got a tail. Sybil was entrusted with having it sent to London for mounting.

When he finished *Alexander*, his hopes high for a favorable reception of this "intelligent epic," he went back to Hollywood for another Fox film, *The Rains of Ranchipur*. The studio had resurrected the story from a film it had made in 1939 under the title of *The Rains Came*, from a Louis Bromfield best-seller about a Hindu doctor with high ideals, and an adulterous married woman in need of spiritual enlightenment. Richard would play the good Dr. Safti, Lana Turner the spoiled married Anglo-Saxon lady. Turner had passed her peak of stardom at MGM and was suffering the indignity of being loaned out to another studio; she was also suffering a back problem caused by a fall in a bathtub. She was not in the best of humors. The studio was counting less on the star appeal of Turner and Burton than on the CinemaScopic special effects that included torrential downpours, an earthquake, and a collapsing dam. Jean Negulesco was the director, a charming man with a fine sense of humor. A visitor, watching a scene being played stiffly, asked him if he thought the picture would turn out well. "This," said Negulesco with a straight face, "will be a *wonderful* picture."

Richard was given a special imported turban expert for the headpieces he wore; another expert tried to give him a Hindi accent. Best of all was the presence of several dusky little ladies in supernumerary roles. He thought they were delightful, and he entertained them in his dressing room so often he was hardly ever seen on the set except for his necessary scenes.

His attitude toward the script was understandably lofty. Lana Turner remained impervious to his charm, and neither could get any real feeling into their love scenes. There was joking about his favorable image of himself, and it was suggested that wardrobe ought to make him larger turbans. Negulesco tried to coax a more realistic performance from him. "You're supposed to be an East Indian," he said. "You're not sounding like one."

BURTON

"I am *not* an Indian," Richard replied.

"For someone who didn't like playing an Indian," Lana Turner remarked, "he did seem to enjoy playing *with* them."

A producer said about Richard that "He is probably the most notable seducer of our times. He is sexually inexhaustible, and apparently gives a satisfactory performance anytime, anywhere, and under any conditions." He didn't seem to make passes. "He's just there and the ladies are there. He has a kind of availability and the girls come running. And when he rejects them, they all go away." They respected him too much, he said, to bother him with hurt feelings.

Raymond Massey was in one of Richard's films and was asked if Richard had missed anyone. "Yes," he said, "Marie Dressler."

"But she's dead."

"I know," Massey said.

Yet, Richard had energies left over. When his brother Ifor and Ifor's wife visited him, he stayed with them in a small Santa Monica hotel. While there, he discovered surfing, and was so active at it that Negulesco asked him to hold off until the picture was finished.

Richard couldn't wait for his chore on the picture to end. "It was beyond human belief," he said of it, and coined the phrase "It never rains but it Ranchipurs."

He was due back in London for another try at *Henry V* at the Old Vic. But he had to hang around Hollywood in case he had to redub any of his lines. He went to just about every party being held in the town, winding up at the Humphrey Bogarts' house in Holmby Hills. The phone rang at three in the morning. The producer was trying to locate him to tell him he was free to leave. Sybil had already left for New York with the Jenkinses. Richard stayed up the rest of the night and caught the first flight for New York. When he arrived twelve hours later, he stayed up the following night, too, celebrating the return to England.

This time around, his Henry V won the plaudits of most of London's critics. Tynan made it official that Richard was now "the natural successor to Olivier." In time, he said, he would be regarded as the greatest living classical actor. At the present stage of his career, wrote Tynan, "The open expression of emotion is clearly alien to him. He is a pure antiromantic, ingrowing rather than outgoing.

BURTON

Within this actor there is always something reserved, a rooted solitude which his Welsh blood tinges with mystery. Inside these limits, he is a master."

In January 1956 the London *Evening Standard* gave Richard its award for his Henry V as the best stage performance of the year. A month later, Richard took on the strenuous challenge of alternating Othello and Iago.

The Rains of Ranchipur and *Alexander the Great* were released in quick succession, and neither did Richard any good. *Time*, while deriding the first, failed to notice that Richard was in the film. *Alexander* was a bigger flop, because it was more expensive. The speeches Rossen had given Richard came out hollow and pompous. The pace was agonizingly slow, the battle scenes stodgy. So much for fidelity to historical truth. Audiences fell asleep.

Why would Richard, after these, continue to make films when he was now clearly one of the great English stage actors? He and Sybil were reasonably well off. A notable stage career lay ahead if he wanted it. And yet, as soon as the chance came to do another film, he leapt at it. This one, *Sea Wife*, was offered to him by Fox. To do it, he cut short his stay at the Old Vic.

In terms of financial independence he still felt insecure. And he was angered by the British taxes he paid. He spoke of it often—the large amounts he got, and the small amounts left over. While in New York, back in 1949, he had met a lawyer-accountant, Aaron Frosch, who at the time worked with a famed theatrical lawyer, Arnold Weissberger. They handled several British clients. When Frosch went out on his own, Richard had him handle his tax problems. Frosch suggested Swiss residency. Other American and British film stars were taking advantage of favorable Swiss tax treatment. Richard made the decision to become a Swiss resident. A few more films and he could be free of money worries for the rest of his life. With Sybil he set sail for the *Sea Wife* location, Jamaica.

The new project looked to have possibilities. The great Italian Roberto Rossellini would be directing *Sea Wife*, about a nun and three men marooned on an island after their ship was torpedoed by a German sub. Richard's role was that of an RAF officer; young and pretty and wild Joan Collins would play the nun. The British had fun with that. She was being called "Britain's bad girl" at that time, and when she was cast as a nun, a newspaper headlined her as "Sister Sizzle." The studio didn't like the connotation. Rossellini was told that there was to be no kissing between Richard and Collins. Sure, sure, said Roberto, and assured Zanuck that the script would contain no unchaste scenes. But the lack of love scenes seemed unnatural to Rossellini, and he and Zanuck got into arguments. Zanuck won. The first day of shooting, Rossellini was gone, and another director was in his place.

This didn't bother Richard, as Joan Collins wrote in her aptly titled memoir, *Past Imperfect*. "He had a take-the-money-and-run attitude toward it, which I found depressing." And the money, this time, was earmarked to be squirreled away in Switzerland.

She described him as "about thirty-three years old [he was thirty] with thick, light-brown hair, intense, strong features and eyes of a piercingly hypnotic greenish-blue. . . . His back and shoulders were deeply pitted and rutted with pimples, blackheads, and what looked like small craters." She assumed these blemishes had come from years spent working in coal mines.

More accurately, she divined that he had "intentions" toward her. During a lunch break on an offshore diving raft he made the first pitch, which was well in line with his standard technique. Touching her neck as they both absorbed sun on the raft, he said, "Did anyone ever tell you you look pretty with short hair?"

"Yes," she said, firmly moving the hand that was beginning to roam. She went on to mention her very rich boyfriend, Arthur Loew, who was *extremely* jealous. This did not deter Richard. "My dear," she reported him saying, "what the eye does not see the heart does not grieve for," upon which he bestowed a salty kiss on her lips. She quickly informed him she wasn't in the mood for an involvement with "a married Don Juan," and he gracefully retired, implying that she, too, would fall, like so many others. In fact, he listed for her his many conquests of "all the actresses he had worked with on stage and screen."

"They always succumbed to you finally?" Collins asked.

"Always, even if they were not receptive at the outset."

She was not, but she noticed that others were. "Some were reasonably attractive, and others, to put it bluntly, were dogs!" She witnessed a middle-aged toothless Jamaican maid leaving his quarters early one morning. "Richard," Collins said later in the day, "I do believe you would screw a snake if you had the chance."

"Only if it was wearing a skirt, darling," he replied. "It would have to be a female snake."

After eight weeks of location shooting, crew and cast returned to England to finish the film at the Elstree studios. And after a visit to his relatives in Port Talbot and Pontrhydyfen, Richard was next heard from in Switzerland.

It was not only himself and Sybil and eventually their progeny Richard was thinking of when he made the move. He wanted to improve the lot of his brothers and sisters, all of them now with families of their own. One by one he bought for them the houses they lived in, including his father's in Pontrhydyfen; he financed them into new trades and professions, and settled semiyearly incomes on them. There was a streak of quixotic generosity in his nature, as when a professor came to him asking for a donation to help reopen the Oxford Playhouse. Richard quickly made out a check to him for two thousand pounds—well over five thousand dollars.

He could boast to a reporter who came to see him in Switzerland that he now had well over a quarter of a million dollars set aside and well invested, which would see him through any financial shoals for a long time to come—and his tax rate was now a minuscule few thousand dollars a year.

The villa he purchased in the small village of Céligny, twenty minutes or so from Geneva, was more comfortable than large or ornate; it was close to the train station—more a stop than a station— and the house was set back a good fifty yards from the road that led to Lake Geneva, a half-mile away. The village probably had no more than five hundred residents; white peaks could be seen in the distance; the air was bracing.

Sybil, he said, loved Switzerland—the quiet, the food, the people. Here he could store the books he collected. Later he would build a small chalet as an addition to the property. A high chain fence would go up around the property.

From Switzerland, leaving Sybil—now pregnant—behind, he journeyed to North Africa for another inconsequential film, *Bitter Victory*. Again he seemed to be guided more by the director than the

BURTON

material—Nicholas Ray this time; he had made *Rebel Without a Cause*. The lead role in David Lean's *Lawrence of Arabia* had been dangled before him, although a first choice was Marlon Brando, who had refused it. As it turned out, the part went to Peter O'Toole, who ran with it into fame and stardom. More wisely, Richard turned down the role of the Earl of Warwick in Otto Preminger's production of *Saint Joan*. Preminger had assumed that Richard had agreed to play it and complained bitterly that he had not told him about deciding otherwise. Richard's reply was that he had indeed sent word of his decision, but he admitted that Preminger's choice of the neophyte Jean Seberg to play Shaw's martyred heroine had worried him. It turned out that he was right.

Sitting in Switzerland after finishing *Bitter Victory*, Richard looked back on a film career that appeared to be over. There were no offers; there was no stage work because of his necessary tax-induced exile from England. In any case, the British hadn't taken kindly to his leaving, especially after he remarked to a reporter that he wasn't against the high taxes in England. "I believe," he said, "that everyone should pay them—except actors." It was a sour joke, and it didn't go down well with the public.

In May 1957 his father died at the age of eighty-one. Neither Richard nor his brother Ifor, who was staying with him in Céligny, attended the funeral. "My father would be shocked," Richard explained, "if he knew I had traveled seven hundred miles to go to his funeral." Richard would more and more reveal an aversion to sad occasions, to unpleasantnesses in general. Drinking can of course help to drown sorrow, at least temporarily. He and Ifor toasted old Daddy Ni on his way to his beery heaven.

Milton Sperling, an independent American film producer, made his way to Céligny to see Richard. It was a role in a stage play, however, he wanted him for. He had already gotten Helen Hayes for Jean Anouilh's *Time Remembered*, and he needed an actor of high caliber to play with her. Sperling was wise enough to know that Burton's film career was in the doldrums, and his timing proved to be right. Richard was ready and willing. He agreed to fly to New York in mid-September for a Broadway opening in November. The day before his leaving, Sybil providentially gave birth to a daughter, who was named Katherine and immediately called Kate in Shakespeare's honor.

Sybil was not due to follow him for eight weeks, and Richard at once made up for lost party time. There was a large British contingent on Broadway at the time—Noël Coward, Peter Ustinov, Laurence Olivier, and Laurence Harvey among them. Philip Burton was there too, now living in New York, and eventually to become the director of the American Academy of Dramatic Arts. It was like old-home week for Richard. And for his favorite form of amusement besides drinking he had a new little playmate, nineteen-year-old Susan Strasberg, the ingenue of *Time Remembered*.

Susan, pretty and diminutive, was the daughter of Lee and Paula Strasberg, brought up among theater people, with all their vagaries. (When she was thirteen, at dinner while her parents entertained some Broadwayites, she wondered, after hearing the conversation, "Who will my husbands be?") She already had star quality from her playing of Anne in *The Diary of Anne Frank*. She was fresh and perky and perhaps more callow than she realized. At rehearsals, at first, she was a touch fearful of Richard because of his lady-killer reputation, but admiring him at the same time. In her memoir, *Bittersweet*, she recounted her growing passion for him. He called everyone "luv," but she thought there was more meaning in it when he called her that. Soon he took to swinging her in the air at rehearsals and calling her "my beautiful little Jewish princess."

From rehearsals in New York, the play moved on to Washington, Boston, and New Haven for its tryouts. In the frothily romantic play, Richard was a prince moping over a lost love, Helen Hayes his worried aunt, and Strasberg a little milliner and lookalike for his dead sweetheart. By the end of the play the milliner (hired for the task) has weaned the prince from his grief and won him for herself.

Perhaps Strasberg had visions of something similar happening in real life; moving from city to city, the relationship became more intense and also difficult, because, as she confessed in her memoir, she hadn t brought her diaphragm along. For Richard, without knowing the cause of her carnal hesitance, it was "let us not to the course of true love admit this impediment." He became, wrote

Strasberg, all the more persistent, in spite of the fact that mother Paula was hovering about constantly, keeping an eye on both her daughter and her performance, and sharing the hotel suite with her. Susan, once her mother was asleep, would steal into Richard's room, bringing her alarm clock with her to make sure to be back in her own room by dawn.

Upon reaching New York, the diaphragm problem was solved, and the play opened to good reviews. The New York *Times* said that "Mr. Burton's grave, handsome, manly prince—drawn between sulkiness and egotism—is ironically entertaining." The play settled in for a run, and now that Sybil had arrived with daughter Kate, Richard and Susan took to meeting in their dressing rooms before the performances. After the show they went out on the town. "Sybil was somewhere with the children." (There was only one.) They dined together in restaurants, went to nightclubs. Susan had her own small apartment within the large, sprawling Strasberg apartment on Central Park West in the Sixties. There, around three in the morning, she would quietly let her lover in. In time they became bolder. Mother and Father Strasberg blandly looked the other way. Lee, the master of Method, knew that emotional problems could be worked out eventually through psychoanalysis. Susan had a fight with Richard over attentions he paid to another woman and went home alone. Richard rang the apartment doorbell at five in the morning, bellowing out Shakespeare in the hallway. Lee Strasberg took it all as a matter of course.

According to Susan, Richard felt he could learn something from Strasberg. He had agreed to play Heathcliff in a television version of *Wuthering Heights*, and he asked Strasberg's advice on some problems he was having with the part. If a review of the production is to be trusted, either the advice wasn't helpful or Richard ignored it. "As Heathcliff," said the *Times*, "Richard Burton virtually exhausted himself. At Catherine's deathbed, he was panting, with decibels to spare, and his final wail in the cemetery was not in the least heart-rending."

Through a friend, an apartment was rented for Susan and Richard where they could have their tête-à-têtes in complete privacy. Richard gave Susan satin lounging pajamas that made her feel like a mistress. When Christmas came he presented her with a white mink scarf and

BURTON

muff, but she was distressed when she learned he had given Sybil a full-length mink coat.

There was no satisfying the young lady. When she turned twenty, Richard arranged a surprise party for her at an unoccupied theater. The cream of Broadway stardom was in attendance, but she was furious because her hair wasn't fixed and her makeup applied beforehand.

The Burtons were known more for being entertained than entertaining, but Susan reported a "Hawaiian luau they gave in a hotel; portable swimming pools were set up, and guests entered on a slide." One of them broke a leg. Richard was also generous in another way. A group of Broadway actors got together on Monday afternoons to become more adept with Shakespearean verse. They persuaded Richard to become their teacher. In the group was the delightful Tammy Grimes, and they were occasionally seen together. She reported afterward that the first few days with Richard were full of sparkle and wit, but that soon repetition of his stories caused them to turn flat. But not for the adoring Susan.

She grew more desperate. What would happen when the play was over? She wrote him notes and poems, and spent sleepless nights when it became apparent that Richard was seeing her less and less. He wrote her a letter telling her about his need to stop drinking: "Because if I don't, I shall die, and if I die, I shall not see you again. . . ." His drinking continued, however. And one night he took her riding in a horse and carriage through Central Park to tell her he was returning to Switzerland as soon as the play closed down. Susan was disconsolate, but he assured her they would see each other again, somehow, somewhere. It was not a bad performance, all in all, except that the blanket that covered them in the carriage was infested with fleas.

But as Milton Sperling, the play's producer, said, though Susan broke her heart over Richard, "she's broken her heart frequently." More distressing to him was that the play lost money—the salaries for the three principals proved to be too high to sustain the run. Helen Hayes was not amused by Burton's behavior, which included not only his affair with Susan but also much noisy camaraderie in his dressing room. "You can't build a career on shenanigans," she told a reporter.

BURTON

*　　*　　*

Back "home" in Céligny, Richard expansively told reporters who came to see him, after it had been announced that he would play the "angry young man" lead in the film version of John Osborne's *Look Back in Anger*, that for the first time in his life he had no money worries. He pointed to the new Cadillac convertible parked outside the inn where they drank wine and talked. Once started on wine, a reporter could count on Burton going on for hours. Inevitably the subject would wander back to his early days in Wales, when his family seemed to get more and more poverty-stricken. "Our whole family," he said, "had to exist on five shillings a week. Now I have enough money in the bank here never to have to work again. Though it's tempting," he continued, "to try for a million [pounds]. I've thought about it a lot. All those noughts. Do you realize you couldn't count it all if you had a million?"

About the Swiss banks, he told the awed reporter, "You don't use your name—just a number. Heaven help you if you lose it. Mine is written down in Welsh all over the place."

He admitted that his Hollywood films had gotten worse and worse, but attributed it to his having been under contract to a studio. To be a truly big star he would have to stay in Hollywood, and he didn't want that, preferred to be classed along with the Michael Redgraves and "not the Rock Hudsons." He mentioned that he had been approached to be in another epic, *Solomon and Sheba*, "with Gina Lollobrigida and that actor with a face like a Toby jug—Tyrone Power."

Toward the end of August 1958, he was in England filming *Look Back in Anger*, being directed by a first-time director, Tony Richardson. In the film with him was old friend Claire Bloom. And one day at the studio he received a call from a young friend, Susan Strasberg. She was in Brussels rehearsing a play to be presented at the World's Fair there. She had a day and a half off and would fly to London to see him. She had taken the role for the express purpose of being able to meet up with Richard. After presentation at the Fair, the play would be done for English television. She couldn't wait to see him again.

Richard failed to meet her at the airport, and sent a car for her instead. She was driven to the studio, where she found Richard in his dressing room. His greeting lacked passion, and he explained that

BURTON

his costar, Claire Bloom, would be coming in a moment to talk about their next scene. He hoped she wouldn't mind waiting in the bathroom for a few minutes.

Were Richard and Claire more than merely costars? When Richard rescued Susan from her bathroom hideout, he took her for a drink at a pub, and then to her hotel. He didn't dare walk her through the lobby, because someone might see them, nor would he be able to see her later that night. It was a dreary reunion all around.

In Hollywood, Milton Sperling ran into objections from the Warner Brothers studio when he cast Richard in his film *The Bramble Bush* as a young doctor involved in a case that had to do with a patient's death. Warner's view was that Burton was looking more and more like box-office poison. Sperling, on the other hand, thought that Burton still had unexplored possibilities as a romantic leading man. Daniel Petrie, who had directed Richard in the TV version of *Wuthering Heights*, wanted to direct *The Bramble Bush*, although he had not yet directed a film. If it was all right with Burton, Sperling said, it was all right with him.

Petrie cabled Richard, and Richard cabled back saying that Petrie was acceptable to him. "He knew," said Petrie, "that it was a major opportunity for me, and it did start me off on my Hollywood career. But I have to say, in spite of Richard's own statements, that the script and the people involved with the project didn't count as much as did the money. At that time, if he was free and you could come up with the money, you got him.

"But I will still say that, even then, pound for pound in terms of voice and acting equipment, he was among the best in the world."

Petrie knew something of Richard's drinking habits, but when he had begun rehearsals for *Wuthering Heights* he learned something odder about him: his aversion to certain actresses.

"We imported this actress I won't name to play Cathy," he remembered. "Her look was quite wonderful—the sort of wild look we wanted Cathy to have. Then we discovered she didn't have quite the sensitivity we wanted. In those days of TV you suffered through things like that. But on the second day of rehearsing, Richard took me aside and asked me how I felt about 'that girl.' I told him I wasn't too happy with her, but I couldn't do anything about it."

BURTON

" 'Do you know of Rosemary Harris?' he asked me. I told him, only vaguely.

" 'You wouldn't think of her as Cathy,' Richard said, 'but she's good.' "

Petrie got the hint, but didn't act upon it. Richard then told him, "Either get rid of the girl, or I'm out. I can't act with her. She even smells bad."

Faced with that ultimatum, Rosemary Harris—another of Binkie Beaumont's ten-pound-a-week discoveries around the same time as Richard—replaced the original Cathy.

"It wasn't done meanly," Petrie insisted. "Richard was just saying, 'Please understand,' and at the same time he supplied an alternative."

When *Look Back in Anger* came out in England, Richard's good reviews buoyed his confidence in himself. It was as though he had broken through some invisible barrier. He supplied the press with some copy. "The film has a sex message," he said. "Sex is the overwhelming urge and driving force in all human beings." And he reiterated that he couldn't act with a woman unless he was powerfully and sexually interested in her. Indirectly, he could be said to be complimenting the Misses Bloom and Harris.

In Hollywood once more for *The Bramble Bush*, he insisted on having two Cadillacs made available for himself and family. Sybil and little Kate were with him. While in England, he had purchased a Rolls-Royce, which he grandly drove to Wales for a family visit, mentioning that he had a Cadillac in Switzerland. And he now had a valet and general all-purpose assistant—in British theater parlance, a "dresser." Bob Wilson was his name, and he would be part of the Burton entourage from then on.

While working on *The Bramble Bush*, Richard told Petrie that he would not touch a drop until five in the afternoon. But the working day went until six o'clock, Petrie pointed out to him. Richard told him that he could still work if he began drinking at five.

"He had a trailer both on the set and on location," Petrie said, "and on the wall a big round clock with a sweep second hand. When that second hand coincided with the minute hand precisely at five o'clock, Bob Wilson would slip a drink—vodka and tonic, generally—into his extended hand. I was there one time when Bob was a few seconds late getting the drink to him. Richard exploded. 'Dammit, Bob, it's five o'clock!' But though he had a temper, he seldom lost it while working. On the set he was a total professional, giving value, in a sense, for value received.

"There was no question that he was determined to be rich, and I'd say it was his problem as an actor. He said to me once, 'Look at Larry,' meaning Olivier. 'All he has is a house in London and a Rolls. I'm not settling for that.'

"There were a number of ladies who came to see him, happy to be in his company, but none from the cast [it included two young lovelies on their way to stardom, Barbara Rush and Angie Dickinson], and after we became friendly, he liked to talk about his affairs. On the other hand, when he was with Sybil, he was warm and gentle with her. They called each other 'Boot,' and they were good to be with because of their loving and endearing give-and-take when in social situations. I knew he was a bit of a rake, but I didn't think it would ever endanger his marriage."

When they left Hollywood for the location work in Maine, Petrie and Burton took the same plane and sat together. They were served by a splendid-looking and well-proportioned stewardess. "By God," Richard said, "she's gorgeous, isn't she? Too bad there's a rule they can't go out with passengers."

Petrie had been on a plane with another star, and knew that the rule, if there was one, didn't hold true. "Ask her for a date," he suggested.

Richard did, and sure enough, the stewardess was happy to accept.

"A few weeks later," Petrie said, "we were on the set up in Maine, when I noticed a stranger looking on. This wasn't supposed to be, so I went over to the young woman. She looked vaguely familiar. 'Don't I know you?' I asked. 'Yes,' she said. 'The 707 to New York— remember?' I realized it had been more than a single date for Richard."

When Richard returned to Hollywood, there was a message for him to call Moss Hart, who had written the screenplay of *Prince of Players*, the ill-fated film in which he had starred five years earlier. Hart was to direct a musical, then called *Jenny Kissed Me*, based on T. H. White's *The Once and Future King*, being written by Alan Jay Lerner and Frederick Loewe. All three had agreed that Burton would make for ideal casting as King Arthur to Julie Andrews' Queen Guenevere.

But could he sing? Hart wondered.

"Oh, yes," Lerner said. He had been at a party at the Ira Gershwins' and had heard Richard and Sybil sing some charming Welsh songs together. When Richard met with Moss, he expressed doubt about his vocal fitness for the role, but said he would think about it. First, however, he checked with Laurence Olivier on whether he thought he ought to do it. A figure of four thousand dollars a week had been mentioned, along with a percentage if the musical was a hit. And why shouldn't it be, since it was a follow-up to the fabled *My Fair Lady*?

"The money's good," Olivier told him, "so I should say nothing and carry on."

But rehearsals were not to begin for several months, and meanwhile an opportunity came to earn more good money. Warner's had something of an expensive lemon on its hands, the Edna Ferber novel *Ice Palace*, which had apparently been purchased on the strength of the author's name. The script was so poor that it was doubtful that stars could be obtained for it. But Robert Ryan and Martha Hyer were persuaded to appear in it—and Richard Burton, in spite of the studio's poor opinion of his star quality. His price was another $125,000 for deposit in his numbered Swiss account, with penalties if the schedule went beyond eight weeks. Shooting in Alaska began in early August 1959 and lasted well into the fall.

"Here we are," Burton told a drinking companion, the actor Jim Backus, "sitting on top of the world, having a drink at three in the morning, making this piece of shit." If Warner's wanted to keep paying him outrageous overtime sums, it was their problem.

On the other hand, the penalty for him was further damage to his screen reputation. His reviews in England were favorable for *Look Back in Anger* but less so in the United States, where many critics landed on it. Everything about his performance as Jimmy Porter was wrong, they said: his age, his voice, his personality. The producer of the film, Harry Saltzman, blamed Burton for his taking a loss on the picture, the American market being crucial to its success. He and a partner had acquired the rights to Ian Fleming's James Bond series, and they were looking for a suave and ruggedly elegant actor for the 007 role. Burton might have seemed an ideal candidate, but he was passed over in favor of the far-lesser-known Sean Connery.

Nevertheless, *Camelot* loomed.

PART
TWO

While Richard was in Alaska, Sybil was in Switzerland, with Kate, awaiting the birth of another child (Jessica). When Richard was back in Hollywood for the remaining scenes of *Ice Palace* at the studio, gossip about him flourished once more. One name mentioned was the underage Diane McBain, who was in the film with him. The eagle-eyed Hedda Hopper came across him in the Brown Derby holding hands with another young actress, Roberta Haynes. "You can say that Richard and I are very close friends," she informed Hedda, and added, to Richard, "Aren't we?"

And there was still the wonder about Sybil, who might have come across such items in the gossip columns. Did she know, and if she did, how much did she care?

When Richard finished his work in *Ice Palace* he returned to Switzerland, where he more or less stagnated for a few months. Some English reporters found him. He told them he had given his word that he would be in the Lerner and Loewe project when they were ready for him, and that Marilyn Monroe was talking about their doing a movie together. Independent production was the new thing in the movie business, and producers were running over half the globe trying to put packages together—that is, bundling together a couple of name stars with a director and screenplay. Several of the

BURTON

type came to see Richard, and he mentioned to the reporters that certain deals were in the works.

At the same time, he spoke witheringly about the films he had made in Hollywood, blaming contractual obligations. It was enough to make a man think of retiring from films altogether. He could afford it now.

Early in 1960 he went to London for a few weeks of BBC television work, and while there worked out an arrangement to provide the voice-over for a twenty-six-episode documentary on Winston Churchill. In the United States, ABC would air the series. The money, as Olivier might have said, was good—$100,000. Richard mentioned to reporters that he had been selected by Churchill himself, but the producer of the series said: not so; *he* had selected him.

Soon after, Richard was called to the United States for *Camelot.* He would fit in the Churchill speeches while on the road with the play.

Alan Jay Lerner and Frederick (Fritz) Loewe had acquired partial rights to T. H. White's fanciful Arthurian series, *The Once and Future King,* and based their story on the marriage between Arthur and Guenevere, and Guenevere's later romance with Lancelot. There was never any doubt that Guenevere would be played by Julie Andrews, the delectable star of the same team's earlier *My Fair Lady.* The attempt to equal that fabulous success put heavy pressure on the lyricist and composer. Loewe had suffered a heart attack two years before. Lerner, who had had a series of unlucky marriages, was having another with his wife of the moment. Moss Hart, the director, was a survivor of a recent heart attack. A wit, soon enough, termed the forthcoming musical a "medical."

During the time Richard vegetated in Switzerland he added to his estate there by building a cottage for visiting family members, and refashioned a garage to hold his growing library. He read voraciously, and continued his diary, which, he said, no one but himself would be able to read because it was written in his own invented hieroglyphics.

The script, the lyrics, and the music of *Camelot* were shaped during the early months of 1960; casting was begun and completed, finally, with the opportune discovery of Robert Goulet for Lancelot.

BURTON

Rehearsals began in New York in September 1960. Five weeks later, the company moved to Toronto for the first out-of-town opening. Lerner and Loewe, their own producers, had been intrigued there by a lucrative offer to open a new theater called the O'Keefe Center, a cultural undertaking of the O'Keefe Brewery Company. It was large, and, as was soon discovered, had terrible acoustics. Lerner was the first to collapse. His marital problems had brought him to the point of nervous exhaustion. Drugs had been given him to get him through the rehearsal and tryout period. When the drugs were withdrawn he was to adhere to a strict eating regimen.

"Two days before the Toronto opening," he recalled, "I was carted off to the hospital with an internal hemorrhage. I was there for ten days, and as I was going out I saw someone on a table being wheeled into the room I had vacated. It was Moss Hart, with another heart attack."

Lerner took over the direction of the show, even though he was already saddled with rewriting chores. He didn't know if he would be able to handle the responsibility, and he confided his doubts to Richard, who said, cheerfully, "Don't worry, luv, we'll get through." He assured Lerner that he would support him in every way possible.

"I can't recall any actor," Lerner said at a later time, "who was loved by a company as much as Richard was."

Richard saw that Lerner was again wearing himself out directing the show by day and rewriting by night. "He came to me, saying, 'Listen, luv, you're not going to have time to rehearse the understudies, so I'll take that for you.'" From then on, Richard coached the understudies.

Lerner knew of Richard's close relationship with Philip Burton, and asked him if he might feel more comfortable having him around during rehearsal periods. "He wasn't pushy about it," Lerner said, "but he said, yes, I think that might be a nice idea."

However, Philip Burton had nothing to do with Richard's performance. It was more a matter of coming in during the trying period after Moss Hart's illness and making suggestions. Most of them had to do with the staging of the crowd scenes.

Lerner, in his autobiography, *The Street Where I Live*, gives a clue to Richard's ability to affect an audience. In rewriting a scene, he gave him a new line in a scene played with Roddy McDowall as the villainous Mordred. The line referred to an early scene in which Arthur mentions how Merlyn turned him into a hawk and allowed him to fly around free as air. Now, embattled and in trouble, the new line for him went, "Merlyn, Merlyn, make me a hawk and let me fly away from here."

At the first reading, Richard smiled at McDowall and said, "Well, luv, it's every man for himself."

"He knew perfectly well what he was going to do with it," Lerner wrote. "With that incredible voice of his, the line exploded with a cry of anguish that almost cracked the rear wall of the theater."

For Richard, the excitement of the theater was just that, the competitive aspect, the match—every man on the stage for himself. The thrill of self-created power.

Lerner said: "I've never known anyone else with that kind of presence on the stage. There was a moment when he was merely standing by the fire, supposedly in deep thought, while others in the scene were speaking. But I saw that no one was interested in what was being said. His peculiar power of concentration was so great that he just sucked all the energy of the stage into him. I spoke to him about it and he told me he had done a play once that had failed for that reason. I rewrote the scene to eliminate many of the lines of the others, and made sure to include him in it."

From Toronto, the musical moved on to a four-week run in Boston. The stresses were still great. The show ran until nearly midnight. The New York opening was looming, and rumors were spreading that *Camelot* might well be one of the world's great fizzles, in spite of an advance sale well into the millions. And the rumors about dissension between writer and composer were all too real.

"God knows what would have happened if it were not for Richard Burton," Lerner wrote. "If ever a star behaved like a star, it was he."

Richard would not allow doubts of the play's success to change his mood. Instead, he continued outwardly to show complete faith in it, and his conviviality and geniality during tryouts were so great that he infected everyone else. Just before the Boston opening, Lerner gave him several cuts and changes. He simply accepted them and went to work. His powers of memorization were such that it was

BURTON

not the chore for him it might have been for others. In the middle of the Boston run, while performing the original material at night, he rehearsed a radically changed second act by day. When other actors grew panicky over the changes, Richard calmed them, telling them all would work out well.

"In simple language," said Lerner, "he kept the boat from rocking, and *Camelot* might never have reached New York if it hadn't been for him."

Lerner knew, as did almost everyone else, that Richard would drink before, during, and after performances, and there were stories that he continued drinking well into the morning hours.

"I decided to see for myself," Lerner said. "So I went out with him one night, determined to stay by his side. We visited a couple of bars, and while I nursed one drink, he would down double vodkas with beer chasers at an absolutely incredible rate. I've never in my life seen anyone drink like that.

"Finally, I gave up. It must have been three or four in the morning, and I left him in the bar of our hotel. I came down again at noon, and there he was, still at the bar, still drinking, with an entourage he had collected."

After one of those bouts and a nap he came into the theater before the performance. Lerner took a look at his face and asked: "How are you, Richard?"

"Fine, luv," Richard croaked in a voice barely above a whisper, "how are you?"

"Richard," said Lerner, "for God's sake, you can't go on with that voice."

"Don't worry, luv, don't worry," Richard croaked.

In trepidation, Lerner waited for him to come on the stage. Sure enough, the first words he spoke came out low and gruffly; then, almost miraculously, his normal voice returned, and remained for the line-perfect performance.

"I would have matched him," Lerner said, "drink for drink against anyone in the world. If anyone had watched and clocked him, he would have made the *Guinness Book of Records*."

Lerner discussed Richard with a doctor friend in Boston. The doctor had come across such cases before. "Welsh livers and kidneys seem to be made of some metallic alloy," he said, "quite unlike the rest of the human race. One day, like airplanes, they eventually show metal fatigue."

According to Lerner, every young leading man who goes into the theater falls in love with the leading lady. "That's *de rigueur*. Automatic, happens every time." He was not speaking of Burton but of Robert Goulet, who as Lancelot fell in love with Guenevere and in real life with Julie Andrews. There had been expectations among many that sparks would fly between Julie and Richard, but this was not the case. She had recently married the talented scene designer Tony Walton, and while he was away from her often, her faithfulness to him was rock-bound. Goulet made his pitch again and again, and failed again and again. In despair he went to the master himself, Burton, whom he vastly, almost slavishly admired. Richard told him that so far as Julie was concerned he had no workable remedies to offer.

"I tried everything on her myself," he told Lerner later. "I couldn't get anywhere either."

By the time the show opened in New York on December 3, 1960, it was already being redubbed "Costalot." The reviews reflected the change in mood from the lilting first act to the sober second act, and most of the praise was reserved for the performances. Richard, *Time* said, "gives Arthur the skillful and vastly appealing performance that might be expected from one of England's finest young actors."

Walter Kerr went further. Richard's syllables, he wrote, "sing, the account of his wresting the stone from the sword becomes a bravura passage of house-hushing brilliance, and when it is time for Mr. Burton to join Julie Andrews in 'What Do Simple Folks Do?' there is at once a sly and fretful and mocking accent to take care of the humor without destroying the man."

With reviews like those, no wonder that Richard was soon being called "The King of Broadway." Yet, for its first three months the show subsisted on its huge advance sale rather than continuing lines at the box office. Moss Hart returned and redirected the show to shorten it by a half-hour. It was Ed Sullivan who helped in the rescue. He wanted twenty minutes of Lerner and Loewe on his television hour, and he allowed them to be devoted to *Camelot*. Most of the

BURTON

twenty minutes were given to Richard and Julie Andrews. The next day lines developed at the theater, and *Camelot* was off on a more than two-year run.

Soon enough, Richard made excellent copy for the press. Now that *Camelot* was secure at the Majestic Theater, he complained about his dressing room and the fact that he and Sybil had spent seven hundred dollars to clean it up. He didn't like the benefit audiences, wondered why he couldn't budge a laugh from them. "Would you laugh," Robert Coote explained, "if you paid fifty dollars for a ticket?"

His dressing room became a favorite gathering place for several current Broadway denizens, among them Alec Guinness, Mike Nichols, Tammy Grimes, Lauren Bacall, Jason Robards Jr., and Robert Preston. They called it "Burton's Bar." Why shouldn't the room be filled constantly, especially between matinee and evening performances? "It's the cheapest bar in town," Richard said.

The celebrated mingled with secretaries. Next door *An Evening with Nichols and May* was playing. "I was good friends with Julie Andrews, too," Mike Nichols remembered. "Our group would sometimes include her, and sometimes Elaine May. Robert Goulet and Roddy McDowall were with us often. We would do things after the show. One place we went to a lot was a small restaurant, Mont St. Michel, which Richard loved. He had a lot of girls. None of us knew whether or not Sybil knew. I think there was a way in which Richard managed it without her knowing. It seems hard to believe, because it was so open, and there was so much to talk about.

"Sybil was and is such an extraordinary woman. Her sense of family—Richard's extended family of all his friends in the theater—provided the glue in his life. We were all glued together by Sybil's concern with people, her vitality and love. It was Sybil who would call you back, Sybil who would suggest a trip to New England—this was a very important part of any friendship with Richard."

Noel Behn, who was Philip Burton's partner in the acting academy they had started, remembered seeing Richard at Downey's, a popular hangout for actors in the theater district. "The place," he said, "was filled with young actresses and chorus girls, and Burton seemed to have the pick of the lot. One of his close friends was the actor Robert

BURTON

Webber, who was a friend of mine, too. When Bob was on the West Coast, he would lend us his apartment. I wrote my first novel there [*The Kremlin Letter*] and I used to think that enormous energy flowed from the bedroom, where Richard Burton had entertained so many women." An apparent favorite of Richard's, seen frequently with him at Downey's, was Pat Tunder, a beautiful blond dancer from the chorus at the Copacabana.

Barbara Gelb of the New York *Times* visited him in Burton's Bar, and reported: "He drinks more or less steadily, and has now reached Phase 2: Charming-and-Witty (the characterization is his own; Phase 1 is Warm-and-Cozy; Phase 3 is as yet unsuspected, let alone defined)."

She noticed that the drinking did not affect his performance, that there were always one or two unattached women hovering, that on matinee days he seldom returned home. "His wife, Sybil, and their two small children have learned to go about their business without him."

Richard's ability to drink and perform well impressed his Broadway colleagues, and Robert Preston proposed a bet: that he could not drink a fifth of hundred-proof vodka during a matinee and another during the evening performance without noticeable effect. Richard promptly took the bet, and others clamored to get in on the action.

In Richard's account, "I popped off the stage every so often, and there was a glass waiting for me. The unknowing judge was Julie Andrews." After the performance, he asked her: "Julie, how was I today?"

"Rather better than usual," she replied.

During the run of the show, Richard often made extemporaneous remarks that struck his colleagues as rather too casual. Daniel Petrie came to a performance, and during a scene in which Richard and Julie were watching a parade, he leaned forward to Julie and said: "That's Dan Petrie out there." Petrie was pleased but at the same time appalled by the breach of theater etiquette.

Ms. Gelb attempted a psychological profile of Richard. With considerable perceptiveness she wrote: "A tug-of-war began in him at the age of two [referring to the loss of his mother], and the two sides of his nature have never been reconciled. He appears to be at once

BURTON

self-possessed and uneasy with himself, unsure where the caustic Welsh clay stops and the silken veneer begins. He is simultaneously the dark and self-destructive Celt and the glossy idealization of classical actor, circumspect and disciplined. In his bemusement over which of these selves to champion, he often takes refuge in a third and safer self—the little boy lost."

In England, Twentieth Century-Fox was desperately engaged in revamping its problem-laden production of *Cleopatra*. The original director, Rouben Mamoulian, bowed out, and Joseph L. Mankiewicz was lured in to take over the direction and refashion the screenplay. Mankiewicz felt compelled, as the renowned screenwriter he was, to measure up to such illustrious predecessors as Shakespeare and Shaw, both of whom had dramatized the story of the Queen of the Nile and her relationships with Julius Caesar and Mark Antony. He wanted actors who would be able to handle the rounded characters he was recreating. Soon enough, this need led to Rex Harrison for Caesar and to Richard Burton for Antony.

The film's producer, Walter Wanger, was willing to use Burton instead of the earlier choice, Stephen Boyd, for Antony, but objection was made by Fox's chairman of the board, Spyros Skouras, who pointed out Burton's poor box-office record. And who would be able to understand that accent of his? He gave way, however.

(Later, when meeting with Burton, Skouras made the same comment in his own thick Greek accent. "Like I can't understand you?" Richard asked.)

In mid-June 1961, six and a half months into the New York run of *Camelot*, Walter Wanger presented himself in Burton's dressing room. They went out for dinner and a talk. Wanger told Richard about the marvelous screenplay Mankiewicz was writing. The Antony role, in particular, was being developed into a fully rounded characterization, with interesting psychological overtones. This would be no ordinary spectacle picture. This would be *the* spectacle. Richard was not in the habit of quibbling about a script, especially with Mankiewicz doing it. Was the money good? It turned out that it would be very good.

Fox was in a bind. A false start and production delays had lost the studio millions already. They didn't quibble, and made Richard an offer of $250,000—more than he had ever received before—for four months' work, with provisions for overtime. But he would be needed soon, and he was committed to *Camelot* through November 1962.

With Loewe and Hart in Palm Springs looking after their bad hearts, Lerner was "running the store" on his own. Richard went to see him and told him of the *Cleopatra* offer. *Cleopatra* was being shifted to Rome, and he would be wanted there no later than mid-September.

"Richard asked me if he could be let go in time to accept the *Cleopatra* offer," Lerner said. "I told him, 'Richard, of course I'll let you go, but let me try to make something of it.'" Lerner would have had to double Richard's weekly take of four thousand dollars if he stayed with the show for another year. A replacement would cost a lot less.

"I had my lawyer call the Fox people," Lerner said. "I knew they were spending money as though it had gone out of style." The lawyer requested fifty thousand dollars for the loss of Richard's services. Fox paid it without a peep. "When I told Richard about it," Lerner said, "he roared with laughter."

Richard made sure that his publicist let the press know that Fox wanted him so badly that they had paid an extra fifty thousand to get him. The year was turning out to be his most remarkable yet. In April he had won the Tony Award as "Best Actor in a Musical." The Kennedys had seen the show and he had been invited to the White House. The record album made from the show was soaring to unprecedented sales heights. Richard had even been made an honorary fire chief for helping to put out a fire that had started backstage.

And now he was about to play opposite the world's most fabled screen star in what everyone said would be the mightiest spectacle yet.

"She was splendid to see and hear," a Roman scribe wrote of Cleopatra, "and was capable of conquering the hearts which had resisted most obstinately the influence of love." Movies were in their infancy when the same lady attracted filmmakers. In 1899 she was the subject of a short film by Georges Méliès. Helen Gardner played her in the United States in 1912, Theda Bara in 1917, and Claudette Colbert bathed in milk in Cecil B. DeMille's 1934 extravaganza. In 1946, Vivien Leigh was cute and coquettish in a British film made from Bernard Shaw's *Caesar and Cleopatra*.

The historically based story contained a good many of the elements filmmakers have traditionally looked for: seduction, sex, love, power, the fate of empire. Cleopatra was a queen and also the world's preeminent vamp. When Julius Caesar conquered her domain, Egypt, she seduced and conquered him. When Caesar was assassinated the Roman Empire was split between the inheritors of his power, Mark Antony and Octavian. To ensure state harmony, Antony married Octavian's sister, but left her for Cleopatra, whom he eventually married. This precipitated a war between Octavian and Antony and Cleopatra, who lost, and took their own lives. Cleopatra used a novel suicide method, the bite of an asp.

It was Walter Wanger's idea to make another *Cleopatra* as an epic based on historical sources. Always central to his notion was Elizabeth Taylor in the key role. He envisioned Laurence Olivier as Caesar, and even in the developmental stages of the project, Richard Burton as Antony.

Wanger met opposition on all three from the Fox executives. "Who needs Elizabeth Taylor?" one of them asked. "Any hundred-dollar-a-week girl can play Cleopatra." A bunch of other names came up for the three roles, among them Cary Grant as Caesar and Burt Lancaster as Antony. For the lady, the names tossed around ranged from Brigitte Bardot to Marilyn Monroe. Lost in the mists of history is the name of the executive who proposed model Suzy Parker.

Wanger, however, was adamant about Taylor, and he phoned her in London, where she was filming *Suddenly Last Summer*. More jokingly than seriously she said she might do it for a million dollars. While commonplace today, such amounts were unheard of then, although stars who traded a salary for a profit percentage occasionally breached the barrier.

The studio eventually met Taylor's terms, which guaranteed her the million, plus a percentage of the gross return. Rouben Mamoulian was hired to direct the film in Rome. The studio changed its collective mind and switched it to England. Having splurged on Elizabeth Taylor, Fox was cutting costs elsewhere. Thus Peter Finch for Caesar and Stephen Boyd for Antony.

From here on, as plans for the production proceeded, corporate comedy was intermixed with personal near-tragedy. The film was to start production on September 30, 1960, at which time Elizabeth Taylor came down with a viral infection. The production was stalled until November, when Taylor was laid low again with an abscessed tooth, and soon after again with a meningeal infection. Three months after the start of production, only ten minutes of film had been shot, none with Taylor. By this time the screenplay had had several writers. When Taylor saw her new lines she said they were awful, and said the picture needed Joseph L. Mankiewicz to rewrite them. The sorely tried Mamoulian resigned, and Fox made overtures to Mankiewicz, who was writing another film in which he hoped to direct Elizabeth Taylor.

The studio was already in a deep financial hole with the picture. Lots of money changed hands, and Mankiewicz forsook his pet proj-

BURTON

ect—Lawrence Durrell's *Justine*—and came on to rework the script and direct. He looked at the ten minutes of film that had been shot and said they were worthless. He looked at the sets and said they were cheap and garish. Everything had to be rebuilt. Soon after his arrival in England in February 1961, Elizabeth Taylor developed Asian flu, and such severe inflammation of her breathing passages that she turned blue and was on the point of expiring. To keep her alive a tracheotomy was performed. If Elizabeth Taylor had been famous before, she was far more now, as the real-life drama of her struggle for breath and life was portrayed on the front pages of newspapers throughout the world. Her return to life had miraculous overtones. The public disapproval of her so-called private life turned to sympathy.

In the eyes of the public Elizabeth was a sultry and voluptuous beauty—some thought the most beautiful then on the screen. Developed and coddled early on by the MGM studio, she had risen to a dizzying height of stardom. Married at age nineteen to Nicky Hilton, she grew careless and sulky about her career, drank to excess, was noted for her bawdy vocabulary, and yet, when once committed to a role, worked with professional skill. After divorcing Hilton, she married the much older Michael Wilding and had two sons by him; then, after divorcing Wilding, she married the even older Mike Todd, converted to Judaism, and bore him a daughter. Soon after, Todd perished in a plane crash, and Elizabeth was comforted by Todd's close friend, singer Eddie Fisher. The relationship became too close for comfort for Debbie Reynolds, Fisher's wife at the time, and she sued for divorce, after which Elizabeth married Eddie. Not even Cleopatra had led such a hectic life, transportation being slower in those days.

Now, though, as a kind of reward for remaining alive, the Motion Picture Academy voted her the Best Actress award for an at best middling performance in a mediocre film, *Butterfield 8*. All of which made her more valuable than ever to Twentieth Century-Fox, now persuaded that by spending more money it could get back some of the money it had already wasted. The overworked Mankiewicz was hurried into putting his unfinished new script into production where it had been originally scheduled to be made—Rome. He demanded Richard Burton for Antony, and got him. It was against this back-

BURTON

ground that Richard Burton found himself in Rome late in September 1961, once more to portray a great historical figure.

At Cinecittà, the large studio built at the behest of Mussolini, huge sets had been erected; farther south, at Anzio, a private beach had been rented for the mock-ups of Alexandria, into which Caesar (Harrison) would make his entrance. Back at the studio, a building was set aside for Elizabeth Taylor and her personal staff—secretary Dick Hanley, a maid, a hairdresser, and a husband, Eddie Fisher, who was given his own office. It was as though the fate of the production, even of the studio, was dependent on her health, happiness, and ability to work. And, in a sense, it was. Fox was in financial trouble, its films were laying eggs, and the bloom of CinemaScope had faded. The president, Spyros Skouras, and all the vice-presidents were feeling heat from the stockholders.

Amid all the hurry, Richard idled away his well-paid time in Rome. The early scenes mostly had to do with the relationship between Caesar and Cleopatra. For nearly four months, his contractual period, he was before the camera only five or six days. When he was on the set, he was mostly, as he put it, peeking around pillars. The enforced idleness, however, was easy to take. Living expenses were taken care of, and overtime work would make him considerably richer.

During his first day on the set he paid his respects to Mankiewicz, Taylor, and Wanger and posed for the obligatory publicity photographs. With him was the film's publicist, Jack Brodsky, who was taken with his "charm and overall niceness." Burton agreeably posed with Taylor and Mankiewicz, after which Brodsky suggested Richard be taken alone. "I saw him staring at Elizabeth," Brodsky remembered, "with a strange expression. Something a little envious, a little greedy in his eyes. 'They don't want me,' he said, 'they just want Elizabeth Taylor.' I had the sense that he was struck, at that moment, by the glamour of her stardom, the kind he would have wanted for himself."

Elizabeth Taylor remembered that first meeting, too: "He said hello to Joe Mankiewicz and everyone. And then he sort of sidled over to me and said, 'Has anyone ever told you that you're a very pretty girl?'"

If he was using his standard approach and signaling to her that he had fun and games in mind, she failed to respond.

BURTON

Taylor recalled: "I said to myself, *Oy gevalt,* here's the great lover, the great wit, the great intellectual of Wales, and he comes out with a line like that. I couldn't believe it. I couldn't wait to get back to the dressing room and tell all the other girls." Still, she admitted to a certain resentment of him, "because I envied his Shakespearean background, and the fact that he was not a movie star but a genuine actor."

Jack Brodsky, by this time, was disenchanted with Taylor. She was, he admitted, "an extraordinarily beautiful woman with magnetism, but I was put off by her cackle of a laugh, her language, which was foul, and her drinking. It's not something you like to see happen on a movie set—especially this one, with a whole company in dire trouble. It was wine mostly, a lot of it consumed at lunch, and sometimes champagne or bourbon."

This indulgence did not noticeably affect her performing, but did cause problems for the costume designer, who constantly had to remodel as the star went up or down in weight (she loved to eat, too), and the weight changes were bound to be apparent when the film was finished.

Off screen she lived lavishly with Eddie, the three children, and a menagerie of dogs and cats, in the Villa Papa on the Appian Way. The pink marble mansion had fourteen rooms, the grounds had a tennis court and swimming pool, and all was surrounded by several acres of pines. Not far away, Richard had a villa too, which was considerably smaller, but roomy enough for himself and Sybil, the two small children, and for Roddy McDowall and a male friend, who were also assigned to the villa. It was largely at Taylor's request that McDowall, a longtime friend of hers, had been given the role of Octavian, and was pulled from *Camelot* at the same time as Richard. McDowall liked Richard and was especially fond of Sybil.

During the first few months of the production, the Burtons, the Fishers, and McDowall and his friend went out for dinner frequently. Mankiewicz worked on the lengthy script by night and filmed scenes by day. Eventually, Caesar was assassinated and the time came for Antony to replace him in Cleopatra's affections. Richard and Elizabeth would be working in close quarters with each other. The night before he was to have his first love scene with Elizabeth, Richard was out all night. Elizabeth recorded his arrival on the set in her memoir.

She had never, she said, seen anyone so hung-over in her life. "He was quivering from head to foot." To still his trembling, he asked for coffee, and Elizabeth helped him put the cup to his mouth. His need for mothering endeared him to her. His very vulnerability made her want to hug him. When he blew his first line—this great actor— her heart "just went out to him."

Richard liked to entertain friends in his dressing rooms. Burton's Bar was transplanted to Rome, and Elizabeth joined the group of frequenters. Taylor was anything but stuffy about drinking. Eddie Fisher, on the other hand, would try to regulate her amount of wine consumption and to get her home to bed at a reasonable hour. She found this irksome, especially when Richard was with them. She loved listening to Richard tell his stories about Wales, about his father's escapades, about London theater life. Richard never worried about getting home to bed. On one of these evenings, Fisher prodded Elizabeth about getting back to the villa and stopped her from re- filling her wineglass. Richard engaged him in conversation while surreptitiously substituting his filled glass of wine for her empty one. "I absolutely adore this man," she thought. Love was blooming.

Still, it took a while for Eddie or Sybil, or anyone else, to notice that something more than mutual admiration and professional respect was happening between the two stars. Sybil, according to a close friend, noticed something going on at a party that struck her as significant. "I suddenly looked at Rich," she told him, "and saw him looking at Elizabeth. It was the way he kept his eyes on her—and I thought: hello!"

Eddie, too, at a party, noticed something. Richard and Elizabeth were doing an inordinate amount of giggling together, but as he said in *his* memoir, "It never occurred to me they were falling in love."

There was another hint when Elizabeth arrived on the set for one of her scenes; her makeup lady brought along a bottle of Coca-Cola for her. Eddie was thirsty and borrowed it for a sip. The Coke turned out to be brandy. "What's going on here?" he asked Mankiewicz. "Eddie," Mankiewicz replied, "she hasn't the faintest idea of what she's doing."

A friend telephoned Fisher and asked him if he was aware that

BURTON

Richard and Elizabeth were becoming unusually friendly. That same night, in bed with her, he asked her if something was going on. The answer, given softly, was "Yes."

Rashly, Eddie packed a bag and moved to a hotel, and the next day went to Mankiewicz for advice. Joe's word was that he better get back to the villa before he found himself charged with desertion. Mankiewicz conferred with Wanger. This was a serious matter. Elizabeth's reputation had been sullied in the past. If something was going on between her and Richard, and it got out, public moral outrage could endanger the financial prospects of the film. Neither man was unused to stars utilizing their dressing rooms for romantic interludes between takes, and the custom was simply to look the other way. When the transgressors were married, efforts were taken to shield them from public view. Wanger and Mankiewicz decided that Eddie Fisher—and Elizabeth, too—required talking to before rumors surfaced in the press.

Several visits were made to the Villa Papa in attempts to calm the troubled marriage, or at least to keep it from snapping asunder. Unfortunately, the rumors were already out in the open. People on the set were talking; so were hired help at the villas. Fisher tried to bear up under the painful situation until a friend in whom he confided suggested he get hold of a gun and threaten Richard with it. Although admitting the foolishness of the notion afterward, he did obtain a gun, and stashed it in the glove compartment of the Rolls, then mentioned it to Wanger, who was precisely the wrong person to tell. Wanger had a police record. He had spent a few years in jail after shooting the lover of his then wife, Joan Bennett—a storied Hollywood scandal. Let there not be another such! Pressure was quickly brought on Fisher to get out of town.

The Fishers owned a chalet in Gstaad, Switzerland. Eddie decided to hole up there for a while, but now Elizabeth asked him not to leave. She and Eddie had only recently adopted a German baby whom they named Maria, in honor of Maria Schell, who had found the child for them. Elizabeth needed Eddie to stay around to demonstrate that she was a proper mother for the child.

And certainly, in a sense, she was. The baby was born with a serious hip deformity, and if she were ever to walk would need a series of operations that the original parents could not have afforded.

After the birth of Liza, her child with Mike Todd, Elizabeth had undergone surgery that precluded her conceiving again. She wanted more children, and keeping Maria was all-important to her.

Eddie remained for a few more days, but the affair with Richard had gone so much to Elizabeth's head that she boldly brought him to the villa one day after both had been imbibing freely. "Who do you love?" Richard asked her in Eddie's presence. "You," she said. "That's the right answer," Richard agreed, "but it wasn't quick enough."

By Fisher's account, Elizabeth became hysterical shortly afterward and left the villa, while Richard stayed on, drinking Fisher's brandy and confusing the poor man with charming apologies one moment and insults the next.

Did Sybil know? She seemed to be above whatever might be happening at the studio between the two stars. If she had inklings of the affair, she wasn't taking it seriously. In mid-February 1962, Fisher thought it time to break the news to her, which he did by telephone. In the words of Jack Brodsky, "Fisher started squawking."

Sybil paid a visit to Cinecittà and had some stern words with Richard. What made both Elizabeth and Richard furious was that it was Eddie who was the villain by betraying them. Those privy to what was going on could only shake their heads in bewilderment.

To Mankiewicz and Wanger in her dressing room Elizabeth said, "I love Richard and I want to marry him."

"Mank and Wanger died," Brodsky wrote Nathan Weiss, his PR colleague in New York.

"At the outset," Brodsky recalled, "it seemed to me that Burton was half in love with her and half in love with the idea of what the relationship might do for him. In the beginning, it was simply that she was one more leading lady he was having an affair with. It seemed it was something he expected. He was always involved with his leading ladies, with a couple of exceptions."

But this affair was different. He was suddenly famous as he had never been before. With an avalanche of publicity, whether wanted or not, he was for the first time a genuine international movie star. He felt a new sense of power. The love he made on the screen was repeated more intimately in the dressing room. Even when Elizabeth

BURTON

was not scheduled to work, she was so in thrall that he told a friend, "She'll be on the set every fucking day I'm on."

Fisher packed his bags again and this time made good his threat to leave for Gstaad. Elizabeth didn't try to stop him. She could be ecstatic one moment and full of remorse the next . . . and plunge into the depths of despair. A day after Eddie left Rome, so did Sybil. Roddy McDowall, the distressed man in the middle, came to the studio and told Richard that she had gone to the house in Céligny.

Richard was shattered; never had any of his affairs threatened his marriage to this degree. For years, Sybil had weathered the stresses in their marriage, which she regarded as inviolate as he did. But now the brutal media glare that fell on her as well as the guilty couple was too much for her to handle. So she fled to Switzerland.

After speaking with McDowall in a corner of the soundstage, Richard went to Elizabeth and asked her to come to his dressing room. "She turned white," said Brodsky, who was observing a drama that was already more absorbing than the one that was being filmed at such enormous cost. But it was his job to publicize the lesser of the two, not the other.

What transpired in the dressing room shocked Elizabeth. He would not allow his marriage to break up. Sybil had to come first, even if it meant breaking off the affair. For him it was a good moment to draw back and let the air clear, for he was to leave for Paris to make a cameo appearance in Darryl Zanuck's film *The Longest Day*.

In Brodsky's less-than-sympathetic words, Elizabeth "went coconuts. She wants to junk everything. Imagine a guy turning her down!"

For Wanger and Mankiewicz it was a grave crisis; the entire production could collapse if Elizabeth Taylor defaulted. Together they labored to calm her down. On her return to the villa she was sedated by her personal physician. Wanger visited her and found her still in a highly emotional state, upset about the hurt she had caused Sybil as well as to herself and Eddie. How many sleeping pills Elizabeth took after Wanger left her is not known, but when it appeared she had taken an overdose, she was rushed to a hospital. A story was quickly concocted that she was suffering from food poisoning.

On the way to Gstaad, Fisher had changed his mind and instead headed for Milan with the idea of catching the first plane for New

York. He went by way of Lisbon, from where he decided he would call Elizabeth. When he learned she was in the hospital, he flew back to Rome, although, he said, no one around his wife had urged him to do so.

During the next several days it was like filings on a magnet settling into new patterns. Eddie stayed around his wife, even buying her a diamond ring for her thirtieth birthday, February 27. A gift of jewelry, he said, could improve her disposition for days. Nevertheless, Elizabeth remained in a flutter over Burton, who had returned from Paris bearing in tow, Brodsky reported, "his Copa cutie, an ex-girlfriend." She was Pat Tunder, the girl he had seen a good deal while he was in *Camelot*.

Rather cruelly, he flaunted her by bringing her to the set to watch him work with Elizabeth. "Taylor and Burton a riot on the set," Brodsky wrote Weiss. "She's looking daggers at him, mixed with steamy, passionate stares." Elizabeth informed Richard that Pat Tunder's presence on the set annoyed her. Richard warned her, "Don't get my Welsh temper up."

March 1 was St. David's Day, the traditional Welsh holiday, and Richard's contracts always specified he was to have the day off. He celebrated it this time with Pat Tunder, staying out the entire night and bringing her with him to the studio. Fuming, Elizabeth waited for him to come out of makeup to the set. "You kept us all waiting," she told him. "It's about time somebody kept you waiting," he replied. "It's a real switch." And it was. Elizabeth could keep everyone waiting for hours if she felt indisposed, or desired alterations on her costume, or whatever.

Brodsky asked Mankiewicz how he was able to work and put up with the problems caused by his temperamental stars.

"When you're in a cage with tigers," he said, "you never let them know you're afraid of them or they'll eat you."

Mankiewicz related differently to each of his stars. With Elizabeth he coddled and soothed, flattered and cajoled, and sympathized. At the same time he told a writer friend that he would hesitate before ever attempting to plumb what went on inside that beautiful head. With Richard, on the other hand, he was dealing with a man whose mind he could respect and whose acting abilities were beyond challenge. And Richard had equal respect for Joe, who was at least as deeply read as he was and who was making every effort to give him beautiful lines to say.

Those in a position to watch the development of *Le Scandale*, as Richard took to calling it, found themselves grudgingly admiring Elizabeth as she went after what she wanted—Richard. She not only knew what she wanted, she knew how to get it. Within a matter of days the affair was on again and Tunder was gone. Sybil fled farther, this time to London, to seek emotional solace from the man who had brought her together with Richard—Emlyn Williams. Suddenly the newshounds were barking outside his house. At the same time, Eddie finally got the message when one night Elizabeth didn't even bother to return home.

In London, as Sybil unfolded the whole sorry tale to Williams, he realized the dimensions of the scandal created by Richard and Elizabeth. He was outraged by Richard's behavior.

"I felt responsible," he recalled. "I had introduced the two of them. I was so fond of Sybil. She was a perfect wife, completely with him and devoted to him. She was heartbroken, of course. And I was godfather to their little Kate."

Williams took a plane to Rome. He was playing a very bad part in this domestic drama, he thought; he wasn't cut out for it and, worse, he was paying his own fare. Richard met him at the Rome airport with a car. Both avoided the subject while driving back to the city. Then Richard suddenly stopped the car and looked straight at Emlyn, the man who had begun his career, who was his mentor and friend. Emlyn thought this was the moment to begin the lecture he had prepared, but Richard spoke first, in Welsh: *"Dwi am briodi'r eneth 'ma."*

Williams was stopped short by what Richard had said. Translated, the words meant "I am going to marry this girl," and the fact that they were said in their native language convinced Emlyn all the more that Richard was serious. This one was not another temporary infatuation. He flew back to London with his gloomy report, but not before leaving behind a letter making it clear to Richard and Elizabeth how pained he was by their behavior.

Yet, most people around them thought it was Richard who had

sent Sybil to England to wait it out until the picture was finished, after which point their marriage could return to normal. To Mankiewicz, though, Richard confided that he was falling more in love with Elizabeth each day. The news was not without its positive side. If the two stars could be kept happy, the picture could move along faster.

Fisher, who had meanwhile flown to New York, ostensibly for recording sessions, held a press conference shortly after his arrival. He still felt his marriage could be held together, and he put in a call to Elizabeth in Rome to prove it. He wanted to put a reporter on the line, but she was uncooperative. "I can't do that, Eddie," she said. "I just can't do that."

It was page-one news the following day in papers all over the country that Fisher had lost his last battle.

With Sybil in London and Eddie in New York, Richard and Elizabeth for the first time felt free to appear together in public. As Richard told Brodsky, "I just got fed up with everyone telling us to be discreet. I said to Liz, 'Fuck it, let's go out to Alfredo's and have some fucking fettuccine.'" Oddly, while with Elizabeth, his language became saltier, and she began developing an English accent.

Wearing a leopardskin coat and a matching cloche, Elizabeth strolled arm in arm with Richard on the Via Veneto. At Bricktop's, a popular nightclub then, they stayed until three in the morning. The paparazzi were beside themselves with joy; it was like finding money on the street. Just being seen out together was enough, as Burton said, "to knock Khrushchev off the front page. . . . Jack, love," he said plaintively to Brodsky, "I've had affairs before. How did I know the woman was so fucking famous?" He protested too much. It was his macho side showing again.

But he was equally famous, as he discovered when he flew again to Paris for another scene in *The Longest Day*. No one had asked to interview him on his previous trip. This time several dozen reporters and photographers were waiting for his arrival. So was Sybil, who had flown from London.

Was it another change of heart for Richard? Or was it Zanuck (who was in a power struggle for control of the beleaguered studio) who had asked him to cool things down? Certainly there was worry that the affair and its notoriety could endanger the enormous investment in the film. The Vatican press was accusing Elizabeth of erotic vagrancy and of being the wrong mother for the adopted child. Elizabeth later related that she and Richard had doubts. "My God, we told each other to leave a hundred times."

On the other hand, it was Eddie she officially left, by issuing a statement that they were divorcing. Then, as though playing a game with the gossips, Richard took Sybil to dinner at Maxim's and strolled with her on the Champs-Elysées. He issued a statement, too—that there were no grounds for the current rumors. Then he fired the press agent who had written the statement.

On the set he and Elizabeth were in each other's arms. The love scene looked all too real. "Cut!" said Mankiewicz. The embrace continued. "Cut!" he called again. "I feel," he told them, "as though I'm intruding."

The conflicting statements and rumors about the breathtaking affair confused both press and public. An Italian paper claimed it had "the true story." It was not Richard and Elizabeth, but Mankiewicz and Elizabeth who were having an affair. Burton, the story went on, was "a shuffle-footed idiot" who was merely serving as a shield for Mankiewicz.

When Richard came across the story he shuffled over to Mankiewicz and said, "Mr. Mankewicz, do I have to sleep with her again tonight?" Elizabeth screamed with laughter.

The Associated Press called Brodsky, and asked for a comment on the story from Mankiewicz. "The real story," Joe told Brodsky, "is that I'm in love with Richard, and Elizabeth is the cover-up for us," and added: "Send it out." Brodsky did, and the new story duly appeared in several papers.

In late April, Richard and Elizabeth, in separate cars, stole away (or thought they did) to Porto Santo Stefano, some eighty miles from Rome. But getting away from the photographers was about as easy as robbing Fort Knox in broad daylight. They stayed in a cottage on the grounds of a hotel favored by European royalty and were caught by photographers embracing and nuzzling among some rocks overlooking the Tyrrhenian Sea. Just as this was happening, Sybil decided to return to Rome. Walter Wanger tried to reach them

BURTON

at their tryst, but didn't have the telephone number. United Press International obligingly furnished it. Richard was all for heading to Rome at once. Elizabeth wanted him to stay. The fierce argument was complicated by the steady drinking he had done. Richard stormed back to Rome in his car, she in hers. Her face was bruised when she arrived—from a car accident on the way, she claimed.

Filming was set back another ten days while Elizabeth recovered, and when she returned it was noticed that her eyes were red and swollen from weeping. Richard comforted her, but he also placated Sybil by arranging for them to be interviewed by David Lewin, a friendly British reporter.

They blandly made the following points to him:

1. There never had been a question of a divorce between them, and there would not be one.

2. Sybil and Elizabeth were very good friends, so Sybil said. "Should Rich ignore her?" she asked. "Certainly not."

3. Richard had gone to Porto Santo Stefano to "read Aldous Huxley and learn *Hamlet* in Italian." Elizabeth merely came for a day and had an accident on the way back.

4. Sybil said she would continue ignoring all the rumors, since none of them were true.

Lewin filed the story, like the good friend he was.

A period of relative peace and harmony ensued between Richard and Elizabeth. She had a favorite jeweler in Rome, Bulgari, where she had seen a lovely emerald brooch. She told Richard how much she admired the brooch, and, with someone to point it out to him, he went to Bulgari, gave a whistle at the price—$150,000—and bravely purchased it. Elizabeth was so overjoyed with the gift that she generously suggested he also buy something for Sybil. Richard did so. He found something very nice for Sybil at a quarter of the price.

Sometime later he told David Lewin, "I introduced Elizabeth to beer. She introduced me to Bulgari."

Lewin also recalled a moment with Burton in Rome when he spoke of having seen Taylor's contract for *Cleopatra*. "Do you realize what she's getting?" he said. "And all the things they're paying for? I want to have all that too." Lewin sensed in him "an absolute fascination with money."

BURTON

Just as strong, or more so, was his fascination with Elizabeth, so apparent to Sybil that she withdrew to Céligny when the cast and crew left Rome and descended on the pretty island of Ischia, near Naples. The island and its surrounding waters were the locations for the planning and the action of the climactic Battle of Actium. Once filmed, Elizabeth's work would be finished. Richard, however, had more scenes in Rome and on location.

For the battle, a fleet of gold-painted barges, war galleys, and smaller vessels were anchored offshore. There was another fleet present, too—small boats carrying photographers with long lenses.

Elizabeth was installed in a lavish suite in the palatial Regina Isabella Hotel, Richard in a plainer apartment on the same floor. It was tacitly understood he would be sharing Elizabeth's quarters anyway. The hotel was part of a resort complex owned by the publishing tycoon Angelo Rizzoli. Fashionable Romans came there for the mudbaths that Ischia was noted for. Rizzoli was a film personality himself, since he was the producer of Fellini's *La Dolce Vita*. He owned a luxurious yacht on which he liked to entertain, and Richard and Elizabeth were invited to spend a day at sea with him and other guests. While at lunch, Elizabeth heard a familiar whirring sound. On investigation, it turned out to be a newsreel camera. Quite rightly, she was furious with her host.

While on Ischia, Elizabeth seemed to accept the fact that Richard was not going to make an abrupt move to end his marriage. Yet the two of them gave the appearance of a settled couple, and everyone around them accepted them as such—for the time being. They were given a cabin cruiser for privacy—and to escape photographers who sometimes leapt out of bushes at them. They had long afternoons to themselves, because much of the activity had to do with technical details of staging the battle.

Weiss had replaced Brodsky as the on-site publicist. He felt that some attention should be directed on Mankiewicz; he was convinced that Joe was writing and making a masterpiece. Correspondents from all over the world were clamoring to interview Richard and Elizabeth, but they were off limits to the press, except for a writer from the New York *Times* and myself, from *Saturday Review*. We were invited to Ischia for the express purpose of interviewing Mankiewicz.

BURTON

One penalty was that we had to read his screenplay—by this time almost as long as *War and Peace*. Mankiewicz was particularly proud of the way the character of Antony had developed; Richard's role was enlarged as a result. With an actor of classical ability such as Burton, he had an instrument for lines of dialogue worthy of Shaw— Joe being no mean wit himself. It was to clarify Antony's motivations and illuminate his tragic end that Burton was to remain with the production until its finish.

When I read the screenplay, I couldn't see how the film could run less than six hours. Would anyone be able to sit that long through the mixture of historical facts and fancy, stretches of elegant repartee, moody lovemaking, and scenes of spectacle?

Surprisingly, Mankiewicz told me that a film should not run longer than the time an average member of the audience could refrain from leaving his seat for a visit to the rest room—about three and a half hours. He revealed what he had in mind, not one *Cleopatra*, but two—each running about three hours in length. This meant that Burton would appear very little in the first, which made neither Burton nor the Fox executives happy. Joe's idea was that the two films would be shown on succeeding days. Patrons would have to buy two tickets to see the entire picture—a concept new to the industry.

While the Battle of Actium was being fought, so was the battle of how long the picture would be. It was Burton who would emerge as the shining star of the piece if Mankiewicz's version won out. Mankiewicz suggested to me that he could arrange a talk with Richard, if he so desired, and Elizabeth too.

I was rather doubtful that the readers of *Saturday Review*, a magazine inclined toward serious cultural matters, was the right audience for an exclusive interview with the notorious couple, but Ischia being a lovely sun-drenched place at that moment, and a yacht anchored in the blue waters offshore designated as the place for the interview, I agreed.

I watched as, in a pause between shots (the battle was being planned on a seaside cliff), Joe took Richard and Elizabeth aside. First he spoke to Burton, who nodded his head. Richard then spoke to Elizabeth, who shrugged, as if it made little difference either way. Joe came back to me and said all was arranged.

"What did you tell him?" I asked.

"That *Saturday Review* sometimes placed a film on its cover, and that he was the likely candidate for the photograph. Richard likes to be on magazine covers."

I obligingly spent three hours of the next afternoon with the two of them on the thirty-six-foot cabin cruiser, wondering uncomfortably what I ought to talk about. It was the rarest opportunity, Weiss had assured me, that anyone had had to talk with Elizabeth and Richard.

To me, it was not the most inspiring or drama-filled occasion. If this was the most earth-shaking love affair of the time, all seemed surprisingly muted. The two didn't seem like guilty lovers, more like a pair who had been through a year or two of marriage. Richard did the talking while Elizabeth sunbathed in a shocking-pink one-piece swimsuit on the roof of the cabin, a glass of wine in her hand, silent most of the time.

Richard told me about the fine script Mankiewicz had written. But he was already thinking beyond this picture. He had to get back to the stage, stretch his muscles. He was thinking of another *Hamlet*; Elizabeth wanted him to do *Hamlet* again. And, eventually, *King Lear,* a challenge that it was important for an actor to meet. Marlowe's *Dr. Faustus* was something else he would like to do, perhaps direct it himself. He was being the great actor, I decided, not the star, nor the lover. Elizabeth seemed subdued. When she did speak, she said: "Richard, throw me the oil.". She meant the suntan tube. Her voice was querulous. The ordinariness of the scene contrasted with what was happening at a considerable distance; hundreds of boats had cameras trained on them. "Can they get anything?" I asked. "Not likely," Richard said. "They'll be stopped if they come closer."

Elizabeth's last day on the film approached. There was speculation about what would happen next between Richard and Elizabeth. The betting was that Richard would tell her it was all over. He wouldn't break up his marriage. No one thought Elizabeth would go back to Eddie.

Elizabeth's departure day was not publicized, at her request, for fear, it was said, that the news would bring Sybil back from Céligny. She finished her last scene as Cleopatra, on the royal barge, and at dockside, came aboard the launch that Mankiewicz used for hurried script changes, and, as it happened, interrupted a conversation between Mankiewicz and me. "May I use your john, Joe?" she asked. She did, and returned to the hotel. I thought she looked depressed.

The arrangement was for a helicopter to come for Elizabeth the next morning and carry her to Naples, from where she would head for Rome. Neither she nor Richard had indicated their intentions to anyone, but it was speculated that all would come to a head that night. Inside the gates of the Regina Isabella Hotel an ambulance was parked throughout the night, a driver at the wheel. A precaution? Against what? No one said.

The next day dawned, the helicopter came, Elizabeth left the island, and the ambulance was driven away. Richard said not a word of what he and Elizabeth may have talked about. But their story was to have many more chapters.

A week before, Alan Jay Lerner had been vacationing on nearby Capri. Richard and Elizabeth paid him a visit. "They told me an extraordinary story," he said, years later. "I've never forgotten it, and I think it says something about their relationship. Richard said that the night before they came to see me he had dreamed he was in a boat with Elizabeth, rowing, and the boat capsized. He was in a terrible panic because he couldn't swim, but he knew he had to, in order to save her. But he couldn't find her in the water. He kept calling to her. Elizabeth suddenly woke up. She had been dreaming too, and was awakened by hearing Richard call her name. She had been dreaming that she had been in a boat that capsized and that she was looking for him.

"I can't believe they made it up," Lerner said, "and it indicated to me that there was more closeness between them, a merging far beyond what most people assumed. I very much doubted after that day that they would leave each other."

Some ten months after his arrival in Rome, Burton completed his final scenes at Cinecittà. "I never want to see the place again as long as I live," he told writer John McPhee. He had had his fill of flashbulbs in his face in the dead of night, cars, Vespas, and motorcycles following him by day, diatribes in the newspapers, household help selling their "revelations" to the same papers.

Richard claimed that after *Cleopatra* he "couldn't get a job at all for months," meaning that his star status had not risen because of the notoriety surrounding his affair with Elizabeth. But of course it had. *Cleopatra* was a long way from release, with fill-in scenes still being shot on the sands of Egypt, but Hugh French, his agent, announced that Richard's asking price for a film had jumped to a half-million dollars. But was anyone asking?

Richard retreated to his home and family in Céligny. He was rich enough now. By the time all his overtime on *Cleopatra* was added up, his earnings came to $750,000. But his life was emptier than it had been before. The focus of public attention had shifted away from him; he had enjoyed being a sort of storm center in a swirl of all-too-public events. He had had just about all he had hungered for—fame, riches, and the love of one of the world's most beautiful women. He felt dissatisfied. Something was missing in his life—Elizabeth.

They had quietly agreed between them during his last days in Rome (she had stayed on to be with him) that they had damaged too many lives already. Elizabeth put her thoughts in a letter to him. In sum, they had to leave each other. They were last seen together (then) at an opera performance at the Spoleto Festival on July 11, 1962. Elizabeth went to her chalet in Gstaad, he to his in Céligny. Was this proximity to each other prearranged?

It was Elizabeth's contention that she went to Gstaad (instead of returning to California) because her children were enrolled in school there. During the summer months? On the other hand, temptingly close was Richard, only seventy miles away on the north side of Lake Geneva. It was more like a waiting game between them. She wasn't going to make the first move.

The board revolution that had been brewing at Twentieth Century-Fox ended with the ascension of Darryl Zanuck as president and head of production. One of his tasks was the assessment of the Taylor-Burton hullabaloo on the box-office prospects of *Cleopatra*. Nearly forty million dollars of the corporation's wealth had been sunk into its filming.

A decade earlier Ingrid Bergman had been drummed out of Hollywood because of the public outrage over her desertion of her husband and child for Roberto Rossellini. But hers had been a different image from that of Elizabeth Taylor. (Not in private, though; Bergman was all too fond of her leading men.) Elizabeth Taylor was already regarded as tempestuous and spoiled, a sort of serial polygamist from four marriages before she was thirty. From Zanuck's viewpoint, the sanctimonious criticism of her behavior could be disregarded—too small a market. In the United States a few self-serving bigots and lawmakers had gotten themselves some attention, but little support. Obviously the public had hugely enjoyed the affair, getting vicarious satisfaction from the kind of behavior they did not (or did) indulge in themselves. The Kinsey reports had appeared and clearly indicated that adultery, if not quite as common as apple pie, was certainly close in popularity.

Darryl Zanuck thus told a meeting of the Fox board: "I think the Taylor-Burton association is quite constructive for our organization." This may have been a signal. Producers suddenly appeared at Richard's doorstep.

Producer Hal Wallis and director Peter Glenville were preparing a production of the successful play *Becket,* in which Laurence Olivier had taken the title role, then switched with Anthony Quinn and played the king. The historical Becket was a far younger man than Olivier, so the choice for the film fell on Richard. He was cool to the idea at first. He would have preferred the more colorful and younger role of Becket's friend, the king, but, for that, the choice had already been made—Peter O'Toole. Soon enough, though, Peter Glenville obtained his agreement, but not before receiving a telegram from him asking for a guarantee that he would not fire him again, as on *Adventure Story.*

Another offer came from producer Anatole de Grunwald, who was preparing *The VIPs* for MGM from a Terence Rattigan script, a kind of *Grand Hotel* story about a group of fog-bound travelers in the VIP lounge of London's airport. The lightweight screenplay was also by Terence Rattigan and Burton was wanted for the role of an oil tycoon at odds with his wife. The morally renovated Ingrid Bergman and Sophia Loren were prominently mentioned for the latter role.

In spite of his sedentary sojourn in Céligny during this period, Richard felt his life was being torn apart. He still had his protective feeling for his family, hit now by a tragic circumstance. Little Jessica never spoke a word, and it became clear that she was not only severely retarded but also would need special care for the rest of her life.

"The shock to me," Richard said afterward, "of being told my child had the intelligence of a reasonably clever dog, was considerable."

Sybil, said a friend, had at first thought Jessica's condition had been made worse by scares caused by the constant presence of people of the press. Frighteningly, they would peer in through the windows late at night. A further strain between the couple came when Richard insisted, over Sybil's objections, that Jessica be placed in an institution for the retarded. One was eventually selected in Pennsylvania, and Kate, a bright, happy child, grew up with little knowledge of her unfortunate sister.

Richard made the first move. Two months after their last meeting he suggested that Elizabeth meet him for lunch. They were about seventy miles away from each other. He drove one way, she the other; they met at the Château de Chillon overlooking Lake Geneva.

"His eyes were like bright blue bulbs," Elizabeth recorded of the meeting in her ghost-written life story. Other details were more homely. They had both washed their hair. His was "all shiny." Another time she described his hair, which she liked to comb, "as soft as a baby's bum." There was a moment's discomfort between them, as though they were on their first date; then they relaxed and had their lunch. She described the meeting as entirely chaste, not even a kiss. There were subsequent meetings, apparently less chaste. Richard described them to David Frost, in an interview, as not "strictly what you'd call Byronic," nor romantic, but "as a desperate rush for lunch to . . . uh . . . get home." He also spoke of runs up to Gstaad, and racing back to Céligny and Sybil in the early-morning hours. Elizabeth made her decision. Her love was so desperate that she would "be there whenever Richard wanted to call me."

In October 1962, the two of them were called to Paris for redubbing some of their scenes in *Cleopatra*. De Grunwald met there with Richard, and, as Elizabeth told it, she casually mentioned in a joking way, "Why don't I do it too?" The suggestion electrified de Grunwald. Visions danced in his head about having the fabled lovers together again in a film that could be made for a tenth of the cost of *Cleopatra*.

But getting Elizabeth Taylor into a film was easier said than done. Not that she wasn't eager to do it—and to stay with Richard for yet another production—but there was her price, the cool million, and the percentage of profits, and the housing and expenses, and her entourage. Richard's agent had already asked for and gotten him his half-million. De Grunwald frantically traveled between London and Paris, made a few dozen phone calls to the head honchos at MGM in Culver City, and finally put the pieces together.

Elizabeth's waiting game had paid off. Her "joking suggestion" not only brought her together with Richard again, but established them—as it would turn out—as a team of enormous box-office power. The pressures created on them by this power could hardly be resisted.

★　　★　　★

BURTON

On December 6, only two weeks after they agreed to appear together in *The VIPs*, Richard and Elizabeth arrived by way of the night ferry and train at Victoria Station in London. The press was there in force, but they were spirited quickly into separate cars and taken to the swank Dorchester Hotel on Park Lane, where adjoining penthouse suites were provided for them. At the studio, Elstree, they had side-by-side dressing quarters.

Two weeks later Sybil arrived in London with the children to stay over the Christmas holidays in the house in Hampstead. Richard's brother Ifor was there too, doing his best to preserve the strained marriage. Richard did spend several days with his family. He took Sybil out to a theater and supper. The strain showed. He drank heavily again. On one stretch of three or four days he did not return to the Dorchester.

Elizabeth, left alone at the Dorchester, was in a fury. When Richard finally returned she was "in one of her spitfire rages," if the gossip writer Ruth Waterbury was to be trusted. "She began throwing things at him." Richard was well able to deal with her tantrums, and the upshot was that he spent two or three days a week with his family.

Richard in this period was in a state, "maddened with guilt," according to John McPhee. Elizabeth clearly wanted marriage, and she made sure to be with him every hour that it was possible, going with him on his pub crawls, at his side at the rugby matches he attended. Ifor, trusted and respected above all others by Richard, was vehemently opposed to his leaving Sybil and marrying Elizabeth. Family members in Wales were equally opposed.

There were shafts taken at Richard by colleagues, and they hurt. A friend, Harvey Orkin, who had worked for him as an agent, said publicly, "Here is a man who has sold out." Richard lashed back, saying that Orkin was an embittered, failed writer. John Gielgud worried: "When the movie career is finished he will have lost his romantic years, his vigorous years." Olivier warned: "Do you wish to be a household word or a great actor?" British writers, remembering his glory days on the stage, seemed overly worried about what looked to them like a retreat from his promise. Somehow they had forgotten the lackluster films he had made earlier.

The darts at his integrity bothered both Richard and Elizabeth, her perhaps more than him because of the implication she was the cause of his change in career direction. "Listen, I'm just a broad, a star," she told Peter Glenville. "You win a few, you lose a few. But now these critics are talking about a great actor."

To one of his critics, Burton asked plaintively, "Did Olivier sell out when he made *Spartacus*?" Many stage greats, he said, would be happy to do films, if only they were asked.

But after taking on the potboiling *VIPs*, he was considerably more choosy about his roles, and gave credit for this to Elizabeth. "Before I met her," he said, "I was making any kind of film in sight, just to get rich. Then Liz made me see what kind of rubbish I was doing." There was some irony behind the statement, because no matter what he did, he continued to get richer.

Yet, when Kenneth Tynan interviewed him during this period, he said, "I've learned that you can't become a great actor nowadays. It's impossible. You aren't allowed to develop in peace. Public attention is too concentrated, too blazed, too lighted, too limned." He was rationalizing, obviously. Public attention was giving him the power of choice.

During this "Dorchester" period he made his choice between Sybil and Elizabeth. Quietly Sybil returned to Switzerland with the children. There were negotiations, but nothing was heard of them until April. Richard had grown tired of, as he said, "skipping back and forth," and was willing to pay whatever price was necessary to gain peace as well as freedom. The separation agreement was worked out by Aaron Frosch, a condition being that Sybil would stay away from London while Richard and Elizabeth were there. The one bitter remark that was said to come from her was, "The father of my children will never be Elizabeth Taylor's fifth husband."

Sybil had maintained an admirable reserve and reticence throughout the whole trying and indecisive time. Having lost Richard, she was determined to cast him out of her life entirely. She refused to discuss him publicly, and it was two years before she told her friend Elaine Dundy about her mood while waiting it out in Switzerland.

"My lowest point came," she said, "when I'd read myself out. Reading had always relaxed me. There I was in Céligny and I looked down at the page and couldn't read it. Then I knew I was really in trouble. It was awful. When I felt I was finally out of the woods was when I made my decision to go to America. Such a relief to have made up one's mind. I decided in a moment. That was it."

Elaine Dundy was impressed by her ability to be objective, and her strength and positive spirit. As for Sybil's daughter Kate, the older she grew, the more it was left to her to see or be with her father when and if she wanted to. "There was nothing about taking sides," Kate said to me in her maturity years later. "It made it so much easier for me. But at the same time she protected me from all that outside fuss, and helped me understand it and see it in perspective."

Richard paid a high price for his freedom, just about all he had in reserve—a million and a half dollars. But there was no lien put on his now huge earning power. "I gave away everything I had," he said later. "I wanted to start again from scratch." Some of what he gave away then and later went to relatives in Wales in the form of retired mortgages and pensions. There were a lot of relatives, and some of them were not bashful about wishing to be included in his generosity.

Elizabeth raged about one omission in the agreement. There was no provision for a divorce. Richard raged back, and went to Wales for a few days to calm down.

Sybil found New York City congenial and decided to live there. She had good friends such as Philip Burton and Roddy McDowall, and the latter located an apartment for her in the building he lived in on Central Park West. New York was refreshing and exhilarating after those dreary months in Céligny. And she was an almost instant celebrity! Before long, she was busier than ever, both in a social sense and professionally.

At the Dorchester, Elizabeth at last had Richard solely to herself, and she doted on him to the extent of grooming his hair and helping him select his clothes. She read and advised him on the screenplays offered to him. He said she was partly responsible for his decision to play Becket, who became the Archbishop of Canterbury and was canonized. He wasn't sure he was suited to play a saint. Elizabeth catered to his love for reading by making him a gift of five hundred books, custom-bound in leather, then went out and bought a Van Gogh for a quarter of a million dollars and placed it in his suite at the Dorchester. She became infected by Richard's love of poetry and took to reading it herself.

Very little emanated from the set of *The VIPs* because of a strict clamp-down on access to them by the press. The idea was to make it fast and get it out in time to take advantage of the *Cleopatra* publicity. *Becket* went into production almost immediately after the picture's finish. Elizabeth was there on the sidelines, a constant observing presence. Neither liked the reports they were hearing as the release of *Cleopatra* approached. Darryl Zanuck was now personally editing the film.

He had rejected Mankiewicz's proposal for a two-part release. Instead he chopped away at the nearly six hours of film footage, and the more he chopped, the more Richard's role felt the blows. Zanuck told Mankiewicz, "If any woman behaved to me the way Cleopatra treated Antony, I would cut her balls off." Mankiewicz could only despair as he saw much of his work and sweat landing on the cutting-room floor.

In London, Richard and Elizabeth came to his support. "You can easily see where my loyalties lie," said Richard. "I think Mr. Mankiewicz might have made the first really good epic film." Elizabeth said, "What has happened to Mr. Mankiewicz is disgraceful, degrading, humiliating, and appalling."

"Burton suffered most in the cutting," Mankiewicz said. "He gave a brilliant performance, much of which will never be seen."

The Bolshoi Ballet was in London late in the spring of 1963, and the British embassy asked Elizabeth to play host for the members at an advance screening of *Cleopatra*. "I couldn't very well say no," she said. What she saw horrified her. "When it was over I raced back to the Dorchester and just made it into the downstairs lavatory before I vomited. The only things I am proud of, Fox cut out with unerring accuracy." Mankiewicz, she said, had built Antony into a strong figure, but with a flaw that caused him to disintegrate. But in the final cut of the film, "all you see is him drunk and shouting all the time, and you never know what in his character led up to it. He just looks like a drunken sot on campus."

These remarks, and the turmoil caused by the affair, resulted in Fox slapping a suit on her for damages—a way of delaying, at least, the several million dollars owed to her.

Eighteen-year-old Richard in 1943, while an air cadet.
The Springer/Bettmann Film Archive.

Elizabeth thought her marriage to Michael Wilding would be her "happy ending." Not so. *Museum of Modern Art.*

Alan Jay Lerner, librettist and producer of *Camelot,* with his stars, Julie Andrews and Richard Burton. *The Springer/Bettmann Film Archive.*

The nascent triangle, Rome, February 1962. Richard would soon replace Eddie in the catbird seat. *The Bettmann Archive.*

Love, power, jewels, and beverages—all in a single shot from *Cleopatra*.
Photo Museum of Modern Art, courtesy of Twentieth Century–Fox.

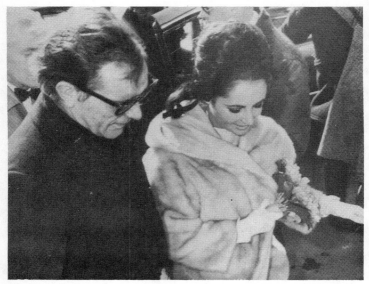

They made it legal on March 16, 1964, in Montreal.
UPI/Bettmann Newsphotos.

Sybil, now married to rock
singer Jordan Christopher,
twelve years her junior.
*The Springer/Bettmann
Film Archive.*

With his third wife, tall, willowy Susan Hunt—one of three
"fragile, beautiful, but strong-willed women" who tried
to save him.
UPI/Bettmann Newsphotos.

Elizabeth with Number 6, John Warner.
The Springer/Bettmann Film Archive.

Kate outside a Broadway theater with her father.
The Springer/Bettmann Film Archive.

Attending the post-premiere party for *Private Lives* with Sally. The reviews spoiled the occasion.
UPI/Bettmann News-photos.

Richard taking direction from John Gielgud for his 1964 run in *Hamlet,* which sold out and broke a Broadway longevity record.
UPI/Bettmann Newsphotos.

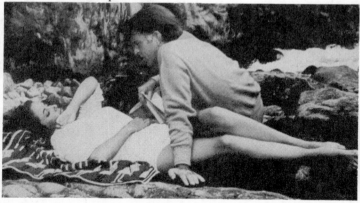

At least they were frank about why they made *The Sandpiper.* "For the money," said Richard, "we will dance."
Photo Museum of Modern Art, courtesy of Metro-Goldwyn-Mayer.

About his performance in *Equus* a critic wrote: "He is the most promising middle-aged English-speaking actor of his time."
The Springer/Bettmann Film Archive.

BURTON

Richard claimed never to have seen the film, but he reviewed himself while talking with Kenneth Tynan: "In Mankiewicz's version, Antony is a man who talks excessively to excuse his own failure to become a great man. He's extremely eloquent, but at times inarticulately eloquent. The fury is there and the sense of failure is there, but sometimes all that comes out is a series of splendid words without any particular meaning."

Charges and recriminations filled the air. Mankiewicz blamed Zanuck for not seeing the need for character motivations. Zanuck blamed Mankiewicz for the skyrocketing cost of the picture. He had kept Burton and McDowall hanging around Rome with nothing to do for months. Mankiewicz blamed the Italians who had worked on the picture for kiting costs to the tune of an extra five million. No one seemed to know exactly how much *Cleopatra* had cost, although eventually it was said the money was gotten back.

At its first showing the film ran a few minutes over four hours. Mankiewicz made a turn-around and helped cut twenty-one minutes from it. Then Rex Harrison sued Fox for breach of contract. He was supposed to get equal billing with Elizabeth and Richard, but there was that huge sign on Broadway: Richard and Elizabeth in a languorous pose took up most of the space. Up in a corner, like a postage stamp, was Harrison staring down at them.

Harrison, though, came out best in the reviews. Taylor, *Time* wrote, "to look at is every inch a morsel for a monarch, but when she plays Cleopatra as a political animal she screeches like a ward-heeler's wife at a block party."

Richard, the same magazine said, "staggers around looking ghastly and spouting irrelevance, like a man who suddenly realizes he has lost his script and is really reading some old sides from *The King of Kings*."

The reviews around the country ran a gamut, as reviews do, and the public made its own decision. Whether they came to see the movie or to see Richard and Elizabeth make love remains a moot point. *Cleopatra* went into cinema history as one more overblown and overpublicized film. What it had fostered was far more lasting: continuing public fascination with the romance between Richard Burton and Elizabeth Taylor.

PART
THREE

12

A film like *Becket* could hardly have been better calculated to restore—or enhance—Richard's prestige. As a play on Broadway it had won kudos for Olivier and for Anthony Quinn. For the film, Hal Wallis and Peter Glenville gathered some of the most famous names in British theater: in addition to Burton and O'Toole, John Gielgud as Louis of France, and others such as Donald Wolfit, Martita Hunt, and Pamela Brown. It was a stylish production all around.

For Elizabeth it was a time to admire—all these great players gathered together in a story of substance. For Richard, the presence of O'Toole was a bonus—a friend, a gifted and flamboyant actor, and a fellow drinker. Richard vowed he would not drink when due on the set, and much of the time he kept to the promise. Glenville on the whole found him conscientious and disciplined. O'Toole was somewhat less dependable. "He was a binge-type drinker," Glenville remembered, "but only a couple of mornings' work were lost because of it."

When the drinking was done, it generally began during the lunch break when Richard, Elizabeth, and O'Toole would wander off together. Wine and champagne were the beverages of choice. At the workday's end, Richard and Elizabeth would head for a pub, where they mingled with the simple folk and where Richard switched to

BURTON

stronger stuff, washed down with beer. Elizabeth made it her concern to guide Richard back to the Dorchester, after more stops on the way.

Glenville, intent on getting performances, seemed curiously oblivious of the off-set roistering by his stars, perhaps because in the earlier scenes, Thomas à Becket and the young king were boon companions in hunting, dining, wenching, and wining and were supposed to be in high spirits anyway. What mattered more to Glenville and pleased him was the fierce but friendly competitiveness between the two actors.

Richard, benefiting from tips by Elizabeth on film acting as opposed to stage acting, restrained his performance, while O'Toole went as bravura as he might have had he been on the stage of the Old Vic. The contrast between the two performances favored Richard. O'Toole was colorful as he ranted and swaggered, while Richard intoned his lines dispassionately, almost coldly, and was more effective. He made the scene in which Becket is murdered a model of restrained but emotionally chilling acting. In that moment he achieved a touch of greatness.

The contrast in real life was something else. During the production, Michael Mindlin, Paramount's publicity man, was bewildered by Richard's anything-but-saintlike behavior. Never in his experience on film sets had he seen so much drinking. He had arranged for Richard to be interviewed by Ed Sullivan, who flew to London to film a segment for his television show. But Richard was missing at the appointed time. Mindlin was pacing the lobby of the Dorchester late one afternoon when Richard and Elizabeth came in.

"They sat down for a drink," said Mindlin. Dozens of tourists having their tea or cocktails in the lobby bar stared at the couple. Richard, after a few drinks, began reciting the verse of Dylan Thomas—always a reliable sign that he was well on the way—when suddenly, without warning, he threw up over himself, the sofa he was seated on, and the cocktail table. Immediately, Mindlin said, Elizabeth went to him, put her hand on his forehead, and for the benefit of the onlookers, said loudly, "Oh, my dear. I think you have a fever. You haven't kicked the flu yet."

Otto Preminger, the director, chose this moment to enter the lobby and noticed Richard and Elizabeth, whom he knew. He went over to pay his respects, but Burton only glared at him and yelled: "Fuck off. Just fuck off." Preminger fled.

Elizabeth later sent word to Mindlin that Richard would do the interview the next day at the studio after filming. This time Mindlin arranged to have Peter O'Toole present. Richard's condition was hardly better than the day before. When Sullivan asked him if this was the first time he and O'Toole had worked together, Richard said, "Yes, and it will probably fucking be the last." Sullivan flew back to New York with a film that was unusable.

Glenville felt he never fully understood Richard. "The man," he said, "was imaginative, highly intelligent, scholarly, a brilliant and serious actor." Then there was another side. "He was curiously fixated on obtaining wealth—not just to be well off, but really wealthy. And yet without much purpose of what he would do with the wealth if he obtained it. The more he was with Elizabeth, the more he seemed to change in this direction. If there was a catalyst, it was Elizabeth." Glenville also saw a hidden aspect to his personality, as though there was something he did not want to face, and which drinking perhaps covered up. "He will always be a mystery to me," Glenville concluded.

While Richard was doing *Becket*, Elizabeth was approached to be a kind of tour guide for a CBS television special on London. The $500,000 she got for it was the highest fee paid to that time. What American viewers saw in addition to the sights was a gracious lady-like Elizabeth, speaking in a newly cultured accent that was somewhere between American and British. She might have been on her way to have tea with the queen.

It was due to her urging that Richard began seriously to consider a new *Hamlet*. An American producer, Alexander Cohen, was in London looking over the theatrical scene, and lunched with John Hayman, who managed some of Richard's affairs, and was looking into producing himself. He mentioned that Richard might be interested in doing a *Hamlet* in New York—but it would have to follow his film commitments, which, at this time, included not only *Becket* but also John Huston's production of Tennessee Williams' *The Night of the Iguana* in Mexico. Cohen perked up his ears. He would be interested too, he said.

Soon Cohen was dealing directly with Richard. "He was all business," Cohen related. "When you have a conference with him there are no interruptions, no phone calls, no visitors. Now and then Richard would be reminded of a story, or do an impersonation of an actor suggested for the production, but he knew precisely what he wanted." Cohen, already on his way to achieving one coup, was hopeful for another. Wouldn't it be wonderful if Gielgud could be gotten to direct? Richard agreed that it would be, and said that if the moment seemed right, he might ask him.

That moment occurred while *Becket* was on location in the north of England. On a cold, gray day in late August, when Richard and John Gielgud were between takes, Gielgud asked Richard if he planned to do anything for the Shakespeare Quattrocentennial in 1964. Casually Richard said: "I'll do *Hamlet* if you'll direct it."

"Where?" Gielgud asked.

"New York."

"Very well," Gielgud said. "Who shall produce?"

"Alexander Cohen," Richard said.

"Good," said Gielgud.

Richard's memory was hazy when he wrote sometime later that it happened more through impulse than by design, for he had already committed himself to Cohen, as well as promising Elizabeth he would do *Hamlet* in the spring. Gielgud simply fell into the net. But then, as Philip Burton said more than once, Richard was not always truthful.

Once an agreement was reached, discussions went on between Richard and Gielgud about the form the play would take. Both preferred not doing a traditional mounting. Richard did not want to play Hamlet in doublet and hose. Gielgud suggested performing the play as though it was a final run-through, out of costume, before the opening night. Actors could wear whatever rehearsal clothes they felt comfortable in. Richard made no objection; his concern was making the play as immediately understandable as possible.

Before leaving England for Mexico he took Elizabeth on a visit to Wales, describing it beforehand to her as "a squat and ugly place full of rain." She didn't find it so; in fact, she was enchanted by the seaside town of Port Talbot and the tiny village of Pontrhydyfen, even to the little house in which Richard had been born. She met sisters and brothers, and visited the local pubs, where she was gawked

BURTON

at like some celestial visitor from another planet. One grizzled miner reached out and parted her lips to examine her teeth. "Just like they were looking at a horse they bought," she said afterward. Richard took her to a rugby match and, afterward, to a pub. Suddenly a large hand grabbed her backside as though demanding a pound of flesh. "You were asking for it," Richard said, referring to the tight white ski pants she was wearing. Elizabeth was less understanding. She stung the man's face with a resounding slap.

Before Richard and Elizabeth left England for Mexico and *The Night of the Iguana,* the two Wilding boys were sent off to school in California, while the adopted Maria stayed behind in London with a nurse for another in a series of hip operations. Liza Todd was with Richard and Elizabeth when they arrived at Mexico City's airport on September 22, where a huge crowd awaited them. Elizabeth balked at leaving the plane and facing the mob, while Richard was anxious to get off. There was a shouting match between them, interrupted by a large man wearing a sombrero and pistols at his hips, who took Elizabeth by the arm and commanded, "Follow me!" Not knowing the man was John Huston's assistant director, Emilio Hernandez, Elizabeth rent the air with screams.

"Get this maniac off the plane," Richard yelled, "or I'll kill him!"

Finally, the two were calmed down and led off the plane, but not without loss to Elizabeth while making her way through the throng— her purse and both her shoes. They were found later.

Richard and Elizabeth, understandably ruffled after their ordeal by arrival, refused to attend an arranged press conference. Richard sent a statement, however: "This is my first visit to Mexico. I trust it shall be my last."

A week later they were at the location headquarters in Puerto Vallarta, an as-yet-unspoiled fishing village on the rugged west coast three hundred miles north of Acapulco. Hardly luxurious, it was far less so at the principal location, a tiny settlement on the Mismaloya peninsula where bungalows had been built high on the hills as quarters for the crew and cast. Noticing the lack of a bar, Burton went to Huston and convinced him that having one would add to company morale. The main set, a down-at-heels hotel, the center of much of the action, was also built at Mismaloya.

BURTON

Difficult as the location was to reach, and in spite of heat, humidity, and a variety of insects, reporters and gossip writers poured in, attracted more by the possibility of drama off screen than on. In the cast with Richard were seventeen-year-old Sue Lyon, the svelte Ava Gardner, and the ladylike Deborah Kerr, all of whom would have a go at him in the film story. And, in the wings, so to speak, watching, was Elizabeth Taylor.

And there was a kind of incestuousness in the private pasts of many of those present. John Huston had once been married to Evelyn Keyes, who was presently married to Artie Shaw, who had once been married to Ava Gardner. Deborah Kerr's husband, Peter Viertel, had once worked as a screenwriter for John Huston, and had afterward published a novel, *White Hunter, Black Heart,* in which the unfavorably portrayed main character bore a keen resemblance to Huston. And then came Michael Wilding, former husband of Elizabeth Taylor, who was now allied with Hugh French, Richard's West Coast agent. It was all very cozy, and possibly incendiary.

But harmony, for the most part, reigned. Wilding had located a pleasant house in Puerto Vallarta with room for Liza's nurse, Elizabeth's personal secretary, a cook, and a chauffeur. The house was four stories high, on a steep hill that gave a view of the bay. Richard eventually bought it, in spite of his remark about never returning to Mexico. John Huston settled there, too. The avalanche of publicity that hit the town later boosted it into a popular tourist place.

During the making of the movie Richard captured attention both off and on the set. He enjoyed the raffish local bars, and welcomed company. "There's nothing nicer," he told a visiting reporter, "than sitting at a bar and drinking and swapping stories. I can never drink at home. I can't understand people who do. My father, great boozer though he was, never brought beer into the house."

In a philosophical mood one evening he said, "The only thing in life is language, not love." This made Elizabeth weep. If true, where did that leave her?

Richard's reputation as a robust drinker did not suffer in the least in Puerto Vallarta. A recipe for a Richard Burton cocktail made the rounds: "First take twenty-one tequilas . . ."

Elizabeth had the job of dragging him back to the house in the early hours of the morning, and consequently she slept late. But she was always up in time to reach the location promptly at noon, bearing a basket of hot lunch for Richard, which her cook had prepared. Since much of the filming took place at Mismaloya she hired her own launch, *Taffy*, for the twenty-minute ride across the bay. After tying up the boat to a floating dock, she was faced with a twenty-minute climb to the location. She was rarely late, but a few minutes' delay and Richard would loudly complain.

Afternoons she would retire to the beach, where she displayed one of the forty bikinis she had brought with her. Unkind onlookers noted a roll of fat around her middle. In street dress she sometimes looked as exotic as a toucan. On one occasion she wore on her head large black flowers made of human hair, a green-and-white Mexican shift over her bikini, and beaded thongs of turquoise on gold.

There was a wealth of women in the cast, and Richard must have felt she was keeping a possessive eye on him, for he once asked her if she'd mind his taking a picture of the nubile Sue Lyon. "Of course," she said. "Why do you ask me?" "Because I'm afraid of you," he answered.

She made it her business to manage his hair, fussing over it after his hairdresser had arranged it. For a scene that was to take place in the rain, the hairdresser fixed him a wet look. Elizabeth didn't like it, and annoyed the hairdresser by doing it over. Richard ended the matter by grabbing a bottle of beer and pouring it over his head.

Yet, as the weeks wore on, he spent more and more time with Elizabeth in the house, showing every sign of domestication while, to reporters, he would not admit that marriage was in the offing.

However, his negotiations for a divorce were proceeding. Sybil gave way first. Richard had said earlier that he didn't like the idea of a Mexican divorce, "but we must work something out soon." The transfer of money and assets was agreed to, and Sybil granted Richard free visitation rights to the children and obtained a divorce in Guadalajara on December 5, 1963. The grounds were abandonment and cruel and inhuman treatment. When Elizabeth heard the news she called Irene Sharaff, her designer for many years at MGM, to set to work on a wedding dress.

She was still not legally free from Fisher, who balked at the divorce papers sent him by her lawyers. She wanted just about everything they had in common—the green Rolls-Royce, the house in Gstaad, his gifts to her in jewelry, and the profits from their mutual corporation. She also wanted Maria and Liza, he being the adopting father of both. He gave way on Maria but insisted on remaining Liza's legal father. Mike Todd would have wanted it that way, he said.

Some sort of settlement was made, but only after Richard chose a curious way to enter the fray through an angrily worded letter he wrote to Dick Hanley, Elizabeth's secretary. In it he accused Eddie of being laggard and ungentlemanly about a divorce. The letter was quickly made public. Elizabeth was lashing out at him too: she had never loved him, he was a weak substitute for the sainted Mike Todd, her marriage to him was the biggest mistake of her life, et cetera, et cetera. Under the onslaught Fisher retreated, and she filed for divorce in Puerto Vallarta, and received it in January 1964. She also got to keep just about everything she wanted to keep.

These quickie divorces caused some unfavorable comment in the press. When a reporter brought this up, Richard said, "If you come down to it, Liz may not have been married to Mike Todd after the Wilding divorce. So that means no one was ever married to anyone really, and we might just as well all start again and get married and divorced on the Koran."

While divorcing tactics were going on, so was the making of the movie, and in John Huston's capable hands, Richard was molding a fine screen performance. When *The Night of the Iguana* was released several months later, most critics lauded his portrayal of the shabby Reverend T. Laurence Shannon. *Time* said, "Burton makes more sense in this movie than he has in his last half-dozen efforts. He has a light in his eye, a line to his mouth, and the carriage of a man who believes in what he is doing."

Time also said: "He is the new Mr. Box Office." This judgment was affirmed further when he was listed fourth in a theater owners' poll of male film stars. Ironically, Elizabeth dropped to seventh on the female list.

Hamlet had not been forgotten while Richard was in Mexico. Gielgud auditioned potential cast members in New York before leaving for an Australian tour during November and December. Communication and exchange of ideas between them was by cable. By the time Huston called out his final "Cut!" on December 30, arrangements were completed for rehearsals and the opening of the play in Toronto.

Richard and Elizabeth did not leave Puerto Vallarta until her divorce papers were safely in her hands; then on January 22, 1964, they checked in at the Beverly Hills Hotel for a brief stay before leaving for Toronto.

Crowds were gathered outside the King Edward-Sheraton Hotel in Toronto on January 28, hoping to catch a glimpse of the famous pair before they checked into their five-room suite. Not all of them were fans. There was hostility. Insults were hurled by supposed guardians of morality. One crackpot virtually picketed the hotel for days with a sign that read "Drink not the wine of adultery." Elizabeth seldom left the hotel during the rehearsal days because of the constant presence of crowds outside and wherever else she was likely to be.

Richard was less disturbed or at least better able to bear up under the scrutiny of a phalanx of reporters and photographers, the fans and the demonstrators. "I've been in the most expensive musical," he cracked, "the most expensive movie, and now the most pressurized *Hamlet*."

When Elizabeth did manage to get to the O'Keefe Theater, she was respectful, even studious as she watched the play taking shape under Gielgud's direction. It was her first close-up experience with classic stage acting; she took to reading books on *Hamlet* and its varying interpretations. Richard was serious, although not solemn, as he worked out his interpretation with Gielgud, sometimes differing with him on little points, but never to the point of real argument.

As the first performance approached, Elizabeth saw a tenseness developing in Richard. She decided to take action. From the hotel suite she telephoned Philip Burton in New York, diffidently introducing herself. Philip had made it very clear to Richard his disapproval of his affair, and had been helpful to Sybil and the children in New York. They had not spoken for two years. "I wish you'd come," Elizabeth said. "He needs you."

If he was needed, it was less for his help than for his reassuring presence. Philip discussed with Sybil whether he should go or not and, nice lady that she was, she advised him to go to Toronto.

By the time he got there, the play had already opened. Philip took in two performances, and gave Richard his comments. Although he took a dim view of *Hamlet* being performed in rehearsal dress, he was approving of Richard's performance. He became aware of the stress on them caused by the avid public attention. And he was won over by Elizabeth, and saw, too, that Richard was clearly in love with her. Peace was made, and Philip's relationship with Richard was reestablished. In a way, it was a gift from Elizabeth to Richard.

As for John Gielgud, never had he rehearsed and gotten a play ready under such extraordinary conditions. To be alone with his star was an undertaking in itself. The corridor on which Richard's and Elizabeth's suite was located was guarded by a man with a machine gun. To walk her dogs, Elizabeth had to use the roof. At lunch or dinner they were accompanied by several people who were there only to keep other people away from them. Gielgud thought it remarkable the way Richard was able to handle it all gracefully. The other actors liked him enormously, and the luckier ones among them were treated to his store of theatrical anecdotes when invited to his dressing room.

A benefit performance, for which glittering Canadian society turned out, was held the evening before the official opening on February 26. There was a delay in curtain raising of more than a half-hour because of another show—Elizabeth's arrival. As she made her way down to a seat in one of the front rows, most of the audience stood to see her. A good many perched on their seats to look over the heads of the standees. Afterward, when she attended performances she stayed at the rear of the theater.

For the official opening, critics came from Canada, the United States, and Britain. The Toronto critics were three in number, and managed to differ with one another about Richard's performance, for which he wore a simple costume of black sweater and trousers. One said he was masterful, another said he was disappointing, and the third was in the middle. Much of the criticism was directed at the set and costumes, but, undismayed, Gielgud and Richard continued to define and refine their conception of the play.

After the second night's show, a party was held on the stage in celebration of Elizabeth's thirty-second birthday. Locked in the hotel much of the time, now she had her moment. A huge flower-bedecked cake had been commissioned for her, with words on it: "To our mascot and den mother—love and happy birthday—The Company." She went to the prop table, grabbed Hamlet's sword, and in imitation of Richard's reading intoned, "Now might I do it pat, now he is a-praying—and now I'll do it." With that she swung the sword over her head and cleaved the cake in two.

On Friday, March 13, John Springer, the personal publicist for Richard and Elizabeth, planned to fly from Toronto to New York. He and his wife, June, were giving a party on Sunday. They had invited favorite friends and clients, among them the Paul Newmans, Myrna Loy, and Sylvia Sidney. And Sybil Burton.

But on that Friday, Richard called Springer and delayed his trip. "Luv," he said, "Elizabeth and I are going to be married on Sunday. We're flying to Montreal. Will you come with us and deal with whatever has to be dealt with?" One of the responsibilities of a publicist of Springer's caliber was to be on call for his clients—especially those as famous as Richard Burton and Elizabeth Taylor. Manfully, he had striven to control rumors and deal with avid columnists and reporters during the *Cleopatra* brouhaha. Now he must sit for two days on a story that much of the world would regard as earth-shaking news.

Montreal was chosen as the marriage site to avoid the crowds that would inevitably accompany a wedding in Toronto. Hume Cronyn, their pal from *Cleopatra,* was in the *Hamlet* cast as Polonius. He had a relative, a high Canadian government official, who promised to help keep the arrangements secret. Sunday morning, March 15, a chartered plane carried Richard, Elizabeth, her parents, John Springer, and a few others to Montreal. Richard was already drinking and had gone without breakfast. "I don't know why he's so nervous," Elizabeth said. "We've been sleeping together for two years."

The promised secrecy had developed a leak. When the plane landed a crowd was waiting. Richard, Elizabeth, and Springer made it to a limousine and sped to the Ritz Carlton Hotel, where Suite 810, the bridal suite, had been set aside for the ceremony. An English Unitarian minister had been found who was willing to perform the ceremony, after several other clergymen had turned down the opportunity.

Elizabeth had already established a tradition for being late for marriages, and this occasion was no different. Richard kept drinking to calm his impatience. But after nearly an hour went by and still no wife-to-be, he grumbled, "Isn't that fat little tart here yet? She'll be late for the last bloody judgment!"

When she appeared she was as gorgeous as might have been expected, wearing a yellow chiffon gown and a headdress of Italian hairpieces entwined with hyacinths and a yellow ribbon. She had on the emerald-and-diamond brooch Richard had bought for her in Rome, and matching diamond-and-emerald earrings and necklace—his wedding gift to her. She had no maid of honor, but Richard's dresser, Bob Wilson, served as Richard's best man.

After a ten-minute ceremony, Richard authorized Springer to say in his behalf: "Elizabeth Burton and I are very, very happy."

"God, yes,"echoed Elizabeth. "I'm so happy you can't believe it. This marriage will last forever."

Edging himself away for a few moments, Springer called Sybil Burton in New York. He told her about the marriage, said he would be flying to New York in time for the party, and that some people of the press would be there, and others undoubtedly would try to come uninvited. Sybil decided it would be best for her to stay home. When Springer arrived at his party he had very little time to enjoy it. Newspapers and the world's wire services kept his telephone busy.

Aaron Frosch by this time had dealt with the problem of the newlyweds' combined earnings and assets, which showed every sign of becoming enormous. Both assured him that the matter was academic, as they firmly intended to stay married to each other all their lives. "Of course," Frosch said. He realized how devoted they were to each other and probably always would be, but as a lawyer, accountant, and tax specialist he always counseled premarital agreements just in the unlikely event something might occur to separate them. They reluctantly agreed to follow his advice, and he set up separate trusts for their holdings and earnings.

After taking curtain calls for the Monday performance following the wedding, Richard brought his new wife onstage and presented her to the goggle-eyed audience. Then he recited a line of Hamlet's to Ophelia: "I say we will have no more marriages!"

"It was madness such as you've never seen," John Springer said.

He was attempting to describe the scene at Boston's Logan Airport on Sunday, March 22, when a chartered plane landed carrying the Burtons and the *Hamlet* company.

Richard had hopes that after the marriage and the end of their "state of sin," the curiosity about them would diminish. Boston surely would be less intrusive than the relatively unsophisticated Toronto. But no—three thousand Bostonians were at the airport on their arrival, and so enthusiastic that they broke through the barriers at the terminal and surrounded the plane. It took an hour to clear the field enough for the plane to taxi into a hangar where limousines and police escorts were waiting to speed them to the Copley-Plaza Hotel.

"At the hotel," said Springer, who was with Richard and Elizabeth in one of the limos, "there was a solid wall of people. The police tried to open a pathway for us. Richard and I were on either side of Elizabeth with our hands on her back to protect her (she's always had a bad back), and hands were reaching out and grabbing at us. The sleeve was torn off my coat. Richard's coat and jacket were ripped. Worst of all was the way they kept pulling at Elizabeth's hair, yanking her head back each time."

BURTON

The lobby, too, was crammed with about a thousand people. "Elizabeth's ear was bloody," Springer said, "from someone pulling at her earring, trying to rip it off. Three policemen trying to clear a path to the elevator were knocked down. We later heard a girl had her leg broken in the crush. By the time we got to the elevator Elizabeth was screaming, with sheer terror, I'm sure."

Finally Richard, with a shove that came from his rugby-playing days, got them into the elevator. When the doors shut on the bedlam in the lobby, Richard said: "Do you think this is how it's going to be?"

They took deep breaths when they reached the safety of the hotel suite, where bar service had been provided. With drinks in hand they sat down, and then all three broke into waves of hysterical laughter.

The two-week Boston run brought full houses and universally admiring reviews for Richard. The performances were fine-tuned for the Broadway opening on April 9, a Thursday.

In New York, Richard and Elizabeth were installed in an eight-room suite—named the Princess Grace suite—on the twentieth floor of the new Regency Hotel on Park Avenue. This became their home during the run of the play, and it provided them with about all the conveniences they might want: three bedrooms, three baths, a forty-foot living room, a well-equipped kitchen, servants' quarters—all done to a designer's taste that ran to Louis XV and XVI, in pinks, oranges, and whites.

In this pleasant abode Elizabeth was able to say: "Richard has given me a sense of reality. I am now—above and beyond anything else—a woman, and that's infinitely more satisfying than being an actress. I'm a woman who needs to be dominated." In 1964, that statement did not seem as strange as it might have twenty years later.

The night of the opening at the Lunt-Fontanne Theater, West Forty-sixth Street was wall-to-wall with people from Broadway at one end to Eighth Avenue at the other. First-nighters had to show their tickets to police to get through the barriers in front of the theater. In all the glory days of Broadway, no one had seen anything quite like it before.

Richard had driven himself to a peak of effort for ten weeks to face the celebrity-filled audience and the forbidding New York critics

BURTON

in their aisle seats. This would be proof that those who accused him of selling out were wrong; proof to Elizabeth that he was the great actor she believed him to be; and most of all, proof to himself that he could dominate a stage and hold an audience in this most testing of roles.

On the other hand, he could hardly have calculated a more advantageous venture. If he triumphed he would be vaulted higher in status—and in our society, status is exchangeable for gold. As it was, he was not being underpaid, with fifteen percent of the box-office receipts as his share.

Like others, he had his theory about Hamlet's nature, that Shakespeare, far, far ahead of his time, had created a manic-depressive. This conception was behind the energy and activity with which he played Hamlet. On that first night in New York he was not reassured by the response.

"They were a chill and indifferent audience," he said afterward. "Strange, not normal. There were so many celebrities they hardly had time to notice us on the stage. They did not pay attention."

It might have been that a good many in the audience were anticipating the lavish party thrown afterward by Alexander Cohen at the Rainbow Room, sixty-five stories high in Rockefeller Center. "It was the scarcest ticket in New York," *Newsweek* reported. "Six hundred carefully selected celebrities and celebrity watchers gathered to pay homage to Rich and Liz. Everyone wanted to see her." All had to wait in line, give their names, and produce their engraved invitations. Montgomery Clift, Elizabeth's dear friend, was there, as were Michael Wilding, Margaret Leighton, Billy Rose, Carol Channing . . . The list of well-known names was nearly endless.

Finally came Richard and Elizabeth, he steering her through a horde of photographers. "Mr. Taylor," one called out to him. "Mr. Burton," he corrected, and then said loudly enough for all of them to hear, "Let's get away from this rubbish."

A radiant Elizabeth went from table to table, advising her friends that they ought to see another performance because Richard felt "the audience was a bit tense, and he reacts to his audience."

The cameras and the bulb-popping became too much for them after a while, and the couple made their escape through a kitchen door. Alexander Cohen upbraided his security men. "This party cost me ten thousand dollars and you let the photographers drive them out?"

The reviews the following day were just about all that Richard and Elizabeth could have wished for. The New York *Times*'s critic spoke of "electrical power and sweeping vitality." Another said Richard was "lucid and sensitive." The distinguished Walter Kerr wrote of "Burton's reverberating resources," but complained of a certain lack of feeling. *Time,* on the other hand, said that he had "put his passion into Hamlet's language rather than his character. . . . His acting is a technician's marvel. His voice has gem-cutting precision and he can outroar Time Square traffic."

It was a personal triumph for Richard, but not for the production as a whole. There was carping about other actors, about the rehearsal costumes, Gielgud's direction. The latter eventually excused himself by saying that the theater was too large and that he was forced to use American actors who all worried about their motivations.

On succeeding nights, crowds continued to wait outside the theater for a glimpse of Richard and also Elizabeth. She attended forty of the performances and never showed up dressed twice in the same outfit. Other times she called at the theater in her chauffeured Rolls to pick up Richard after his performance. The crowds never seemed to diminish, and when audiences came out of other theaters the crowds grew even larger. What was clear was that Richard and Elizabeth had become one of New York's nightly tourist attractions. A reporter asked one woman why she was there. "I wouldn't have come to see her," she said, "if she were only married to Eddie Fisher."

"It's all a mystery to me," Burton told the same reporter. "I'm not sure I like it. It's so undignified." Some were reminded of the days when Frank Sinatra crooned at the Paramount and hordes of bobby-soxers waited outside. But Sinatra, visiting Richard backstage, said it had been different. His crowds were smaller, and they didn't appear night after night for months on end. Richard thought it wouldn't have happened if it hadn't been for the affair and the marriage. "Nonsense," Elizabeth said supportively, "you're the one they're coming to see. You're the Frank Sinatra of Shakespeare."

"Get ahold of yourself, luv," Richard replied.

Elizabeth arranged for another reconciliation when she invited Emlyn Williams—who was also appearing on Broadway—and his wife for a meeting with Richard at the Regency. All hatchets were buried. Emlyn knew by this time that Sybil had adjusted well to her life in New York.

"The last time we were together," Williams told Elizabeth, "you met Mr. Hyde. This time it's Dr. Jekyll."

Elizabeth also took it upon herself to call Richard's family in Wales and invite them to New York to see Richard performing on Broadway. She paid for first-class air tickets, booked rooms for them at the Regency, and had them chauffeured to the theater. Cissie, Richard's beloved sister, struck her as a bit dowdy and she arranged to have bought for her a splendid new wardrobe.

If anything marred Richard's triumphant return to New York, it was the constant sense of confinement he felt. He couldn't even cross Forty-sixth Street and enter Dinty Moore's, one of his favorite restaurants. Also denied him was one of his favorite pastimes, convivial drinking in bars. And as large as the suite was at the Regency, it too was confining. Not that this made Elizabeth unhappy. She had Richard with her to watch bad old movies on television, to talk, and, on many occasions, to fight. She declared their fights were fun. Others who overheard their screaming at each other weren't so sure. Elizabeth described Richard's furies as "like a small atom bomb going off—sparks fly, walls shake, floors vibrate."

One night, as Richard was receiving his usual ovation from the audience, he heard a loud boo. He turned pale. After the curtain came down, he told the stage manager to leave the curtain up after the next call. Then he stepped close to the footlights and said, "We have been playing this production for eighty performances. Some have liked it, some have not. But I can assure you, we have never been booed." The audience applauded, but the booer refused to be silent. There were six more, by actual count.

Richard steadied his nerves with several drinks and returned to the Regency, where Elizabeth was in bed with a cold, watching television. He ordered her to turn the set off, but she continued watching.

Then, taking his shoes off, he said, "I was booed tonight." Elizabeth said something soothing. "Do you understand," he said, "that I have been booed? I played *Hamlet* and was booed!"

"Oh, don't be silly," said his wife.

With that he went to the television set, kicked it over, knocking off one of the knobs, then kicked the set again. Unfortunately his toe hit a screw where the knob had been, causing bloodshed. Richard, a congenital bleeder, couldn't stop the flow, and called for a doctor. He played *Hamlet* with a limp for the next few nights.

Alfred Drake, who played the king, noticed that after a time Richard varied his performance. "He had a theory that Hamlet could be played a hundred ways, and he tested every one of them. Within one scene you might get Heathcliff, Sir Toby Belch, and Peck's Bad Boy." Richard himself mentioned that one night he played Hamlet as a homosexual. He also theorized that most in the audience weren't listening carefully, or had no knowledge of the text. As a test of the theory, he inserted lines from Marlowe during a performance, and apparently no one noticed.

Sunday, a day off, made Richard more than ordinarily restless. John Springer was with them in the hotel one Sunday when Richard became distinctly upset because he couldn't even take a stroll in the park like simple folk did. "We can do it," Elizabeth said. "I'll bet we can do it." She borrowed a plain dress from the baby-sitter, put on a babushka and glasses, while Richard pulled on an old sweater over baggy pants and wore dark glasses. They went out through the hotel garage on Sixty-first Street to avoid a group at the Park Avenue entrance, and barely made it to Madison Avenue, a half-block away, before a mob came rushing after them. Elizabeth was less bothered by it than Richard; she had endured such situations for much of her life.

More bothersome to her was the couple who rented a suite below theirs for the express purpose of listening in on whatever happened above. They would stand on chairs and hold empty glasses to the ceilings to listen in. Elizabeth heard about it when the couple told their friends about the dreadful fights the Burtons were having. Elizabeth acknowledged that they must have heard a good many choice four-letter words. "I love four-letter words," she confessed. "They're so terribly descriptive. They just give me a good feeling." Richard attempted to rid her of the habit. In fact, under his tutelage, or perhaps by example, Elizabeth improved her vocabulary, read better books, and became thoroughly familiar with the gloomy poetry of Dylan Thomas.

Philip Burton, these days, was having problems maintaining his nonprofit acting academy. Richard came up with the idea of holding a poetry reading on a Sunday evening at the Lunt-Fontanne Theater for the benefit of the school. He and Philip would stand on a bare stage and read from T. S. Eliot, D. H. Lawrence, and, of course, Dylan Thomas. But he then realized that if Elizabeth were involved, a high-paying crowd could be drawn. "She'll make them come out of curiosity," he said, "like they go to the zoo. Both Elizabeth and Philip were hesitant at first, but then Philip began working with her three hours a night, five nights a week.

On June 21, 1964, Elizabeth took to the live stage for the first time in her life, with Richard beside her. Filling the hundred-dollar seats were many of Broadway's finest, including Bea Lillie, Adolph Green and Betty Comden, Alan Jay Lerner, Carol Channing, Hume Cronyn and Jessica Tandy. Also there were Montgomery Clift, Kitty Carlisle, and two sisters of the late President Kennedy. Elizabeth (who changed during an intermission) appeared in matched Grecian off-the-shoulder gowns, one purple and one white. Her high-piled hair was ornamented with purple flowers. The costume alone was enough to bring on applause.

After a few false starts, Elizabeth was off and winging, to the surprise of the audience, many of whom were waiting for her to fall on her beautiful face. She started one poem, halted, and said, "Sorry, may I start again? I got all screwed up." "I could say that in *Hamlet* every night," said Richard gallantly.

"If she doesn't get worse soon," Bea Lillie whispered, "they'll all be leaving."

But Elizabeth got better and better, and the audience stayed and listened to her read poems by Hardy and Yeats, and in tandem with Richard, T. S. Eliot's *Portrait of a Lady*. As *Time* pointed out, it took courage for them to recite "Thou hast committed fornication, but that was in another country." She went on to Elizabeth Barrett Browning's "How do I love thee? Let me count the ways." He did the St. Crispin's Day speech from *Henry V.* She recited the Twenty-third Psalm in English, and he in Welsh. And they ended with a scene from *The Lady's Not for Burning*.

"I didn't know she was going to be this good," Richard told the audience at one point, and later she told them, "See—you did get something for your money."

The audience stood for a thunderous ovation that Richard said was unlike any he'd had before. "I've never had an ovation, period," Elizabeth said. "I like it."

The evening brought financial stability to Philip Burton's school. And Burton's *Hamlet* continued to sell out for every performance except a matinee and evening when a tonsil infection caused Richard to miss a day. Forty percent of the audience demanded their money back because of his absence. By the time the agreed-on seventeen weeks came to an end, Richard had set a new record for a *Hamlet* run—136 performances. He had established himself as the best and the most famous. Now he went after the riches. The film he chose to do next was a potboiler—*The Sandpiper*.

While he was still in New York an editor at *Glamour* magazine had the bright thought of asking Richard if he might like to write something for the Christmas issue. This encouraged him to try an autobiographical tale about a Christmas in Wales. Written in longhand and in the first person, it was about how a character called Mad Dan had kept his small nephew out late with a group of miners on Christmas Eve. Eventually the boy learned that his elder sister gave birth that night. The editor at *Glamour* was happy with it and sent him a check for five hundred dollars. When word got out, a publisher secured the rights to bring it out as a slim volume for the bookstores. Richard was immensely gratified to be entering the literary ranks— he admired writers above all others.

Given his choices, *The Sandpiper* would not have been his first if it were not for Elizabeth's desire to do it. A clever producer, Martin Ransohoff, concocted the idea himself, and with Elizabeth and Richard in mind. Until then he was best known for some successful television series, notably *The Beverly Hillbillies*. His story dealt with an unmarried woman artist living alone with a son in the Big Sur region of California. As developed by several writers, Dalton Trumbo among them, the boy looks to be headed for delinquency, causing the intervention of a married local minister. This enables him to meet and soon to be involved with the boy's uncommonly voluptuous mother.

Elizabeth had not worked in a film for nearly two years. She was anxious to restock her bank accounts. "Picking up a million here and there is always a bit of a giggle," she was quoted as saying. She was taken by the part of the unconventional woman; Richard was less enchanted with playing another ecclesiastic. Elizabeth was offered her giggle of a million and Richard half that. But Aaron Frosch pointed out a serious problem. Their tax situation meant they would actually lose money by exceeding the limits of tax-free stay in the United States. An accommodation was made: a month of location in the Big Sur region, and interiors to be done in a Paris studio.

Offers were now pouring in for the celebrated pair, and no sooner was the deal made for *The Sandpiper* than Paramount offered him *The Spy Who Came in from the Cold*. Richard had read the book earlier, and made overtures to buy the rights; but by that time director Martin Ritt, with Paul Newman, had acquired it. "I fought to get Burton," Ritt said. "His agents were asking three-quarters of a million for him. Finally Paramount agreed to pay it." Producer Ray Stark, at the same time, was after Elizabeth for the film version of *The Owl and the Pussycat*, and MGM wanted Richard for a remake of *Goodbye, Mr. Chips*, but both fell through.

In late July the Burtons entrained for Los Angeles on their way for a short stay in Puerto Vallarta. While in their compartment on their favorite train, the *Super Chief*, Elizabeth took out a play script and said to Richard, "They've asked me to do *Who's Afraid of Virginia Woolf?*" Neither had seen the corrosive play about an ineffectual professor and his blowsy wife. She read it while he buried himself in a book. After finishing the play she handed it to Richard without saying anything.

"I thought I'd have a glance at it," Richard later recalled. "It was late, ten at night, which is late for a train. Perhaps I'd read an act and finish it in the morning. But I was compelled to finish it."

By then, Elizabeth was asleep. Richard read through the play again, and woke Elizabeth. "I think you're too young for the part," he said. "I don't think you're enough of a harridan. Maybe you don't have the power to play Martha [the acid-tongued wife], but you've

BURTON

got to play it to stop everybody else from playing it. I don't want any other actresses to do it. It's too good a part." They stayed up most of the night discussing it.

Waiting impatiently for the *Super Chief* to make its way across the country was Ernest Lehman.

He was one of Hollywood's most successful screenwriters, and had been assigned both to adapt the play and to produce it. He had been mulling over how to cast the film of the play, which was considered a daring project for that time. The play's harsh language had electrified Broadway, and a prominent Hollywood topic of conversation was who would play the two important roles, and would the language survive? Hugh French, the agent for the Burtons, tested the waters for them (without their knowing it) by mentioning them to a friend of Lehman's. The more Lehman thought about Elizabeth Taylor as Martha, the more he liked the idea, but he could not see the powerful-voiced Burton for George, the professor.

Lehman went to see studio head Jack Warner and told him he wanted to offer the role of Martha to Elizabeth Taylor. "She's too young for it," Warner objected. "And she'll cost too much." Then the idea appealed to him, too, and he gave Lehman the go-ahead to negotiate.

But this was not to happen until the Burtons returned from their brief sojourn in Puerto Vallarta, a refuge from the constant prying attention they received elsewhere. The house he had bought when making *Iguana* he named Casa Kimberley; later he added a second house across the street. To a first-time visitor it was hard to imagine why they wanted to live in Puerto Vallarta. Next to the house was a grocery store. And while they had a view of the sea, they also gazed out over the town's more decrepit quarter. But behind the barbed-wire-topped walls of their house, they had their all-important privacy, and for much of the year magnificent weather.

Late in August, Hugh French telephoned Ernest Lehman and asked him to meet with Elizabeth in the Burtons' bungalow at the Beverly Hills Hotel. Richard let Lehman in, saying Elizabeth was still at her dentist's having a tooth recapped. He explained that she was allergic to the anesthetic, and the procedure was very delicate. He talked

BURTON

about the play and the kind of actresses who might be able to play Martha, but Elizabeth, he said, came through the black box like no one else. "I've told her," he said, "this is your *Hamlet*."

Elizabeth arrived, then Hugh French and Michael Wilding, their agents. Richard repeated what he'd said to Lehman, when Elizabeth stopped him. "Shut up, luv. I don't want to hear it from you. I want to hear it from Ernie."

Lehman had the notion that already Elizabeth sounded a little like Martha. "I have the feeling you're on the same wavelength as Martha," he told her.

"You mean because I use four-letter words?" she asked.

"Not exactly," Lehman said, squirming.

"I don't use them anymore. Richard has broken me of the habit."

"That's right," said Richard. "I've cured her of that unfortunate tendency."

Elizabeth turned her violet eyes on him and said, "You bet your ass." Turning back to Lehman, she said, "That's a three-letter word."

They continued discussing how she might play the role. She would have to deglamorize and age herself, and put on some weight. But when he left the bungalow, Lehman was left uncertain about whether or not she wanted to do the film.

14

During the four weeks the Burtons spent in California's Big Sur region on location for *The Sandpiper*, negotiations continued for Elizabeth to appear in *Who's Afraid of Virginia Woolf?* She was altogether eager to take on the challenge of Martha, but Hugh French negotiated for her as if she were reluctant. But by the time she and Richard returned to Los Angeles for a brief stop before heading to Paris, she was committed to the film. The start date was set back to mid-1965; the major portion of *The Sandpiper* remained to be finished, and Richard would then go into *The Spy Who Came in from the Cold*. Elizabeth did not want to be separated from Richard, nor did she want to be separated from the children.

The boys' schoolwork was suffering from being shifted from place to place and school to school. Liza at seven was still unable to read, and Maria, hospitalized for several operations to correct her deformed hip, spoke no English. A tutor was added to the growing entourage. Richard would have preferred to have the children in English boarding schools during the many months in Europe, and the tutor, Paul Neshamkin, also thought it a poor idea to trot them around. But Elizabeth wanted to have them with her, and when the time came to leave for Paris, the children were packed up too. On their arrival, someone counted 136 pieces of luggage. Their combined staff now consisted of Elizabeth's secretary, the secretary's secretary, a chauffeur, the tutor, a governess, a nurse for Maria, Richard's dresser and personal assistant, Bob Wilson, Wilson's wife, Sally, Richard's makeup man, Ron Berkeley, and a hairdresser for Elizabeth.

But before leaving the country, they stopped off at the Beverly Hills Hotel and met with Ernest Lehman. Jack Warner knew it was foregone that Elizabeth would demand her usual million-dollar fee. This time she wanted more and got it: a million-one, in Hollywood parlance, and ten percent of the gross after ten million return, and approval of a costar and of the director. With the deal made, Lehman was there at the bungalow to discuss the choice of the costar.

Elizabeth, in a dressing gown, sat with Richard while Lehman, embarrassed at having to talk about it in the actor's presence, brought up the names of Jack Lemmon, Arthur Hill, and Peter O'Toole as possible for George.

At the mention of O'Toole, Richard said, "He's got no bottom," by which Lehman assumed he meant he was lacking in depth.

Idly Elizabeth, with a slight turn of her head toward Richard, said, "What about him?"

Lehman quickly told Richard he indeed regarded him as the finest actor in the world, but he was too powerful, too virile, too impressive, and so on.

"I think you're wrong, Ernie," Elizabeth said, "but back to the list." She gave her approval to six of the actors he mentioned. "I know we're not talking about directors yet," she said, "but Richard and I think we can get Elia Kazan to do the picture."

"You and Richard? But only *you* are in the picture."

"We're stopping in New York," Elizabeth said, "and I'm sure we can get Kazan. He would do anything that Richard and I are in together."

Lehman had the sense of a steely interior beneath her satiny exterior. So did Richard. "Ernie," he said, "I want you to really be free to make your own decision. But if you can't get the one you want, I'll always be there in the bullpen, ready to come in if you need me."

Lehman said politely, "You think about the role while you're in Paris, and I'll think about it."

BURTON

As he was leaving, Elizabeth told him, laughing, "Ernie, I'd have done this role for nothing, you know. But Hugh French told me to say a million wasn't enough. We took you, we really took you." She cackled at the humor of it.

From New York Richard and Elizabeth and their entourage set sail for France on the *Queen Elizabeth*. In Paris they settled in at the Hotel Lancaster, a quietly luxurious hotel just off the Champs-Elysées. The rent for twenty-one rooms, and services, came to ten thousand dollars a week. Richard and Elizabeth inhabited the top floor, the children were on the floor below, and had their own school-room. When time allowed, they would be sent for by Elizabeth and Richard.

Their work schedule was arranged for them to arrive at the studio at ten in the morning for makeup, to be ready for the camera at eleven. At lunchtime their chauffeur appeared and whisked them off to a restaurant of their choice, or back to the quiet bar of the Lancaster for meetings with a growing group of agents, lawyers, accountants, and producers. To handle the complexity of their finances, as well as avoiding taxes, they formed two separate corporations. Elizabeth called hers Interplanetary Productions; Richard named his Atlantic Programmes Limited. He thoroughly enjoyed being a corporation as well as a star. He told the tutor, "I want to be rich, rich, rich." And he added that he wanted to be at least as rich as his wife.

Invitations to the toniest social events in Paris poured in to them, and most of these they ignored, but when they did make an entrance, as for an occasion held at Maxim's, Elizabeth glittered and Richard sparkled, as all eyes turned toward them. Yet, they seldom went out, preferring to stay at "home" at the Lancaster or to dine quietly at a favorite restaurant where they knew the management would protect them.

At the studio they now and then deigned to meet with reporters, who usually found them burbling with enthusiasm for each other. "Nothing—we vow, nothing—will induce us to be apart," Elizabeth told one of them.

"We tried to be apart for an hour and a half once," Richard chimed in, "but it didn't work."

"Another thing," Elizabeth said, "since I've known Richard, I've never been seriously sick. A cold, maybe." (A few months later she was in the hospital again.)

He enjoyed making light of Elizabeth's charms. "I think her arms should not be overexposed, because they're not among her virtues. And she should never wear low-heeled shoes." Fondly he would call, "Where is that fat cow of mine?"

On the other hand, he told a writer, "Life with Elizabeth is like waking up and finding a wonderful new toy on your pillow every morning. You never stop marveling or being surprised."

Pausing for effect, he added, "I worship her."

He was bold enough to challenge the film's director, Vincente Minnelli, with objections to the way he set up a scene. Minnelli, a longtime veteran, said it would be done his way. Richard subsided. "For the money," he said, "we will dance."

In Hollywood, Ernest Lehman received a call from Hugh French. "Richard has given the matter of playing George some thought," French said. "Now he is convinced he can do it."

Lehman had earlier decided that Jack Lemmon was his choice for the role. He had sent the script to him, and Lemmon indicated his interest. But a few weeks later, Lemmon's agent called. "I don't know how to tell you this, and I don't know who Jack's been talking to, but he'd rather back away from it."

Lehman never did find out why Lemmon refused to play a role as rich and important as any film of the time offered. "Perhaps someone said to him, 'She'll eat you alive,' or maybe he just didn't want to play a castrated male." And he began thinking: if it were a problem of handling Elizabeth, who would be better than Burton? Jack Warner balked at first, when Lehman made the suggestion to him. The budget would soar even more. But since Burton now wanted the role, perhaps his price could be negotiated downward. Hugh French assured him that Richard was very anxious to play George, and would be cooperative. They negotiated long distance. Lehman lost the battle; Richard would get $750,000 along with a percentage of the gross.

Richard was on the soundstage at the studio in Paris when Hugh French called from California with the news. He hung up the phone and gave a great cheer. "They paid me my price!" he exulted.

BURTON

* * *

Lehman is unsure to this day of the degree of manipulation that led to the teaming of the famous couple in his film. But almost lazily, seeming to make no effort, Elizabeth had gotten her way in having her husband with her in a role more demanding than any she had played. It was as though she was aware of her power, and had become adept at using it. Her agreement was needed not only for the costar but also for the director.

During the Thanksgiving holiday period, as filming on *The Sandpiper* was winding down, Lehman flew to Paris to present some names, prominently that of a sensitive director who had not yet had a major hit. He checked in at the Lancaster and then taxied to the studio, where he found Richard and Elizabeth in a small screening room looking at daily rushes. Each had a bottle of champagne from which they sipped. They sat and watched in silence. When the lights came up, Elizabeth suggested that Lehman talk to Richard about directors.

"Out of the question," Burton told Lehman when the man he wanted was mentioned. "He doesn't know how to tell a story."

When evening came, Lehman joined the Burtons for dinner at an excellent restaurant, La Méditerranée. There was a liberal consumption of fine wine and champagne. The mood was warm. "Why don't you direct?" Elizabeth suggested to Lehman. "I wouldn't do that to you," Lehman said, "or to Edward Albee."

"I want Fred Zinnemann," Elizabeth then said.

Zinnemann had already been approached but had shown no interest.

Richard suggested noted French director Henri-Georges Clouzot.

"You don't know anything about anything," Elizabeth sneered, punching him on the shoulder. "You made *Ice Palace*."

"John Frankenheimer?" said Richard, unperturbed.

"I talked to him," Lehman said. "He insists his name would have to be above the title."

"Fuck him," Elizabeth said.

"Any director should be thrilled to do this picture," Richard agreed. "Under those conditions, we'll forget him."

"You know who's a genius?" Elizabeth asked.

"Who?"

BURTON

"Mike Nichols."

"But he's never directed a picture," Lehman said.

"I'm in awe of him," Richard said. "He's an enormous talent."

"Yes, Ernie," said Elizabeth. "We think he should certainly be considered."

Lehman agreed to consider him, along with a few others that neither Elizabeth nor Richard made objection to. The next morning he heard a knock at his door, and upon opening it, saw Richard. "Elizabeth," Richard said, "has instructed me to come down and apologize to you."

"For what?"

"I don't know," Richard said, "but those are my instructions, so I'm giving you my formal apologies for last evening."

The choice of a director still unresolved, Lehman packed his bags and as he was about to leave for the airport, his room phone rang. The New York call was from Larry Turman, a producer and a good friend.

"Ernie," he said, "I'm calling on behalf of a friend of mine, Mike Nichols. He'd like me to tell you that he's very interested in directing *Who's Afraid of Virginia Woolf?*"

"Whose friend are you, Larry?" Lehman asked. "Mine or Mike Nichols'? He's a comedy director."

"I'm just passing along the message," Turman said.

By this circuitous route, with pressure obviously, but delicately, being applied by Elizabeth and Richard, Mike Nichols became the prime candidate to direct *Virginia Woolf*. It was news to Jack Warner until an agent called him to negotiate for Nichols. On Lehman's return to California he called him to his office. "What's all this about that comedy director?" Warner asked him.

"Look," Lehman said, "the Burtons are in awe of him. He'll be able to keep them in hand. This isn't just another Hollywood film. It can have a touch of Broadway genius."

Warner, seeing in his head the budget rocketing even higher, shook his head, but agreed to go along. Since Nichols was preparing a play for Broadway, and Richard and Elizabeth were locked into filming on other pictures, a start date for May 1965 was tentatively set.

★　　★　　★

While still in Paris, Elizabeth took the step of renouncing her dual American-British citizenship and becoming only British, out of love for her husband, she said. But she assured whoever cared (other than the IRS) that she still loved America.

Her love for jewelry was as avid as ever, and she would make it clear to a likely supplier that she would appreciate a pretty little gift. Martin Ransohoff took a broad hint and presented her with a diamond brooch. But she also enjoyed giving gifts, and those around her often received the benefit of thoughtful generosity. When the book version of Richard's Christmas story appeared in a printing of twenty thousand copies, she had her secretaries scour Paris and London for a writing portfolio for him, bound in calf and complete with such accessories as lined writing pads, blotters, pens and erasers, ready for other masterpieces he would write when in the mood.

At Christmastime she decided he needed a new wardrobe and she spent fifteen thousand dollars for thirty-seven hand-tailored suits.

In January 1965 the Burtons were once more at the Dorchester in London, the first of several locations for *The Spy Who Came in from the Cold*. Martin Ritt, at first meeting with Richard, told him, "The key to the part of Alec Leamas is anonymity. You're playing a spy. You'll have to cut down on your voice, because with your voice anyone would recognize you from here to Glasgow."

"You know what you're asking?"

"Yes," Ritt said. "Play the part. Facelessness—that's the key."

None of his elegant Christmas clothes could be worn for the picture, because Ritt insisted he wear the same seedy suit and shabby raincoat through the seventeen weeks of filming. Leamas, the tired spy, must seem able to be lost in a crowd.

"Are you sure you're right?" Richard worriedly asked Ritt, feeling his personality was being damped down to the point of anonymity. Ritt answered simply that no one could guarantee how a film would turn out.

As the filming proceeded in London, Holland, Bavaria, and Dublin, where Berlin's Checkpoint Charlie was reconstructed—neither East nor West German authorities would permit its use for filming— relations between Richard and Martin Ritt became strained.

"He was uncomfortable with me," Ritt said. "On social levels he didn't find me sympathetic."

Ritt is a burly man, a former football tackle who had been associated with some left-wing causes in his youth and had spent several years blacklisted in television and motion pictures. He was known as an actor's director; his most recent film was *Hud*, with Paul Newman starring.

Ritt was bothered by Richard's drinking, less because it affected the performance to any great degree than "because it lacked a certain kind of discipline. I had made a commitment to the picture, to achieve the most that could be gotten for it, and I wanted the same from everybody.

"And I wasn't sympathetic to his life-style, nor Elizabeth's. She was there much of the time as an onlooker, constantly drinking from a champagne bottle. She'd open a bottle as early as eleven in the morning. Richard was fine until lunchtime, and then he'd join her, and by the time he was back he had a buzz on from too much wine. I'm sure he felt that in spite of his great charm, and his popularity with the crew, I didn't appreciate him enough.

"While in Holland, to make up time on the schedule, I wanted to shoot on a Sunday. It seems there was a soccer game he wanted to see. In front of the crew he made some remarks about me—a man known for working-class sympathies who wouldn't allow the crew to see a soccer game on a Sunday. It was a low blow in view of what I had gone through when blacklisted. He apologized the next day for that, but then there was an occasion when I asked for another take, and he snapped, 'It's good enough for me.' I sensed he was giving a superior performance, but I wasn't going to take that sort of shit. So I snapped back, 'It's not good enough for me, Richard.'

"For a second it looked like he was ready for a fight, but then he said, 'I know you've been an athlete and can handle yourself with your hands, but don't fuck around with me.' Then he cooled down."

Claire Bloom, who had been with Richard on the stage and in films several times before, was cast as his costar. "I was aware that she was an old girlfriend," Ritt said. "He had dumped her, of course. But still he wasn't very nice to her, understandable, I suppose, with Elizabeth there."

Bloom made her feelings known about this treatment to the columnist Sheilah Graham.

"He hadn't changed at all," she told Graham, "except physically. He was still drinking, still boasting, he was still late, still reciting the same poems and telling the same stories as when he was twenty-three. They were both rather aloof to me. During the month's shooting in Ireland I was never asked to dinner by the Burtons. He was interesting, years ago, but now I found him rather boring, as people are when they have got what they always wanted . . . a beautiful wife, money, and a great career. In the early days he would have included a wish to be the greatest actor in the world. It was obvious that he was going to be a huge star, which is not the same as being a great actor. He has confused them. He thinks they are the same."

A journalist showed him Claire Bloom's remarks, and asked him to comment. "I can tell you in just four words," Richard said: "Hell hath no fury . . ."

Richard, now nearing the age of forty, could still take pride in his drinking ability. In Dublin, he told a reporter, "On the last shot of the day I had to knock back a whiskey. I decided to use the real hard stuff. We did forty-seven takes. Imagine it, luv, forty-seven whiskeys." Even allowing for exaggeration, Ritt's disapproving attitude was understandable.

Richard had something new to crow about while shooting exteriors in Bavaria. As a result of the Christmas story, and an article on acting for *Life* magazine, a publisher offered him a hundred-thousand-dollar advance to do a book. "My agent is getting bids for my autobiography," he proudly told reporters. He declined a newspaper offer to do a column, but accepted an assignment from *The New York Times Book Review* to review a biography of Dylan Thomas. His writings were sparse, but what he did was invariably polished and professional.

In spite of the tension and lack of sympathy between him and his nondrinking director, there was little doubt that *The Spy Who Came in from the Cold* was turning out well, and it would bring Richard an Academy nomination. Still the blood between them was bad enough for him to refer to Ritt as "that prick of a director." He made the remark to Joanne Woodward, a good friend of Ritt's, and she quickly made a pithy remark of her own in defense of Ritt, and turned her back on him. In later years, Ritt said, Richard made some kind remarks about him as a director—or so he heard—but looking back on it, "it was not a happy picture."

After finishing work on the film, Richard and Elizabeth secluded themselves for several weeks in a villa on the Cap d'Antibes, soaking up sun. Richard, wanting Elizabeth's boys to have the benefits of a good education, arranged for them to be installed in a private Swiss school. And it was while they were in Antibes that news came that Sybil had remarried. Richard cabled her his good wishes.

Sybil was flourishing in New York. She had quickly proven that she did not require the company of her famous husband to be a social success. Hardly a day went by when she did not turn up in a gossip or fashion column. "It was rather like having a holiday," the silver-haired New York celebrity told Elaine Dundy. A favorite place of hers was a club on East Fifty-fourth Street called the Strollers. It featured the Establishment, a British theatrical group. "I loved them," she told Dundy. "They were English and they were something new for me to get interested in. One of the group kept asking me: 'But what are you going to do, Sybil?' "

Joining the group, she helped conceive the idea of turning the club into a theater. She functioned as co-producer and casting director. Soon enough, the Establishment Theater Company, as it was called, was producing such plays as *The Ginger Man* and *The Knack*. When the Establishment group left New York, she took over the club and turned it into a discotheque, naming it Arthur after a Beatle haircut style in the film *A Hard Day's Night*. It quickly became the most famous, the most "in," the hardest to get into. Crowds gathered outside the unpretentious building each night hoping to get in, and, if not, at least to see those recognizable ones who did.

While auditioning rock groups, Sybil was impressed by a quintet called the Wild Ones, and even more impressed by its twenty-four-year-old leader, Jordan Christopher. "I was attracted to Jordan right off, very strongly," she revealed to Elaine Dundy, "but I couldn't believe it, wouldn't let myself even think about it. It was the age difference that shocked me about my feelings. What I kept saying to myself all the time was: 'Sybil, what *are* you doing, you a simple Welsh Methodist lass, with . . . rock and roll?' "

BURTON

Once inside the club, a patron would find himself in a dark crowded room, colored lights flashing from the ceiling, the amplified music shaking the floor and drowning out any reasonable attempt at conversation. "It's like the Black Hole of Calcutta," one of Sybil's investors said, "only with no air." Yet, in some indefinable way, Arthur was different from other discotheques. It had class, a touch of elegance that came from Sybil's presence and the many friends she entertained there. Then Sybil did something that seemed shocking, and remarkably newsworthy at the time: she up and married Jordan Christopher.

But not without introducing him to eight-year-old Kate first. Kate liked Jordan and gave her blessing to the marriage. It did look a little odd, she white-haired, though only thirty-six; he dark, Macedonian by descent, and twenty-four. "They both worried at first about how long the marriage might last," Kate said when she was grown. "But it did. And he became a remarkably good second father."

15

Early in July Richard and Elizabeth came back to Hollywood like visiting royalty. A mansion had been rented for them and their staff on Carolwood Drive, in Bel Air's Holmby Hills, about as exclusive an address as could be found between Bakersfield and San Diego. It had not just one swimming pool but two. The Burtons made news simply because, like Everest, they were there, but they were also appearing in the most-talked-about film of the year, and there was the intriguing question of how would thirty-three-year-old Elizabeth turn herself into the frazzled mid-forties Martha? It was learned that Edward Albee had not approved of either Elizabeth or Richard for the choice roles; he had wanted Bette Davis and James Mason.

Albee was undoubtedly aware that the Burtons, because of their fame, their notoriety, and most important their great box-office potential, were in a position of such prominence that they tended to overshadow other elements of a production. As one important director put it, "The trouble with the Burtons is that their personalities are so strong that they tend to turn everything into a Liz-and-Dick picture. The story and the meaning and the other characters disappear and everybody just wants to see the sparks fly between Liz and Richard."

BURTON

Would this film be one more case in point? It proved to be the summit of both Richard's and Elizabeth's acting careers.

Ernest Lehman was still having problems assembling his team. While there had been no objection to casting George Segal and Sandy Dennis as the other couple in the lives of Martha and George, he ran into an objection from Richard when he proposed Haskell Wexler, noted for his documentary style, as the cinematographer.

"No, not Haskell Wexler," Richard said vehemently. "He'll make my face look like craters on the moon. Ernie, look at my face." He pointed to his pockmarks. "This is the way he'll photograph me!" Lehman realized he was very upset. But the more he tried to reason with him, the angrier Richard became.

Mike Nichols favored Wexler too, but faced with Richard's objection, he telephoned the canny producer Sam Spiegel and asked him who was the greatest cinematographer in the world. "Harry Stradling Sr.," Spiegel said without hesitation. Stradling at first was agreeable to taking on the picture, but just as three weeks of rehearsals were about to begin, he became stubborn. He had certain conditions. He didn't want interference from a first-time director, Mike Nichols. He didn't want to make a beautiful woman ugly, and he didn't want to work with a drunk. "I'm too old and too rich to put up with the bullshit," he told Lehman.

At this crisis, Haskell Wexler was hurriedly contacted and urged to leave another film he was about to start. When he read Lehman's screenplay, he was anxious to do it, and precipitated a little feud (by ditching the other film) that would last for years. By this time, faced with a *fait accompli,* there was nothing Richard could do about the situation, craters or no craters.

Agreement was more easily reached for an art director, the stylish Richard Sylbert, and, as a matter of course, Elizabeth's favorite costumer, Irene Sharaff. Then, what to do about the press, interest from which was high? One press conference was agreed upon, but after that—here the Burtons and Lehman joined together—it was an absolutely closed set. Mike Nichols was not happy about it. "He loved publicity," Lehman said.

The schedule called for rehearsals and three weeks of filming at the studio, then a location trip to the Smith College campus for the large number of scenes that took place at night. Elizabeth and Richard were given spacious adjoining dressing rooms at the Warner studio, bicycles to pedal between the makeup and costume rooms to the stage.

After their arrival and installation in the mansion on Carolwood Drive, Lehman called to welcome them. A pleasant bantering mood was quickly established.

When Elizabeth came on the phone, Lehman said, "Hello, Elizabeth, how are you?"

"Wonderful. Thank you for all the goodies. They're divine."

Lehman had sent up dozens of roses, a case of champagne, bottles of Scotch and vodka.

"Oh, you're very welcome," he said. "I hear you're in town to make a picture."

"Oh, no," she said. "We called it off. Richard and I just spoke to our lawyer."

"That's nice. Are you enjoying yourselves?"

"Yes, so much that we wish we could just stay at the house and not do anything."

"I have an idea," Lehman said. "Why don't we postpone the picture until 1968?"

"Oh no," she said. "I'll see you Tuesday morning."

"Okay, give my best to your husband."

"Richard sends his love," Elizabeth said.

Lehman was to learn that Richard almost never came to a telephone unless it was mandatory that he do so.

On July 4 Lehman spent a desultory day with Mike Nichols beside the pool of his rented house to talk about the script and the upcoming production. Nichols admitted he was having difficulty conceiving of Elizabeth Taylor as stout-and-frumpy Martha. "It's like asking a chocolate milkshake to do the work of a double martini," he said.

He was showing signs of nervousness, which he would cover up with touches of laid-back humor. The night before rehearsals would begin with the cast, he telephoned Lehman. "You know I'm very nervous about this picture," he said, "and you have to start saying nice things about me. You've been saying nice things about me to other people, but you have to start saying them to me."

On the first rehearsal day, prior to the arrival of the Burtons, their dressing rooms were checked to make sure the flowers, the baskets of fruit, and the bottles of champagne were there. At 10:30 A.M. the Burtons grandly arrived in their limousine, to be greeted by Lehman, who received a polite kiss from Elizabeth and a friendly hug from Richard, who liked writers in general and who felt that Lehman was someone not of the general run of Hollywood types.

Elizabeth loved the flowers—lilies-of-the-valley and white roses—and about the champagne she said: "Somebody knows what I like." Soon enough the dressing room was crowded. John Springer, the publicist (usually the antipublicist) came; so did Hugh French and his son, Robin, both Richard's agents; and Irene Sharaff came in to greet Elizabeth. Bob Wilson and his wife, Sally, were in attendance as usual. Meanwhile, Nichols was waiting for his cast on the sound-stage, where a table had been set up with copies of Lehman's script and pads and pencils for suggested changes.

As they walked to the stage, Richard confided to Lehman, "I like your script so much, it frightens me a little." Nichols, on the other hand, kept asking Lehman to cut pages. For most of the day Nichols kept his cast, which included George Segal and Sandy Dennis, sitting at the table reading through and acting out the script.

"It's the first time I've done this," Elizabeth said, "acting out a complete screenplay at one sitting."

She had a complaint to make about a scene in which she dances with George Segal in a roadhouse. "It's phony," she said, "it has a Hollywood kind of vulgarity." A full-scale argument developed over the point. Nichols tended to agree with her: "I'm not saying this just because you're the star."

To which Richard promptly said, "She's not the star. I am."

Lehman was impressed by how quickly Richard committed his dialogue to memory, although in the early stages he made little effort to get deeply into the role. And Richard, in off moments, would come out with remarks that gave Lehman the feeling that there was a brooding side to his personality. He picked up a prop—a copy of *The New York Times Magazine*—and showed Lehman a photograph of the sculptor Giacometti. "I can't believe," he said, "that a man with a face as beautiful as that could have been the great artist he is." He amplified with, "I believe all great art comes from people who are ugly or have a terrible inferiority complex. I know no one who is beautiful and produces art."

Lehman wondered how he classified himself and Elizabeth.

"People feel that Laurence Olivier is a great artist," Richard went on, "and yet is beautiful, but I happen to know that Olivier has such a terrible inferiority complex that he never liked to play a role unless he could put on something that was not himself. Such as a false nose."

The Sandpiper was about to be released, and he and Elizabeth attended a special charity premiere in Hollywood. After the opening the reviews ranged from middling poor to dreadful. Some audiences found unintended hilarity in a scene in which Burton, as the smitten minister, lies on the sand beside his now mistress and announces, "I have now lost my sense of sin." In *Life,* Eleanor Perry accused Richard of having "danced to the tune of petty pipers."

But at least he had been frank in saying he had done it for the money, hardly a crime in a capitalistic world. He and Elizabeth joined the deriders of *The Sandpipers*. One reviewer thought she had given the best performance of her career, and Elizabeth said she would sue him for libel. "It was crap," she said categorically, "and we did it only for the money."

But when the box-office returns showed they had another hit, the delighted producer, Martin Ransohoff, presented Elizabeth with another piece of jewelry, which she was quick to mention to Lehman.

"What does one give to the woman who has everything?" Lehman asked.

"Another husband," Mike Nichols said promptly.

"Hey now," Richard said, "wait a minute."

"Well," Elizabeth said, "I've just seen a fabulous piece of jewelry designed by David Webb."

"Who?" asked Lehman.

"David Webb. Take out your pen and write the name down, so you won't forget. Look what Richard has just given me." She showed Lehman a beautiful diamond bracelet.

"Lovely," he said.

"I wonder why you haven't given me anything yet," she said.

"Because my wife told me that if I did give you a present she would leave me."

"You son of a bitch," Richard, who had overheard, said. "You'll do anything to get out of giving Elizabeth a present."

He and Elizabeth wandered off, shaking their heads at the meanness of the man. It was supposedly all in fun, but Elizabeth's wheedling for gifts ran like a theme through the days of production. On the other hand, she and Richard evidenced their serious attitude toward the film when they told Nichols that if he needed more than the allotted shooting time they would give him two free weeks at the end. At their rates of pay this was a gift worth a few hundred thousand dollars.

Actual filming of the picture began on July 26. Lehman sent two dozen white roses to Elizabeth and a whip to Mike Nichols. Later, Elizabeth told him she loved the flowers but wondered what he was giving Richard. Lehman said he had promised him a piece of sculpture being used as a prop. "Oh," said Elizabeth. "Aren't you lucky, Richard." And, turning to Lehman, said, "What are you giving me?"

He pointed to the set. "How about the entire house?"

Lehman had received a warning from Irene Sharaff. "I must tell you something about Elizabeth. She will see you as every producer who has ever been in her life. She does the same thing with all of them. She chews them up and cuts them into little pieces, then puts them back together until finally there's some sort of relationship."

Richard commented on the double rope of pearls Ransohoff had given her, and which she sported proudly. She reminded him, he said, of his Aunt Tessie, who was apparently on the greedy side. "The wonderful thing about Elizabeth is that she loves jewels so much that she makes even a stingy man like me want to give her jewelry just to see the thrill when she gets it."

They were not long into the filming when Elizabeth began to demonstrate her ways with producers—and directors, too. She conceived an animus toward the assistant director, who, she claimed, was saying unkind things about both Nichols and Lehman. He was causing "distention" on the set.

Did she mean gas? Lehman wondered. Richard had mentioned that Elizabeth had a habit of mixing her metaphors. "It's now in the lap of the cards," she had told him once.

Of course, Elizabeth had gone on, she hated to see anyone fired, but this person was making both her and Richard unhappy, and there was another assistant director over at MGM she had worked with often and who would be perfect on the picture.

A Machiavellian situation developed, with everyone but Elizabeth refusing to get involved. Lehman received a midnight phone call from her. She had the "new" assistant director with her, she said, and now she'd heard that the old one was staying. It was terribly upsetting for her. What a position to put her in! Lehman suddenly realized that the only one with her at that hour was Richard, and asked that he be put on the phone to inject some realism into the discussion.

Richard came on. "Ernie," he said, "all I have to say is this: this is becoming a dreadful picture. The writing is bad, the acting is bad, the directing is terrible, and the whole thing will flop. That's all I have to say. Now I will return to the billiards table."

The next day at the studio Lehman asked Richard how his billiards game had gone the previous night.

"I was in a bad mood last night," he said, smiling. "I was mad at practically everyone yesterday, and when I'm angry I get rather mean, cold, and rotten. In fact, I was being George."

Lehman told him how much the makeup, the glasses he wore, the clothes, made him seem like George.

"I *am* George," Richard said.

The assistant–director situation simmered, with Nichols in the middle between Elizabeth and Lehman. Since both Nichols and Lehman were on their first outings as director and producer respectively, they may not have been aware of the degree to which stars of Elizabeth's magnitude had been coddled in MGM's glory days. The studio tended to wrap them in a blanket of security, assigning to their films the people they felt most comfortable with. But Elizabeth was not getting her way in this case, and a coolness developed among the parties. This was noticeable when Lehman stopped Richard as he was about to enter the set for his next scene and told him he had seen an assembly of the rushes and thought they were quite wonderful. "How do you like the picture so far?" he asked.

"Which picture? Oh, you mean this one?"

"Of course."

"I like it very much indeed," Richard said coolly, and kept on walking.

BURTON

★   ★   ★

Lehman was learning that producing a picture with the Burtons meant catering to them in every way possible. If their wishes and complaints were not made known to him directly, Elizabeth's secretary, Dick Hanley, brought them to him. Late in August, the production moved on to the Smith College campus in Northampton, Massachusetts. A Boeing 727 was chartered to carry the cast and crew. Richard and Elizabeth became upset over the fact that the plane would make a refueling stop at Chicago. Why couldn't a plane have been found that would take them all the way to Bradley Field in Connecticut? They hated flying, and here they were being forced into an extra takeoff and landing, which they particularly hated.

The airline promised to make every effort to fly without an interim stop. To fortify them against the rigors of the flight, the Burtons asked for double vodkas and tonic before takeoff. With these, and refills, the flight passed pleasantly, causing Nichols to remark, "If only we could stay in the plane and never land."

Then came the game of musical houses. It was not expected that the presence of the Burtons in Northampton would cause any great amount of excitement, and in any case, a force of seventy security guards was enlisted to protect the houses and campus. The closed-set edict was being strictly enforced, although now and then a stray photographer or reporter would be found hovering. The house assigned to the Burtons had a large picture window and fronted on a lake. Mike Nichols was also given a large house, but George Segal and Sandy Dennis were provided with hotel suites.

Nichols liked his house so much that he said he wanted to stay there forever. George Segal and his wife didn't like their hotel suite and said they were going to move into Nichols' house until another could be found for them. But the major crisis came from the Burtons. Hundreds of the local citizenry gathered around their house, preventing Richard and Elizabeth from looking out their windows. The four guards assigned to them couldn't do much about it. Lehman had a house too, and because it had acres of grounds around it, it was suggested he trade with the Burtons.

Soon enough, a convoy of limousines arrived at Lehman's house. He opened the customary bottles of champagne and showed Richard and Elizabeth around. "Not adequate," Richard said. Elizabeth, with

Lehman, explored the grounds. "As far as I'm concerned, it's fine," she said, "but I worry about Richard because he's really bugged by invasions of his privacy." It was her fault; she had selected the lakeside house; she hadn't realized the local people would intrude on them so much.

Lehman thought the solution might be for them to trade with Mike Nichols. The one rented for him was a handsome rambling house set on magnificent grounds with a trout stream; it had fourteen rooms, nine fireplaces, and was furnished in New England charm. The Burtons loved it. Mike Nichols wasn't too happy about the trade, but bore up bravely. Peace, above all. After the Burtons moved in they held a Sunday-evening fish fry—trout that came from the stream behind their residence. Lehman discovered something new about Richard that night: he was as brilliant a Ping-Pong player as he was an actor. And at billiards he was just as good. While waiting for a scene to be set up, he would breeze through the London *Time*'s crossword puzzle, "the world's most challenging," in record time. Later Lehman discovered that Richard had a voluminous knowledge of baseball and could name players all the way back to Ty Cobb. He soon after sent him a book called *Baseball's Unforgettable Games*, which Richard said was so fascinating it kept him up at nights.

Lehman became more and more astonished by the facets Richard revealed of himself. One evening Richard invited Nichols and Lehman into his dressing room and read them something he had just written. It was his review of the Dylan Thomas biography for *The New York Times Book Review*. "I wrote it as though I was George in *Virginia Woolf*," he said.

Both Nichols and Lehman told him quite sincerely, to his delight, that they thought it was brilliant.

Much of the filming at the Smith College campus took place at night, going on until dawn. Richard was usually dependable about keeping to the scheduled hours. He believed they were doing something unusual, even unique with Albee's savage dissection of an academic marriage. The film would be controversial, he knew, especially because of its bitter language, some of it well beyond the boundaries of the Production Code of the time. And he wanted it kept intact.

Called for from him were scenes in which he had to weep bitter

BURTON

tears while his wife lies in bed upstairs with their houseguest, Nick (George Segal); they were done in close-up and were exhausting for him—as Nichols, in several takes, extracted from him all the emotion possible.

The next evening, before filming a pre-dawn scene, Richard asked Lehman to dinner with him and his makeup man, Ron Berkeley, the latter now as constant a presence around him as Bob Wilson. During the course of the meal, Richard said, "Ernie, can you arrange for me to be let off at four this morning? Elizabeth's sons are leaving for school in Switzerland and I'd like to have a few hours with them."

Lehman told him they were trying to make up for lost time; their use of the campus was limited, and Nichols wanted to get this scene in the can. Nichols came into the room, and Richard asked the same question of him. Attempting to avoid a decision, Nichols left it up to Lehman, who wouldn't change his mind.

"You can hate me for three days, if you like," Lehman told Richard.

"Not only do I not dislike you," Richard assured him, "but I think you're one of the nicest men I've ever met. I want you to know I really mean it."

Lehman thought the matter was settled, but at three in the morning Nichols told him they were in for trouble. "Richard's in his dressing room, in tears," he said. He didn't really need to get home to see Elizabeth's boys. He just could not do the scene tonight. "It's no use," Nichols said. Richard remained in his dressing room throughout the night, and when daylight came, apologized to Mike and promised he'd be ready to do the scene in the evening.

"What really happened last night?" Lehman asked Nichols.

"I've decided everyone on the picture is crazy," Nichols told him.

Recently, though, Mike Nichols provided a clearer analysis. "Richard had black days," he said. "It's as simple as that. During the production he had perhaps eight or ten of those days, and they took various forms. This one was the most remarkable, because he simply said, 'I can't act tonight. Looking back now, with my greater knowledge of alcoholic personalities, I think it was somehow connected to the fact that he had either drunk too much, or needed to drink more. He couldn't pull himself away from it and concentrate.

BURTON

"On other days it took the form of being abusive to Elizabeth, which was horribly upsetting to us. It was infrequent, but what happens is that when such a day occurs, everyone's constantly afraid another is coming. I wasn't afraid of Richard, and I'd just tell him he was being a shmuck. But not that night in Northampton, because I saw it as despair and inability. How can you tell him he's a shmuck when he's telling you he's so untalented and hopeless?"

Lehman, on the other hand, wondered if some of the problems—bursts of temper from Elizabeth and frayed nerves in Richard—were caused by Nichols' careful, demanding way of directing.

Nichols explained his method with his actors. "With every scene there was a question to answer: what's happening in this scene? What are you, Elizabeth, or you, Richard, doing here that you're not saying? You give the actors their objectives as they go through the script. What's really taking place that's not in the dialogue? That takes homework, and conferring with each other.

"Admittedly, there were days when Richard could not get a line right through sixty takes, but on other days he was wonderful. I could say, Richard, not like that, say it like this. He was perfectly happy to be told anything you wanted to tell him. If it was a black day, everybody trembled. You knew you weren't going to get much usable work."

Lehman wondered if the corrosive quality of the script fueled their quarrels when they were home. If Nichols noticed Richard being abusive toward Elizabeth, Lehman saw Elizabeth often acting toward Richard as though he was George. "She was constantly punching him," he remembered.

Nichols, on one occasion, received one of her blows. She had misspoken a line, and he burst out laughing.

"Are you laughing at me?" she asked.

"Yes."

"Do you mean that?"

"Yes."

With that she hauled back and landed a blow on his chest. Lehman was aghast—the star punching her director in full view of the entire crew. Nichols, though, thought it was part of the joke, and it saved the situation. He maintained a cheerful savoir faire through the trials and temperaments of the production, but the strain began to wear on Lehman, the strain of having to be ever careful of two stars fully aware of their power, and a hugely expensive undertaking riding on their personalities and performances.

"They had it the easiest of any of us," he said. "All they had to do was show up. There were times when I stayed away from the set for as much as a week."

"Have you been avoiding us?" Nichols would ask after one of Lehman's long absences.

"I think I have been," Lehman said.

But with the return to California and the studio, the atmosphere lightened, and there were even signs of affection and appreciation among the parties. For Richard's fortieth birthday (at a party held on the soundstage), Lehman gave him an original edition of Francis Bacon's essays. He was extremely pleased with the rare volume, but was less so when Mike Nichols presented him with a puppy. He was amused and annoyed by the gift at the same time, his household already full of Elizabeth's pets. In retaliation he made Nichols a present of four mice in a cage. During a pause in the shooting the doors of the stage opened wide. Richard walked out and into his wife's present to him: a white Oldsmobile Toronado, wrapped in a huge red ribbon. With much of the afternoon off, he spent most of it riding the car around the lot and showing it off.

It was a week of birthdays, and Elizabeth must have felt left out, because she asked Lehman: "What are you giving me?"

Lehman knew her birthday was a few months off, but checked to make sure. However, Richard honored Elizabeth for her unbirthday with a pair of diamond-and-ruby earrings. Word was sent to Jack Warner that she would very much appreciate a similarly jeweled brooch to go along with the earrings. Warner was not gallant. "For what I'm paying her," he barked, "she can buy her own brooch."

Parties were held for Lehman's and Nichols' birthdays, too. Elizabeth handed Lehman a gift from the two of them, a rare edition of Bacon's *The Advancement of Learning*. It was obviously Richard's gesture, and the note was his, too. It read: "Dearest Ernie, thank you for asking us to play in this old drawing-room comedy. How Lonsdale will love his return to the center of the stage. Many happy returns of the day and the film. Affectionately, Rich and Elizabeth."

When the film ran over its allotted time and budget, the Burtons kept their word about giving the production two weeks of their services free of charge. But the meticulous Mike Nichols needed three weeks beyond those—and they definitely were not free. The final day of shooting was December 13, 1965. A party was held on the soundstage, but even then most of the cast and crew had to wait until Mike Nichols got one last take with Richard and Elizabeth.

The Burtons gave their own celebration of the finish of the film with a huge cocktail party at their rented mansion on Carolwood Drive, making up for all the social obligations they had either missed or failed to return. Ernest Lehman was invited, and during breaks in the music provided by an orchestra he had a few words separately with Richard and Elizabeth. Both, without hearing what the other said, told him much the same thing: they'd had a curious reaction when the filming of *Virginia Woolf* ended. They missed it terribly. And it was hard for them to adjust to not being Martha and George after those many months.

"I feel rather lost," Richard said.

Richard and Elizabeth resumed their itinerant ways in February 1966, leaving California for England. A promise had been made by Richard to his old Oxford professor Nevill Coghill that he would appear in a university production of Marlowe's *Dr. Faustus*. He and Elizabeth had less than three weeks before they were due in Rome to appear in Franco Zeffirelli's film version of *The Taming of the Shrew*. Even with the limited amount of time—ten days of rehearsal and a week of performing—it was a gift of substance. The money from the performances would go to a fund for the building of a new university theater and arts center.

Richard certainly owed a debt of gratitude to Professor Coghill and the dramatic society. His appearance in *Measure for Measure* at Oxford more than twenty years earlier was at least partly responsible for his postwar emergence on the London stage. There had been the coaching many years before by Philip Burton and his memorizing of the role, which made him think he could handle it with little difficulty. And he was still set on directing a film of the play—the profits here, too, to be donated to the funding of the playhouse.

Those weeks at Oxford, he would tell the press, if calculated in terms of their combined earning power, were worth to them a million dollars and more. Just what would have been sandwiched in before their next commitment, he didn't make clear. The British press was usually kind to him, but also suggested that he would very much like to be knighted by the Queen. It was not hard for them to imagine that Elizabeth, already a somewhat checkered first lady of American films, would enjoy also being known as Lady Elizabeth.

Her charities, and his, were often directed toward England, now her home country too. But neither paid British taxes. Much would have to be overlooked if Richard's name came up at knightly honors time. Churlish newspapermen made unkind remarks occasionally about their seeming graciousness. But Richard enjoyed his return to Oxford; he expansively entertained students in his hotel suite. He worked with a largely student cast, and thrilled Professor Coghill with his performance. But not the critics, who had been invited up from London and other cities. They were even unkind to Elizabeth, who merely had to wander around the stage looking filmy and exquisite. "A sad example of university drama at its worst," the London *Times* pronounced.

But the main goal of their appearance was achieved. During their week, twenty thousand dollars was taken in and earmarked for the new playhouse.

While they were in Oxford, the BBC asked if the Burtons would do a television interview. Elizabeth, congenitally wary of interviews, was doubtful, especially when she heard that the interviewer would be David Lewin, who was known for asking sharp questions. But Richard knew and liked Lewin and convinced Elizabeth to participate. "She was right," Lewin recalled. "One of the questions I put to Richard was if he saw a parallel between himself and Faustus. Elizabeth was furious. Right on camera she spat out, 'You bastard, David. I knew you would ask that.' "

Others asked it, too. It was getting to be a common theme among English interviewers. Elizabeth smarted, but Richard had smooth answers ready. To Lewin he said, "Everyone is offered a choice. Most men, regardless of their backgrounds, are faced at one time or another with an obvious, easy one, or a more difficult, rewarding one." It was by no means selling out, he continued, when one was able to command a larger audience. And his own roots were still in the theater, as he was proving here at Oxford.

But at other times he would say that it was necessary to earn a great deal of money, to keep on working, because their expenses were so enormous. And in Rome, while filming *The Taming of the Shrew,* he stated: "There's only one object to it all, to make money, to earn a few pence."

Franco Zeffirelli was more known for his spectacular opera and stage productions than for films, but he had long had the idea of doing a film version of *The Taming of the Shrew* in a comic Italian style. With all due respect to Shakespeare, he wanted to spank the old warhorse of a play into new life by disregarding tradition. He first talked to Sophia Loren and Marcello Mastroianni about playing the roles, but they wouldn't commit themselves. John Heyman, who was working himself from agenting into producing, was instrumental in bringing Zeffirelli together with the Burtons.

Columbia Pictures was approached for financing, but the firm was understandably leery of Shakespeare. For Elizabeth, the opportunity of playing a Shakespearean role was too delicious to let go. She and Richard made an offer that was difficult for Columbia to refuse. They would forgo their salaries and work for a percentage of the profits. A complicated arrangement was made in which the Burtons and Zeffirelli became co-producers, under the aegis of Royal Films International. This in effect meant that Zeffirelli could indulge himself with vast ornate sets and lavish costumes in Dino de Laurentiis' modern Rome studio.

Richard was given a beard to wear, and Elizabeth a plunging décolletage. Much archaic speech and almost half the lines were eliminated, and action and horseplay substituted. One lengthy sequence had Richard as Petruchio chasing Elizabeth, a snarling, spitting wildcat of a woman, in and over a barn, over rooftops, until both fell twenty feet into a huge pile of hay. (Richard had a fear of heights, and stunt people did the fall.)

Off the set, they stayed in a commodious villa on the Appian Way with their usual entourage, augmented by eight security guards to keep the ever-present paparazzi at bay. When they left their villa, they were followed by a police car. All of this was paid for by Richard.

While they were still at work on *Shrew, Who's Afraid of Virginia Woolf?* had its New York opening, and the reviews were all that

BURTON

could be wished for. Richard, Elizabeth, and Mike Nichols came out with glowing tributes from most of the critics. "Burton," said *Time*, "is superb, shrewdly measuring out his powerhouse talent in a part written for a less heroic actor. Elizabeth Taylor . . . loud, sexy, vulgar, achieves moments of astonishing tenderness." It was a triumph all around. In London, the *Daily Express* lauded them for "acting as standard–bearers in a revolution against the American system of film censorship." And it was a victory, of sorts. Warner's released the film with a stipulation that "No one under eighteen will be admitted," a ploy soon after adopted by the Motion Picture Association. The use of words like "screw" and phrases like "hump the hostess" were heard for the first time on the American popular screen, which was never (perhaps regrettably) the same again.

During that spring and summer in Rome Richard learned that he had lost the Academy Award for *The Spy Who Came in from the Cold* to Lee Marvin for *Cat Ballou*. And Elizabeth received the sad news that her close and troubled friend Montgomery Clift had died in New York. She had hoped to appear with him in *Reflections in a Golden Eye*. Marlon Brando eventually took on the role.

Scripts were pouring in. When added up, the box-office take of their films was so large that it seemed a safe bet to producers to pay the huge salaries they were now asking. Most of the scripts, though, called for the two of them together. This nettled Richard. "I do wish," he told one producer, "you chaps could get it into your heads that although we've done five films together, that doesn't make us Laurel and Hardy."

Quixotically, they next appeared together in the film version they had promised of *Dr. Faustus*, staying on in Rome through the autumn of 1966. This film no one would finance. *Marlowe*, after all? Not daunted, Richard financed it himself, to the tune of a million dollars and a modest commitment from an American distributor. This time he acted as producer, star, and co-director with Nevill Coghill. Elizabeth floated through the film in what seemed like scarves of various colors, and Richard attempted to surmount the mediocre stretches of the play with borrowings from other works of Marlowe and effects concocted out of swirls of mist, guttering candles, and billowing draperies. Everyone involved, mostly amateurs, worked for forty-

five dollars a week. All profits were to go to the Oxford University
Dramatic Society.

Perhaps this altruistic contribution to culture would still the press
hounds who talked of selling out. "And I am not hoping for a
knighthood," he told one of them. But he also said, "Despite my
Welshness and my rejection of royalty, I suddenly saw all the majesty
and brilliance of our Western civilization embodied in Elizabeth."

The writer commented: "To make her Lady Elizabeth—the one
prize he can give her that no one else can."

Richard threw himself with full energy into the production of *Dr.
Faustus*, but afterward said he found he had needed seven heads, and
he wouldn't do that sort of thing again. He and Elizabeth went to
London to appear in a television show that would aid the victims of
a mine disaster in Wales. From there, it was to Paris to meet with
Peter Glenville, who was preparing *The Comedians*, from the Graham
Greene novel.

Graham Greene's characters had long appealed to Richard. "They
are usually going to seed," he said once, "and have a strange desic-
cated quality about them." When Glenville had sent Richard the
script, written by Greene, he didn't bother to read it before wiring
Glenville that he would do it sight unseen. His, the chief, role was
that of Brown, a hotel keeper in Haiti, who becomes involved in
underground activity, and on a lesser level with the wife of an ambassador from a South American country. The latter role was a
relatively minor one for a star of Elizabeth's stature, and he advised
her against playing it. In any case, Glenville had someone else in
mind. Location work was slated for Dahomey, in Africa, Haiti itself
not being available in view of the antigovernment nature of the story.

"But," said Glenville, "she wasn't keen about him going away to
Africa without her. The role of the woman was not large and wasn't
really suitable for her. The wife of the ambassador from a minor
country was supposed to be South American, and it was just a quiet,
tortured relationship between her and Brown. My choice for her
was Anouk Aimée. Obviously it was not a million-dollar role. But
then Elizabeth's agents came along with the suggestion she play the
part on more favorable terms."

Elizabeth's version was different from Glenville's. "Peter conned me into it," she told a reporter, "and got me at half pay. He said, 'You realize of course that Sophia Loren is dying to do it. You wouldn't want anyone else to do those kissing scenes with Richard.' "

Glenville had never considered a star as important as Sophia Loren, but he agreed to use Elizabeth, although with some misgivings that a glamorous superstar might topple the balance of the story. "It didn't really throw the budget out of balance. The extra costs came from such niceties as the special car and chauffeur she insisted on."

An incident, puzzling to him, occurred just before the departure from Paris to Dahomey. Aaron Frosch called him from New York and said that Richard was upset that it was because of his close relationship with Glenville that Elizabeth had been persuaded to take less than she would have ordinarily. "Talk to him," Frosch said, "and tell him that you and I had never discussed salary, or obtaining her." All negotiations had been done through her agents and the releasing company, MGM.

Glenville telephoned Richard at the Lancaster, where the Burtons were staying, and asked if they could meet for lunch at Fouquet, across the Champs-Elysées, a half-block away. "I want to talk to you about something serious," Glenville said.

"Is it something very bad?" Richard asked.

"No, no, just a misunderstanding," Glenville said.

When Richard arrived at Fouquet, "he was white and trembling," Glenville said, "like a scared schoolboy. He needed a drink, and I had to soothe him and calm him down. It was as though he was unable to face any dark clouds on his horizon, any ugliness, or any flat recognition of failure or disappointment. Of course, it was a small matter, really. I just thought it needed clearing up. And he did assure me that he had no problems about what Elizabeth was getting."

The Burtons arrived in Cotonou, the capital of Dahomey, in mid-January and stayed there through February. With them was their chauffeur, Gaston Sanz, who was also their majordomo; Ron Berkeley; and their two Pekingese. In spite of the heat they were comfortable in an air-conditioned bungalow facing the ocean, and for a welcome change, there was no worry from bothersome fans. Few in Cotonou knew who they were. The sleepy town boasted two French-language cinemas, one discotheque, two banks, six traffic lights, and an empty presidential palace. The traffic lights were ornamental, since there was little traffic. The deposed president had installed them to make his capital look like Paris.

"Everyone went home quietly at night," Glenville said. A couple of correspondents flew in for a day or two, and Marlon Brando paid a two-day visit to discuss with Elizabeth their roles in *Reflections in a Golden Eye*. Alec Guinness was there in a leading role, and, long acquainted with Richard, found him "generous and marvelous to work with." Although Richard might boast about his competitive spirit as an actor, he was invariably supportive of his colleagues in his scenes with them. Socially, however, Guinness felt it was as though Richard had constructed a wall around himself. Of the twenty weeks' work on the film, Richard was scheduled for eighteen and Elizabeth for only five, which meant that much of the time, Glenville said, "she was there watching and admiring him. She was never any problem."

In March they moved on to the south of France. Academy Award time loomed. Among the thirteen nominations received by *Virginia Woolf* were Richard for Best Actor, Elizabeth for Best Actress, and Mike Nichols for Best Director.

Elizabeth's work in *The Comedians* was desultory enough for her to promise her presence at the ceremonies. She was the clear-cut favorite in her category. This, as Richard had promised, was her *Hamlet*. She was preparing to leave for Los Angeles when Richard confided to her that he had dreamed about her being killed in a plane crash and that he wished she would not go. He had already decided not to go himself when the New York Film Critics voted Paul Scofield Best Actor for *A Man for All Seasons*, directed by Fred Zinnemann—who, as it happened, had turned down the chance to direct *Virginia Woolf*. The Academy would follow suit, Richard felt.

And there were those who noted that Richard would be most uncomfortable sitting in an audience watching his wife receive an award that he wouldn't get. Anne Bancroft accepted Elizabeth's award for her, and Bob Hope, mastering the ceremonies, quipped, "It must be nice to have enough talent just to send for one. But then," he added, "leaving Richard Burton alone on the French Riviera is like leaving Jackie Gleason locked in a delicatessen."

Richard received a measure of consolation, though, when the British Film Academy voted him its Best Actor award, and in Italy he was voted Best Foreign Actor. And while they were in Paris doing final studio scenes of *The Comedians,* word came that *The Taming of the Shrew* had been selected for the Royal Command Performance at the Odeon in Leicester Square. Richard made it into a family occasion—in fact, invited 150 family members from Wales to come to London for a weekend at his expense. All available suites at the Dorchester Hotel were commandeered. Elizabeth had fresh flowers put in all the rooms. Their suite became the center of hospitality; brothers, sisters, cousins, aunts, and uncles crowded in and spilled into the hallways. They drank whatever was in bottles. At the theater they applauded vigorously when Richard made his obligatory little speech on the stage. Back at the hotel the festivities went on through the night.

On Monday morning Richard and Elizabeth were to catch the ten-o'clock flight back to Paris. Bellhops were carrying luggage out of the suite to place in the waiting limousines below. Richard, however, had not finished his drink. There were several more to finish before he felt able to catch the plane. And why not another party? They arrived back in Paris on Tuesday.

There was another grand premiere of *The Taming of the Shrew* held at the Paris Opéra. The crowds massed as though for one of the city's student riots. Reviews for the film were mixed, but it went on to bring back some fifteen million dollars for its three-and-a-half-million-dollar investment. The Burtons were entitled to twenty-five percent of the take. The gamble had paid off with a bonanza.

Grandly, Richard told a newspaperman that their price had gone up to one and a quarter million for each of them. The prices of everything, including diamonds, were going up, he explained. Meanwhile, in Hollywood, change was in the air, and soon enough they would be affected by it.

There was rebellion in the audience, made up more and more of a young turned-on and dropped-out generation. Mike Nichols was canny enough to sense the change when he made his wildly successful

The Graduate. Films like *Easy Rider* and *The Strawberry Statement* were further evidence of ferment; young filmmakers were coming along, a sophisticated group more likely to come from college film courses than the studio breeding grounds. The older idols were losing their hold on audiences, although the trend was slower in European countries. It was because of their largely *international* name value that the Burtons were able to demand and often get their top-heavy salaries. What might be lacking in the American market could be made up in several other countries.

What became apparent around this time was a change in the attitude of critics toward the Burtons that seems hard to explain, in view of their sterling performances in *Virginia Woolf*. Several critics were more than normally harsh in their treatment of them in *The Taming of the Shrew*, as though waiting for an opportunity to pounce. "I wish they'd leave culture alone," Wilfrid Sheed grumbled in *Esquire*. "Of Miss Taylor there is little to say. Her acting was fixated at the age of twelve in *National Velvet*. Mr. Burton's problem is more complicated. He is still a good actor, with a few ideas or at least memories. What is more depressing is the Pygmalion or Professor Higgins complex which prompts him to bring us all this culture. Mr. Burton is a culture vulture."

But as Sheed made clear in another article some months later, he was not really considering the Burtons as actors or performers, but as "the purest celebrities we have in show business." The tendency would grow more pronounced: reviewing them, their lives, more than their movies.

17

Now that the Burtons had it, they flaunted it. Their next assignment, a film called *Boom!*, took them to the island of Sardinia. But instead of joining the other members of the crew and cast, including Noël Coward, in the provided accommodations, they chartered an old seagoing yacht, the *Odysseia,* and anchored it in the bay below the clifftop location—presumably safe from bandits if not pirates. They liked the vessel so much they purchased it for a mere $200,000.

Richard gave its history. "She was built for an eccentric Englishman in 1906, who installed an organ and used to take her out to sea to play Bach during storms." During the two world wars, the 120-foot motor ship had been used as a patrol boat in the Mediterranean. It was renamed the *Kalizma,* in honor of the children, Kate, Liza, and Maria, and a designer, Arthur Barbosa, was engaged to redesign the ship's interior.

Barbosa had come to Richard's attention because he was the decorator of Rex Harrison's house that overlooked Portofino. Richard much admired the house, as did almost everyone who visited it. Barbosa met with the Burtons at the Dorchester in July 1967 to submit his designs. With *Boom!* on the verge of production, and other films in various stages of negotiation and preparation, the suite,

BURTON

as reported by Barbosa, was crowded with "film producers, various writers, and children in fancy dress."

"Gorgeous, Arthur darling," Elizabeth said approvingly of his designs, "but we must have the bedroom canary and not mustard." So much work was required that Barbosa would need many months to accomplish it, but he did promise to have the main cabin, the saloon, ready in two weeks.

From the viewpoint of the Burtons there was some practicality behind the quarter-of-a-million-dollar refitting of the ship and the $150,000 yearly upkeep. Anyone who tries to take a dog into England knows the score: a six-month quarantine. When the Burtons worked there, their four dogs, and puppies to come, need have no fear of internment.

They also purchased another convenient means of transportation, a Hawker Siddeley executive jet, handy for quick trips to premieres and interesting social events. "Now," Richard said, "we can use it to hop over to Nice for lunch." They used it to hop over to Venice for the annual film festival and the associated parties. They were entertained by Aristotle Onassis on *his* yacht, named after *his* daughter, Christina. The Countess Marina Cicogna (one of the truest of Roman and Venetian bluebloods) gave a party for her protégée, Florinda Bolkan, a lissome Brazilian model and actress, at which Florinda, it was reported, caught all eyes, including Richard's. It was the first public notice that his eye may have begun to wander again. But at the party, all he did was look and dance, under the watchful gaze of both Elizabeth and the countess.

Even though they were spending upwards of a million dollars a year to maintain their life-style, their film earnings left enough over to invest in a banana plantation on Tenerife in the Canary Islands, a horse-breeding farm in Ireland, and a directorship in Harlech Television, a commercial network for Wales and western England. Richard promised to use his influence to have worthy programs on it. Their taxes were minimal, since both were now residents of Switzerland. "They had money and assets stashed over half of Europe," one of the accountants later said. As though to avoid British taxes on his death, it was during this period that Richard changed his Swiss status from resident to domicile. The action would eventually have repercussions.

BURTON

As bad as many of Richard's and Elizabeth's films were, none reeked quite so much as *Boom!*, concocted by Tennessee Williams from a play of his that had failed on the boards. Nevertheless, doing this windy, pretentious "junk," as a reviewer called it, they behaved as though the box-office results were preordained. With them was the usual gaggle of managers, accountants, press and makeup people, and secretaries and assistant secretaries. They made their own working schedules, appeared on the set only when all was ready, and just before taking their positions, without looking, would hold out their drinks, to be taken from them by a makeup man or dresser.

Following *Boom!* Richard was scheduled for a World War II action film, *Where Eagles Dare*, to be made in Austria and England, and Elizabeth for *Secret Ceremony*, also in England. This was in line with their policy not to be separated by film work. With some spare time available at the end of 1967, Richard took a small role in *Candy*, described by one critic as a story of a teenybopper, who seems to be mentally retarded, being molested by "a series of dirty old men in odd clothing." Elizabeth again watched from the sidelines as Richard and several other reasonably respectable actors—among them Walter Matthau, James Coburn, and Marlon Brando—attacked the girl on a pool table, atop a grand piano, and in a police patrol car. Richard's role was that of a drunken long-haired poet. It was later said, after the film's critical pulverizing, that he had been talked into it by Marlon Brando, a close friend of the director, Christian Marquand. Perhaps they were all attempting to raise the flag of the screen's new sexual liberalism. They were a little late; the younger generation was well ahead of them.

The following year, 1968, was one of the busiest for Richard and Elizabeth, one of their most profitable, but a profoundly disturbing one for both. *Dr. Faustus*, *The Comedians*, and *Boom!* came out during the year, and all were box-office and critical failures. Their magic was clearly wearing off, although public interest in them was still at a peak.

This was demonstrated when they flew to New York early in February to help launch the American release of *Dr. Faustus*. The premiere took place at a new "art house" cinema, the Rendezvous, outside of which more than a thousand fans gathered. "Not the usual type," Elizabeth said the next day, "but a young groovy bunch, like hippies almost." Emerging from the theater, she found herself stepping on a man who had been thrown to the ground. Two injured policemen were sent to a hospital. One of Richard's objectives was accomplished at a celebrity ball following the showing: hundreds came, and paid, to aid Philip Burton's dramatic academy.

Richard had already spoken out on the British reaction to the film. "I could have written the notices before they appeared. The English critics are the most snide in the world. They are sneaky, mean, and spiteful."

The Americans, this time, went them one better. Renata Adler, in the New York *Times,* reported that the film "is of an awfulness that bends the mind." *Time* took its wrath out on Elizabeth, although she had done nothing but wander around looking beautiful. "When she welcomes Burton to an eternity of damnation, her eyeballs and teeth are dripping pink in what seems a hellish combination of conjunctivitis and trench mouth."

"People don't like sustained success," Elizabeth told Liz Smith the next day in their suite in the Plaza Hotel. "After all, we make an awful lot of money and some people just resent us." She was not yet aware that this year would mark the end of her sustained success.

Location work for *Where Eagles Dare* had taken place in the mountains near Salzburg. Some spectacular stunts were required, and with Richard's fear of heights, so were doubles. His costar, Clint Eastwood, remarked that the film should have been retitled *Where Doubles Dare.* Studio work was done in a studio near London, where Richard would remain for another film, *Laughter in the Dark,* from the Nabokov novel, and Elizabeth would make *Secret Ceremony* with Mia Farrow and Robert Mitchum.

During the winter, their yacht, *Kalizma,* was being overhauled at Marseilles, and Barbosa, their designer, flew back and forth from England to supervise the interior remodeling. He bought furniture at Christie's, had more specially made, and would take swatches of materials to Elstree, where both Burtons were working, for their approval.

Meanwhile, the dogs had to be housed safely, so in the absence of the *Kalizma,* they chartered another yacht, for some twenty thousand dollars a month, and anchored it off Tower Pier. It was not until the end of May that the *Kalizma* made its way up the Thames. The decorative scheme had yet to be completed. Elizabeth had insisted on making the cabins homey: the furnishings included a rosewood Regency sofa, Louis XVI chairs upholstered in yellow silk, two Chippendale mirrors, twelve dining chairs, and six wall sconces for the dining room, Wilton carpeting, a stereo system, bookcases, linens from Rome, and their china and silver from the chalet in Gstaad. The dogs, unfortunately, were not well toilet-trained, and the carpets needed constant recleaning.

This was the year the Burtons began accumulating diamonds. Richard mentioned to Elizabeth that gold as an investment had begun to wobble. "Would diamonds be a safe bet?" Elizabeth asked. "We checked," Richard said, "and decided they were as good as anything—and very portable." A thirty-three-carat diamond, formerly belonging to the widow of Alfred Krupp, the German munitions king, was up for auction. Richard picked it up for $305,000, and Elizabeth turned up wearing it at a party thrown to celebrate the inauguration of Harlech Television.

Playing an art dealer in *Laughter in the Dark*, Richard was filmed at a real auction at Sotheby's. While at the sale he became intrigued with a Picasso drawing, and got it for little more than twenty thousand dollars. Elizabeth was at the sale too, with their friend the attractive and clever Princess Elizabeth of Yugoslavia. There was a nice Monet she was able to buy for $120,000. She already had a Van Gogh. Richard made a trade with her: the *Kalizma* for the Van Gogh.

It was about this time that things began to go askew for the couple who had everything. He had been working in *Laughter in the Dark* for only two weeks, when, after agreeing to do a Sunday-morning location scene, he strolled up—with little Liza on his arm—a half-hour late. Tony Richardson, the director, was furious, and gave Richard a bawling-out. Richard took umbrage and marched off with Liza. The next thing he knew was that he had been replaced by Nicol Williamson. If there was more to it than that, it's not known. The matter was placed in the hands of lawyers on both sides.

After finishing *Secret Ceremony*, Elizabeth's back problems worsened. The pain was deeper and persistent. She and Richard began to fear cancer. After an exploratory operation, a hysterectomy was indicated. Soon after, she talked publicly about adopting another child, but Richard, though he badly wanted a son, was against the idea of adoption. "We have the money to indulge ourselves with pets," he said in a rather lordly way, "but we can take no risk at all with a child that is going to bear our name."

Michael, one of the Wilding boys, was, at age fifteen, already proving troublesome to him. "Our son is a hippie," he told a reporter. "His hair lies on his shoulders and we can't keep him in school. I tell Elizabeth we should do one of two things—ignore him or kick the living daylights out of him." Elizabeth favored a laissez-faire approach, and she clashed with Richard about it.

During the summer, Elizabeth recovered from the operation, but more bad news came from Céligny. The property there was seldom used, because the chalet in Gstaad was more commodious and better situated socially. Richard received the news that his gardener for the Céligny house had hanged himself. Leaving Elizabeth to recuperate in London, he flew with Kate, Liza, and his brother Ifor to Geneva to attend the funeral. With them, too, was Emlyn Williams' son Brook, who often used the villa and had known the gardener. After the funeral, Liza wanted to see the house that her stepsister Kate had spent her early years in. The group drove to Céligny. It had turned dark, and Richard, who hated flying at night, decided they should spend the night at the house, which was closed up. While Richard waited with the girls in the station café across the road, Ifor, who knew the house well from having stayed there often, went to open it and get its lights on. He had no key, and in attempting to get in through the French windows, caught his foot in a grille over a drain, and in falling, broke his neck on a windowsill. When he was found, he was paralyzed from the neck down.

It was perhaps the worst moment in Richard's life, this tragic accident happening to his revered elder brother, the one member of his family he most listened to and looked up to. Ifor remained paralyzed, confined to a wheelchair for the remaining two years of his life. The story given out was that he had had a car accident. A great fear of Richard's, his daughter Kate said much later, was that he too might end his days shackled like Ifor to a wheelchair. When it was his time, he hoped he would go suddenly.

By the end of that summer, Elizabeth was relatively free of pain

BURTON

and ready to work again. George Stevens had engaged her for *The Only Game in Town,* from a play by Frank Gilroy that had not fared well on Broadway. Richard was teamed with Rex Harrison for *Staircase,* also from a play. Both were Twentieth Century-Fox productions, and were made in Paris studios, although *Staircase,* a story of two aging homosexual English barbers, took place in grimy East London, while the other was set in Las Vegas. The power of the Burtons was still manifest. They had used up their allotment of tax-free working time in England, and had decided they must be based in Paris. Elizabeth, though, generously offered to work two weeks of her valuable time in Las Vegas.

Each received a million and a quarter dollars for their services. There was wonder why both Richard and Rex would undertake such seemingly unconventional and uncommercial roles. "It was a case of I'll do it if you do it," Harrison said, while Richard cited his admiration of his costar. Neither mentioned money. Both pictures went down the tubes, a fact that was not lost on other producers bidding for Richard's and Elizabeth's services. It was about this time in their careers that they stopped demanding their million-plus fees and worked instead for profit percentages.

Richard's black moods became more noticeable, as did his drinking. Social occasions in which the Burtons were involved could be disastrous if Richard had consumed heavily. "You bore me," he snarled to a highly titled Englishman at whose side he sat at a dinner party. In his foggy state of mind it may have been his way of emphasizing his own plebeian origins. Elizabeth attempted to apologize for him, but he then turned on his hostess, too, saying, "I hate all this fucking privilege . . ." Flowers and telegrams of apology were sent the next day by a contrite Richard—at Elizabeth's insistence.

When the Paris filming was completed early in 1969, they flew to Los Angeles, where Elizabeth checked in at the Cedars of Lebanon Hospital to have tests made for her back condition. Rest was prescribed for her, and they went to the villa in Puerto Vallarta and stayed there until May, when Richard was due back in England for his next film, *Anne of the Thousand Days.*

Richard's role was Henry VIII, but the plum role was that of Anne Boleyn, played by the charming Canadian actress Genevieve Bujold. When Hal Wallis, the producer, came to see Richard to discuss the

BURTON

film, Elizabeth had volunteered to play the young girl who failed to bear Henry a son and had her head chopped off in the Tower. Wallis was astonished at the offer. Elizabeth was well into her thirties and decidedly plumpish at that moment. Richard was the one who told her that she would be wrong for the girlish Anne Boleyn. Whether she was determined to stay at Richard's side, or there were no offers made to her, it was two years before Elizabeth would make another film.

While Richard worked with Genevieve Bujold, Elizabeth, ten years her senior, could only watch with jealousy and envy. Richard, when he talked with reporters, loyally spoke supportively of the idle Elizabeth, but he was flowery about the talents of Genevieve, whom he referred to as Gin, and whom he predicted would become a big star. If there was any involvement beyond a comradely one between him and his costar, it was not apparent, but Elizabeth's jealousy was enough to cause Wallis worry that it might affect Genevieve's performance.

However, she, along with Richard, was nominated for an Academy Award and was the winner of a Golden Globe. At that occasion she may have sent a shaft or two toward Elizabeth when in her acceptance she remarked, "I owe my performance all to Richard Burton. He was generous, kind, helpful, and witty. And generosity was the one great quality." Some thought she was being a bit mischievous.

Richard knew that one certain way to keep Elizabeth purring like a cat was to add to her burgeoning jewel collection. But he outdid himself in 1969 when a huge diamond, all of sixty-nine carats, came up for auction at Parke-Bernet in New York. Elizabeth called the firm's jewelry director to find out if the stone was perfect, and was assured that it was. "I want it," she told Richard. "I really want it." Burton ordered Aaron Frosch to bid for it to the limit of a million dollars, which, as it turned out, was not enough. Cartier's topped the bid by fifty thousand dollars.

Elizabeth collapsed into tears at the news, and Richard went to the telephone and ordered Frosch to get the stone at whatever cost. The amount paid was not made public, but Cartier exacted some publicity from the deal by displaying the "Cartier-Burton Diamond" in its window.

Much of the world took notice of this extravagance, and the New York *Times* editorialized: "Actually, the inch-long, inch-thick diamond is a smart buy, because it goes with everything. It won't clash with the smaller Krupp diamond. It won't seem out of place in the yacht parked in the Bahamas or the Mediterranean . . . . In this Age of Vulgarity marked by such minor matters as war and poverty, it gets harder every day to scale the heights of true vulgarity."

To which Elizabeth retorted, "I know I'm vulgar, but would you have me any other way?"

Richard, too, appeared to be unruffled by criticism of their life-style. "We're criticized for owning a yacht," he said. "Who cares? Elizabeth and I walk around it, touching it, caressing it. I can't get over the great wonder of owning a yacht. I still feel the wonder of owning an original Van Gogh. We enjoy these possessions, not for their market value, but because of a great pride in owning something truly beautiful. That's a comfort, you know."

But behind the smooth rationalizations could be discerned some nagging sense of inferiority that accounted for that sort of obvious display by a man of such high intelligence. The jewels, the yacht, were a way of proving not just his monetary worth, but his worth among the few at the top. As one famed movie star said about her jewels, "They are important to me because they prove I belong among all these powerful people." For an insecure man, one way of proving his power—his potency—is to bedeck his lady with furs and expensive baubles and show her off. The wonder is that Richard knew this about others, but not about himself.

After finishing *Anne of the Thousand Days*, Richard returned with Elizabeth to Puerto Vallarta, with nothing in the way of work firmly on the horizon for either of them. Problems had developed with Michael. He was asked not to return to Millfield, an expensive preparatory school he attended with his brother. Elizabeth decided to send both boys to Hawaii, where her brother was a professor of ocean-ography. While there, Michael met a nineteen-year-old keypunch operator, and both set off on an exploration of the Middle East and India. Richard didn't think much of the education the more serious Christopher was getting in Hawaii, and gave him a choice—either a good boarding school or a tutor. Irked by Michael, Richard hoped

BURTON

at least to achieve a proper education for Christopher. About Kate, he had no worries. Sybil had stowed her in the United Nations School in Manhattan, and Kate was working hard at her studies, which included French and Russian. Liza and Maria came to Puerto Vallarta from their schools in Switzerland.

In need of a tutor, Richard wrote to Professor Coghill at Oxford and asked him to recommend one. And in February 1970, twenty-three-year-old John David Morley arrived in Puerto Vallarta to take up his tutorial duties.

Sparked by the presence of the Burtons and other celebrities such as John Huston, Puerto Vallarta had grown from a village of six thousand Mexicans to a resort town of more than twenty thousand. Richard, wanting a place of his own for his moods of privacy, had taken over the smaller house across the street from the larger one and connected the two houses by building a bridge across the narrow street, modeling it on Venice's Bridge of Sighs.

Richard explained the need for the house, though, by saying it was "for friends and reporters who are always ringing our doorbell. They stop for a drink and stay for a weekend." But many of them came and rang the bell only because Richard had an aversion to telephones.

Joyce Haber, the gossip columnist, paid them such a visit early in 1970 and wrote, "Their hacienda stands ten minutes above the sea as the taxi climbs straight up a succession of cobblestone hills. The primitive streets abound with Mexican children and pigs on ropes attached to houses and dogs." Turning the last corner, she came across "two freshly whitewashed buildings, immaculately tiled and shuttered, trailing in bougainvillea."

Inside the main house, all was spacious and airy. The new tutor found that the center of the activity was a large room where the Burtons ate, drank, talked, and recited Shakespeare or poetry. Open windows gave on "a fine view of the mountains that soared out of the ocean."

Morley discovered that Richard was writing two or three hours each morning on some unnamed project. He would carry a portable typewriter to the lower house, and would take the typewriter with him when he returned to the main house, ready for some random inspiration. Most of what came out of the typewriter Richard squeezed into little balls and tossed them on the floor. Morley one day picked up one of the paper balls and flattened it out. The page was blank.

Richard was drinking heavily during this time. And yet, in the midst of a monumental drinking bout, he was able to recite word-perfect, according to Morley, twelve stanzas of an old Scottish poem, culminating with "Timor Mortis conturbat me!" (The fear of death anguishes me.)

At the table Richard would sometimes use words that Elizabeth thought too big and obscure. "That's one of the differences between us," Richard told Morley. "Elizabeth has a very limited vocabulary. I have an immense vocabulary." Elizabeth flounced out of the room.

Richard's drinking grew heavier as Academy Awards time approached. His nomination for *Anne of the Thousand Days* was his sixth, and he badly wanted an Oscar of his own. Elizabeth, who had two Oscars, agreed to be a presenter at the ceremony.

Morley recalled a day when Richard was in such a mean and nasty drunken condition that Elizabeth asked him to keep the boys occupied outside the house for some hours. She would confide to Morley that she worried about losing her husband. She loved him, but she wasn't sure he loved her any longer. "The trouble is," she said, "I think I just bore him." Richard admitted to being bored, but not necessarily with Elizabeth. It was Sybil who once said, "At first he is bored with someone, then he becomes boring, and finally he bores himself." But that was well after their divorce.

The project Morley noticed Richard working on during the morning hours was purportedly a novel, described by Richard as of a semiautobiographical nature. But he also found time to write an article for a British magazine commemorating the hundredth anniversary of the Rugby Football Union. Although somewhat obscure to other than aficionados of the sport, it was thought to be brilliant by those in the know.

In mid-March 1970 the Burtons entrained for Los Angeles and established themselves in their favorite bungalow in the garden grounds of the Beverly Hills Hotel. As *Variety* reported, "The Burtons came to town, quite candidly, for him to win an Oscar." Interviews were scheduled with reporters, they were booked on the David Frost show, and with Charles Collingwood (a neighbor in Puerto Vallarta) on CBS. They also made a brief appearance on a *Here's Lucy* episode.

They were not in town long before an incident occurred that gave them some unfavorable publicity. They were outside a Beverly Hills nightclub, with several onlookers around them, when a verbal fight erupted between them. Ordinarily when Richard was in a tanked-up condition, Elizabeth, as much as she might have been drinking herself, was able to get him to sleep it off. This time the epithets he assaulted her with proved too much to take. "I've had enough of this drunk," she yelled, and raced to their waiting limousine, directing the driver to take her back to the hotel. Richard arrived a few minutes later, but Elizabeth wouldn't let him into the bungalow. He would have to ask the desk clerk for another room.

Richard, in a fury, tried to kick the door in. Elizabeth left the bungalow and went to a friend's house to spend the night. The next day she found Richard in the hotel's Polo Lounge, still drinking. She gave him a resounding slap on the face, after which the quarrel between them was made up. Richard was contrite enough to promise to stop drinking for three months. Elizabeth had begun to accuse him of being an alcoholic, and he wanted to show her that he wasn't, that he could stop whenever he wanted to, that his drinking was a matter of preference rather than need. It was another of his rationalizations. Spencer Tracy, a noted Hollywood alcoholic, could also abstain for long periods, but when he binged, the results were legendary.

Because their spat was recorded in the press, Elizabeth explained to Charles Collingwood in their interview that "fighting with someone you love and are really sure of—and if you're really sure of yourself in your love—having an out-and-out outrageous, ridiculous fight is one of the greatest exercises in marital togetherness."

Collingwood noticed they were wearing chains with symbols around their necks and asked if they were peace or love symbols. "It seems to work," Richard said, "because we haven't quarreled for at least forty-eight hours." He revealed two bones of contention between Elizabeth and himself. "She is never on time and she loves films." One of the perils for him of their visiting Frank Sinatra or Edith Goetz, a close friend of Elizabeth's, was that both would show films for several hours. For his idle hours he preferred reading. He did not mention drinking.

Alone with Elizabeth he would tell her that she drank as much as he, or more. True or not, Elizabeth was much better at controlling her intake and behavior.

Although agents and lawyers were busy with the multifarious affairs of the Burtons, new film prospects were sparse. Not long before, Richard had boasted that he could have had almost any part he wanted, but even if true, this was hardly the case now. The film industry was changing radically. A new generation of film actors was displacing most of the old guard. The "hot" names now were Dustin Hoffman, Jon Voight, Jack Nicholson, Ryan O'Neal, Steve McQueen, and Robert Redford. Most were breaching the million-dollar barrier. The irony was that neither Richard nor Elizabeth could now command their customary figure. The way around their box-office riskiness was to work with little or no fee and take their earnings as percentages of the take.

Richard took a dim view of the so-called generation gap that was manifesting itself among audiences. *"Easy Rider,"* he told *The Hollywood Reporter* during his visit, "is a travelogue with a very weak message." Its success he attributed to the soundtrack with its "forty with-it songs. The gap lot are infinitely squarer than I was at the same age."

However, less trouble with the "gap lot" was being had by such older actors as Peter Finch, Paul Newman, Marlon Brando, and George C. Scott. And it was Paul Scofield, his elder by several years, who took on the *King Lear* that Richard had long announced was one of his ambitions.

Academy night turned out to be a disappointment to him. Grizzled John Wayne took the Oscar for *True Grit,* and Richard returned empty-handed with Elizabeth to Puerto Vallarta. He had even lost, he said, the twenty thousand words of his novel that he had brought with him to Los Angeles.

In Puerto Vallarta during the late spring and early summer of 1970, Richard claimed to be working on his novel (all he had been able to find of it was the first page) and taking a year's rest from filmmaking, at Elizabeth's insistence. His schedule, Elizabeth told an English reporter who stopped by, was to get up at eight-thirty and write until ten. "Then he wakes me up and we go swimming. Then he works through again till lunch." There were always scripts to read, she said, and Richard occasionally went hunting on horseback into the nearby jungle for jaguar, wild boar, and other game.

Richard had kept to his word about not drinking. "We'll never leave this place," Elizabeth told the reporter. "We love it too much. Besides, there's nowhere else to go."

Yet, when an offer came along from Universal to appear in a quickie film, *Raid on Rommel,* Richard accepted, even though there was no money up front. The film would be shot during late summer in a desert area of Mexico on a schedule of only twenty-five days. Universal had been hoarding thousands of leftover feet of film from an earlier desert epic, *Tobruk,* and wanted to use them up. When Richard was bored, as he likely was at the hacienda in Puerto Vallarta, film work was a solution for him, and in this case he took what was available. He seemed heedless of the damage done to his career by making poor films. The plain fact was that he was not bothered about enhancing his career. In any case, it was difficult, he said, "to find worthy material that is pertinent to our times."

In one of its July issues, *Time* magazine ran a list of what it called "the World's Prize Bores." Both Richard and Elizabeth were on it. In England, two young American producers, Alan Ladd Jr. and Jay Kanter, ignored the implied warning and gave Richard the lead in a low-budget crime film called *Villain*. Actually, it was because Richard gave them a better deal than the one they already had with Robert Stack, who wanted $175,000. Richard offered to do the film for a profit percentage only. And if his box-office potential had faded in the United States, it was still strong in England. After finishing *Raid on Rommel,* Richard, with Elizabeth, went to England, where they rented a house in North London.

Family matters had begun to disturb his peace of mind. Young Michael, not yet eighteen, had decided to marry his girlfriend, Beth Clutter. Elizabeth insisted they marry in London, where she had married his father. Richard was best man for Michael, whose hair flowed down to his shoulders and who wore a red caftan for the ceremony. Richard needed strong drink afterward. Elizabeth's view was that marriage would settle Michael down. She gave them a honeymoon in the Dorchester's bridal suite, and Richard found them a house in London. A few weeks later, Beth told them she was pregnant. Elizabeth, not yet forty, would soon be a grandmother.

On his forty-fifth birthday, Richard was honored by the Queen at Buckingham Palace, not with a knighthood, as he had hoped, but with the still prestigious CBE, the next best. With him were Elizabeth and his proud sister, Cecilia. He attributed his lower ranking than Olivier and Gielgud to the fact that he wouldn't agree to changing his residence to England—the back taxes, he said, would have been too much to pay. But court sources denied that such an offer had been made, or would have been made. Richard was developing a slight taste for sour grapes.

While in London with Richard, Elizabeth found work in *X, Y, and Zee,* a film based on an Edna O'Brien screenplay. The roles she and Richard were taking on were becoming more and more curious. In *Villain*, Richard played a cruel, sadistic cockney gang leader, the film hewing so close to the low-budget line that the young director

BURTON

came from television, and a small, simple trailer was used for Richard's dressing quarters in some seedy areas of London. Bare as the trailer was, it still contained a bottle of vodka and a case of tonic. "I used to get a million a picture," Richard told a reporter cheerily, "and on the next I'll be back to the normal rate. I'm not going to quibble when people want to give me money." That next picture was to be an oddity called *Hammersmith Is Out*, in which he would play an escaped lunatic and Elizabeth a waitress in an all-night diner. As for *X, Y, and Zee*, Elizabeth would take revenge on her unfaithful husband (Michael Caine) by seducing his mistress (Susannah York). They were already being accused by critics of taking the money and running. It indeed looked like it.

"Fame is pernicious," Richard told Bernard Weinraub of the New York *Times*. "So is money." Weinraub saw a depressing change in the actor. "The shadows of the past have deepened. The drinker, the lover, the celebrity, have flickered into a surprisingly weary figure."

He revived sufficiently to spend a few days on an adaptation by Andrew Sinclair of Dylan Thomas's *Under Milk Wood*. In 1954 Richard had made a memorable recording of one of the "voices" in the verse play for BBC radio. Now he recorded the voice again for the film and appeared in it (voiceless) wandering around with a pal in a Welsh town. Elizabeth took a minuscule role as a Welsh whore, and Peter O'Toole was seen as an old captain. The critic Stanley Kauffmann found it neither film nor play, but one long lyric. And "two hours," he said, were "a lot of lyric." Moreover, Richard struck him as slightly drunk.

But only slightly, as Richard assured Sinclair. "I am not drinking in your film," he told him. "That means only one bottle of vodka a day. I am sober on two. But when I'm drinking it's three or more." Sinclair's feeling was that he drank to escape from melancholy to sociability, rather than being driven to it.

No sooner had Elizabeth finished *X, Y, and Zee*, than they left London for Mexico. By this time, two more films were in the offing, in addition to *Hammersmith Is Out*. "We must be out of the country by next week," Richard told a writer, "or it will cost us a million or two in taxes."

While still in London and preparing to leave, Richard received a call from the Yugoslav embassy saying the ambassador wanted to see him. There was no time for an appointment, Richard said, because they were in a rush. Two men immediately came over bearing a photograph of President Tito in uniform as a partisan during World War II and another of Richard in his uniform in *Where Eagles Dare*. There was a strong resemblance between the two.

It turned out a state-supported film was to be made called *The Battle of Sutjeska* and Richard was wanted to play Tito as a partisan. Richard rather relished the idea of playing so great a figure, and asked if there was a script. There was, but it happened to be written in Serbo-Croatian, and was 250 pages in length. Another problem was that the picture was to start in three weeks. In what was becoming a habit pattern, Richard agreed to do it after his *Hammersmith* chores, and had a translation of the script sent over to his British manager, John Heyman, who, in his understated way, said, "Really, Richard, you can't do this." But Richard insisted. After all, the money was good, and he seemed intent on gathering it in as though there would be a long winter after a balmy summer.

His faith in Joseph Losey (after the resounding failure of *Boom!*) was still strong enough for him to agree to work into his schedule *The Assassination of Trotsky*. The unstable nature of the projects he was agreeing to was underlined by a delay in starting *Hammersmith*, due to the lack of a guarantee of financing for finishing the film. (In movie parlance, this necessary financial instrument is known as a completion bond, and is one of the headaches involved in independent production.) This was a clear signal that the Burton-Taylor magic was fading fast. The producer taking a fling into films was a manufacturer of mobile homes, a booming industry in this time of social flux. Somehow, the normally astute Peter Ustinov got himself involved as director in the misguided and unfunny dud that resulted.

"Whatever Became of Richard Burton?" was the headline of an article that summer in the New York *Times*. *Villain*, said the critic Vincent Canby, was Richard's "latest and least interesting bad movie." His potential as one of the world's great actors had been taken for granted for so long that it was time for reevaluation. *Time* magazine charged in at almost the same moment with "Burton's voice remains one of the most distinctive and controlled in the world. But he is no longer in charge of his face. The little piggy eyes glisten and swivel in a seamed and immobile background. Dissipation, alas, now seems less a simulated image than a portrait."

"We all talk too easily," wrote Canby, "about corruption by power and material success, especially as it relates to his career, and the failure of a once promising actor. It may be, however, that this is all that Burton ever could have been, that no one has been corrupted, only remarkably lucky for a lot longer than anyone in his right mind could reasonably hope for."

Not all of these shafts reached Richard, or Elizabeth either, because the members of their establishment often clipped out offending items. Publicly, at least, Richard seemed loftily unaware of the denigration of his work. In Europe, with its proliferation of film festivals, there was sufficient ego feeding. A prize of some sort could be tacitly arranged in return for a celebrity's presence. Joseph Losey, whose only good films seemed those made from scripts written by Harold Pinter, had retrospectives given in his honor. Invariably a critic could be found who would point out the delicacy of nuances in a film such as *Boom!*

And wherever the Burtons were, they were still news. Having finished *Hammersmith,* they were in residence on the *Kalizma* in the harbor of Monte Carlo. Richard had stopped drinking, because, he said, "the kids didn't like it." Actually, in their distress, they had cried and pleaded with him to stop. While an English writer was working to make sense out of the Tito script, word came that Beth Wilding had given birth to a daughter. They made a quick flying trip to London, and declared themselves delighted with their grand-daughter, and Richard said this one, Leyla, took the place of the child they had been thinking of adopting.

Elizabeth had been providing support for the young couple, and had gotten Michael work as a camera assistant. But the early hours proved too grueling for the long-haired lad, and he had quit. Now he announced that he did not like his mother's life-style. With that, he gave up the house in Hampstead and took his wife and baby to Wales to live in a commune.

The irony of this was not lost on Richard. "I made it up," he said, "and Michael is trying to make it down. I try not to interfere, but I still get goddamned mad. When I think what it took to climb out." For Beth, life in the commune was not to her taste. She fled to

London, where Elizabeth put her and the baby up for a while in their Dorchester suite, and not long after, Beth also tired of the Burton life-style and retreated to Portland, Oregon, from where her odyssey had begun.

Later that year, the *Kalizma* was berthed in a small harbor near the old city of Dubrovnik. Wolf Mankowitz had managed to make some sense out of the *Sutjeska* script, and the production was under way in the mountains. A military helicopter furnished by the Yugoslav government would arrive to pick up Richard and carry him to the location, returning him to the yacht at the end of the day. While engaged in the making of the film, President Tito invited Richard and Elizabeth for a weekend stay and personally showed them around his estate in a new Lincoln Continental given him by the city of Zagreb. Richard bragged about the visit.

Dissension arose over the way Richard was portraying Tito as a partisan leader. Directors were fired and new ones hired, scriptwriters came and went, and finally the production bogged down for lack of funds. The local actors found Richard aloof, and thought it rather too capitalistic of him to have a butler (Bob Wilson) on hand to serve him drinks in the wilds of Bosnia.

Toward the end of the year Richard and Elizabeth were in Rome, with Richard playing Trotsky under Losey's direction. When Roderick Mann, a journalist, arrived to have lunch with them, he learned that both had stopped drinking. Elizabeth told Mann that she had stopped exactly one week and four hours ago (this was early November) and that it was proving difficult. "I love booze," she said.

Mann wondered: No drinking at all?

"One martini, before lunch, on Sundays," Elizabeth told him. "Richard prepares it with great ceremony an hour earlier and puts it in the refrigerator."

With *The Battle of Sutjeska* unfinished, and the Trotsky film still under way, Richard flew to Paris to meet with Edward Dmytryk, who would be directing him in his next film, *Bluebeard*. The cast of beauties collected for the wives included Raquel Welch, Virna Lisi, Joey Heatherton, and Nathalie Delon, a pretty blond who was estranged from her husband, Alain Delon.

During a lunch at Fouquet, Dmytryk found Richard in an amiable mood, looking fit and quite youthful. "A sweet, likeable man," he said. The period of abstinence had improved Richard's appearance noticeably. He did not seem concerned about the nature or the quality of the script, which Dmytryk had written with two other writers as a black comedy. The arrangement was for the film to be made in Hungary, where labor was cheap. Richard would get eighty thousand dollars in living expenses, and his earnings would come from a percentage of what the film would take in. "There was no way he could lose," Dmytryk said. "Whether the film lost money or not, he was bound to make a large bundle. I was aware that he was working to bring in the money to keep up the enormous expense of their living arrangements. He had made several poor films in a row, but he made no complaints about their quality. Whether it was good or bad, he worked in the same professional way. If he sold himself, he gave full money's worth."

Dmytryk had vivid memories of his time with the Burtons in Budapest. He was a director who had had his own good and bad times. He had done such films as *The Caine Mutiny*, *The Young Lions*, and *Raintree County*, with Elizabeth Taylor. He had also been exiled from the industry for a time during the McCarthy witch-hunt period. The producer of *Bluebeard* was Ilya Salkind; his method of financing was to collect money from distributorships in various countries. The bigger the names involved, the easier to sell the film in advance. Richard's name was a key sales element. But in certain of the countries, some sex was wanted, too. Dmytryk was asked to insert some nudity. "If I didn't do it, someone else would," he said, "so I did a few scenes, but kept it tasteful." Richard, however, refused to disrobe beyond the limits of modesty. A few of the women were more obliging.

In January 1972, Richard and Elizabeth flew into Budapest in their private jet. They now had other small jets, Richard having formed a company that kept planes for charter. (It was said he lost a considerable amount of money when the company was liquidated and the planes sold.) The Hungarians who watched the plane being unloaded of its dozens of pieces of luggage were particularly amused by the case after case of vodka and bourbon brought out for transport to the Intercontinental Hotel, where they stayed.

BURTON

Elizabeth had long been planning her fortieth birthday celebration, and Budapest was a good place for it. In spite of the country's socialist orientation, Hungarians still loved wine, song, and good food. But the party given by the Burtons was so lavish that it irritated the proletarian feelings of some of the journalists. Several of the two hundred invitees received first-class plane tickets after they accepted, and included in these were several members of the Jenkins clan. Princess Grace came; so did Ringo Starr, Michael Caine, Susannah York, Gianni Bulgari (Elizabeth's favorite jeweler), and Stephen Spender. *Not* invited were the female members of the *Bluebeard* cast.

Edward Dmytryk wasn't much of a partygoer, but he had to admit this was about the best he had ever attended. It went on for three days at the Intercontinental Hotel, and included brunches, lunches, cocktail sessions, and evening dances. Elizabeth showed off the fifty-thousand-dollar yellow Indian diamond Richard gave her as her birthday present. But Emlyn Williams' younger son, Alan, put her in tears when he told her he didn't think the lavishness she exhibited was in the best of taste, considering where they were. Later he described Elizabeth's appearance as "a beautiful doughnut covered in diamonds and paint." Michael Wilding Jr. refused to attend at all.

Richard took notice of the brouhaha and announced that Elizabeth would donate an amount equal to the cost of the party ($45,000) to the United Nations Children's Fund. And eventually she did.

Richard's behavior was exemplary during the festivities. He didn't drink, or didn't appear to, and he was at his charming best. The girlfriend of one of the guests danced with him and talked with him for ten or fifteen minutes afterward. She came over to Dmytryk afterward, starry-eyed, and said, "He loves me!"

He had this amazing effect on women, Dmytryk said. "He would talk to them for a few minutes, and they'd be convinced that either he'd fallen in love with them or would very soon. I never could quite figure it out, but it was all in the way he looked at and talked to them."

Richard's eye had begun to rove, and, as Dmytryk said, "at anything in skirts. Of course, while Elizabeth was around he didn't have too much opportunity, but I know he was very much taken with Raquel Welch. Whatever happened between them, I can't say. I wasn't there with them."

BURTON

Richard later said that it was in that period that he became unfaithful to Elizabeth, that he found himself attracted to younger women. But Elizabeth made sure to be there on the set when his scenes involved him in intimate doings with his lovely costars. One of these was with a young lady Dmytryk described as something of a trollop. In total dishabille, she played her bedroom scene with such passion that at its finish Elizabeth gave her a hearty slap on the face. Later Richard got a plate thrown at him for enjoying the scene too much.

The production went smoothly for the most part, though, until Richard's brother Ifor died after becoming hardly more than a vegetable. Dmytryk excused Richard from three days of filming so he could go to England for the funeral. When he returned there was a change that, said Dmytryk, "took me completely by surprise." If he had known Richard better or longer he would not have been so surprised, because it took very little in the way of trouble or problems to upset his calm and tranquillity. Peter Glenville had noticed this long before when a trifling problem had come up. Now, in his sorrow and even guilt, Richard needed to escape.

"Shortly after Richard returned," Dmytryk remembered, "Britain's ambassador to Hungary gave a little party. Among the guests were the Swiss and Dutch ambassadors with their wives, the American attaché, the Burtons, myself and my wife. Richard was already there when I arrived and was reciting Dylan Thomas verse to the teenage sons of the British ambassador. I noticed he had a glass that he kept reaching for, and I thought to myself: I hope that's ginger ale. But it wasn't. By the time we sat down for dinner he seemed to have retreated into himself. He didn't touch his food, but kept reaching for his drink, and I sensed we were in for trouble. It was the picture I was thinking of. Suddenly he turned to the wife of the Swiss ambassador, who was sitting next to him, and said, 'You remind me quite distinctly of a hungry vulture.' The American attaché was about to take offense but the Swiss ambassador quickly changed the conversation. Richard then fixed his gaze on him and said, 'You Swiss are a very bad lot.' Elizabeth said sharply, 'Richard!' Richard mumbled something and said, 'I think I'd better go home.' His chauffeur took him home, while Elizabeth stayed on, being as pleasant as she could under the circumstances."

Commenting on the Burtons' drinking habits at the time, Dmy-

BURTON

tryk said, "Elizabeth seemed to drink probably as much as he did, but she wasn't nearly as much affected by it, so far as one could see. She was stronger than Richard in every way. The one time I saw her at less than her best was when David Frost came to Budapest to do a taped TV interview with her. It had been assumed that he would edit the tape, because while Richard was at ease and loquacious in interviews, Liz was very shy. She had been drinking, and it didn't show at first, but then her speech got slower, and there were long pauses between her words. That was the only sign she'd had too much. Frost could have edited the tape so it wouldn't show, and it was mean of him that he didn't."

The day following the ambassador's party, Richard was drinking steadily. Night shooting began in the streets of Budapest, starting early in the evening. "Just about midnight," Dmytryk related, "Richard and Nathalie Delon were rehearsing their scene together. At one point he was supposed to take Nathalie's arm and walk down the street. He did this, but kept right on walking with her down the street and around the corner. I thought it was a practical joke of his, but he didn't return. I sent an assistant after him, and when he returned he said Richard and Nathalie had gotten into his Rolls and were driven off. I waited a bit, then canceled the shooting for the rest of the night. More than that, I refused to work the next day.

"Late in the afternoon I received a note from him saying, 'Dear Eddie, please believe that the Richard you saw last night is not the real Richard Burton.' He kept calling and calling, and I wouldn't answer my phone, but finally I did, and he apologized profusely, and we went back to work the next day. But once begun, he couldn't stop.

"He had with him Bob Wilson, who had become sort of his assistant manager, and Gaston, a chauffeur and bodyguard, a judo expert everyone called 'Five-by-five,' because that's the way he was built. Richard needed their protection, because when drunk he became nasty, and in the wrong places might have been killed without them. They would literally lift him out of the car at eight in the morning and prop him up shoulder to shoulder so he could walk into his dressing room for makeup. When he arrived on set or location, he'd have a glass of vodka and orange juice and be able to go to work for a couple of hours. We lost time, but in Hungary that didn't matter much. Everyone was on contract, and labor was the least of our costs.

"I had worked with other stars who drank, but none who started as early as Burton did. Tracy's drunks were periodic, sometimes months of abstinence followed by a week or two in which he'd get mean and wild. Gable didn't start his drinking until five-thirty in the afternoon, so you could get a day's work in. He'd stay on double vodkas and orange juice and continue until someone rolled him into bed. Monty Clift didn't get mean; he would just fall apart, and you'd say 'Cut' and wrap for the day."

Richard's daughter Kate and Elizabeth's Liza came to Budapest for a visit and saw what was happening. "One morning," Dmytryk said, "they both came to his dressing room and pleaded with him to stop drinking. He promised he would, but he wasn't able to keep the promise for long. It must have preyed on him, not being able to keep his promise to two such wonderful kids. He hadn't yet reached the point of where he was aware of it, but it was his body's need now. And from his youthful appearance when I first met him, I could see him getting older week by week. We covered it up with the usual lighting tricks."

Elizabeth's entourage in Budapest was much larger than Richard's, and this was a cause of fights between them. He had taken a particular dislike to Elizabeth's Monsieur Raymond, who was her sort of "chief of everything." And there were six others with various capacities. As Dmytryk saw it, "Their job was to see that she always got what she wanted. Like most courtiers they were protecting their jobs, and for them it was easier to keep her under control if she was less than sober. You could see them feeding her the stuff. Richard would say, 'Goddammit, get rid of them!' He fired one of them—a really sleazy fellow—a couple of times, but she hired him right back again. Elizabeth was a very independent lady."

The Nathalie Delon incident was said to have caused her to fly off to Rome for a dinner date—an innocent one—with Ari Onassis. She put up at the Grand Hotel, and at five in the morning called Richard in Budapest and yelled, "Get that woman out of my bed!"

He told Dmytryk about the call, and wondered, "How did she know? She must have this sixth sense, because how the hell did she know?"

BURTON

"Richard," Dmytryk said, "don't *you* know you're being reported on to her every step of the way? You're surrounded by agents."

Shooting was finished with Richard finally, and the last Dmytryk saw of him was his being slowly walked out of the Intercontinental Hotel, with Bob Wilson and Five-by-five propping him between them. He was ashen-faced.

Two weeks later, a friend went to see Elizabeth at the Grand Hotel in Rome, where she was staying while having her clothes fitted for her next film. She showed the friend a huge sapphire she had recently acquired. "This is for Nathalie," she said with a smile.

During Richard's stay in Budapest, an Oxford don who had come for Elizabeth's birthday celebration discussed with him the possibility of becoming an honorary fellow at the university and making some lecture appearances. The idea intrigued Richard enough to make him consider the offer seriously. In London with Elizabeth while she made a film *(Night Watch)*, he talked about it publicly, saying that he and Elizabeth would spend two terms of each year there, and a season in Mexico. In fact, he said, he would be willing to spend the rest of his life at Oxford.

The Wimbledon season was on, and he watched the matches. To reporters he appeared relaxed and in good shape. His next commitment was to film with Elizabeth two plays for television. It was something he owed Harlech Television as a member of the board of directors. He had promised four years before to take an active part in the programming, but he complained that the other members of the board never listened to his suggestions. Lord Harlech, the firm's chairman, took a different view. "The truth is that whenever we approached Richard to do something specific, he was never available. Although he appears willing, whenever we try to get down to details we run into a complete fog."

Richard told the London *Times* he was growing weary of acting. "I have no real appetite for it," he said. "It seems to me the most ludicrous, undignified job in the world—to sit down and learn tedious lines written by some tedious man." Yet he took on his television commitment, and before beginning on it contracted to follow it immediately with a film called *Massacre in Rome*.

The twin plays were titled *Divorce His . . . Divorce Hers*, the story of a marital breakup from two different points of view. Although set in Rome, only a week of exteriors was scheduled there, the remainder of the film to be done in Munich. John Osborne worked up the scripts first, ignoring pointed suggestions by the Burtons that the story be set either in Mexico or the south of France (in proximity to the *Kalizma*). The Burtons hated the script, and it was given to another writer to rework.

Richard had managed to curb his drinking, and in Rome, where the scenes mostly featured him, he was fine, until Elizabeth suddenly arrived early for her one day of shooting. Richard at once went back to his vodka, and stayed on it for the remainder of the filming, much to the dismay of Waris Hussein, the young director. For him the chaotic marriage revealed in the television plays was similar to the Burtons' own. He felt from the beginning that the project was doomed. And as for Richard's pretensions of becoming a don at Oxford, he regarded it as one of his fantasies. Richard celebrated his forty-seventh birthday in Munich, and Hussein noted that Elizabeth, for a birthday gift, gave him an original Goethe volume, as though attesting to his intellectuality. "I don't know who Goethe is," she told Hussein, "but I hope he likes it."

19

The cracks in the Burton marriage were widening as 1973 began. They were in Rome again, with Richard playing a Gestapo officer in *Massacre in Rome* and Elizabeth preparing for her role in *Ash Wednesday*, a soapy tale of a mature woman, neglected by her rich husband, who has an affair with a young man in a posh ski resort. The careers were diverging. Richard claimed later that he was opposed to Elizabeth's doing *Ash Wednesday*, with its emphasis on riches and idleness. He was drinking heavily.

Franco Zeffirelli saw something of them in Rome during the spring and said afterward that he noticed the strain between them. Elizabeth, he reported, bossed Richard around, and Richard, in turn, became aggressive and intolerant. In Cortina, the ski resort where much of *Ash Wednesday* was filmed, Richard had little to do except drink and add to his voluminous diary. He talked afterward about some "cathartic infidelities."

There were times when he was all but unapproachable by those from the outside world. When he was deep in one of his extensive drinking periods, he still maintained sense enough not to do any business. There were always a great many things to look at, to sign, and it was Bob Wilson who collected these and piled them up until the time he could catch Richard when he was sober. Kurt Frings was the agent for both Richard and Elizabeth at this time, and had been wanting to see him for months. Finally, in Cortina, he knocked on Richard's door at five in the morning. "Am I disturbing you?" Frings asked.

"No, fine, come in," Richard said.

Frings noticed he already had a glass of vodka and orange juice in hand, and had been at a table writing. But he was sober, and able to discuss matters with Frings.

By the time Elizabeth finished working in *Ash Wednesday*, the quarrels between them had become so fierce that she left for California by herself, assuming that once Richard came out of his black spell, he would join her there. Both were scheduled for films in Italy again, late in the summer. The marriage was clearly hanging by a thread. While Elizabeth was seen hanging around in Los Angeles with old friends such as Peter Lawford, Laurence Harvey, and Roddy McDowall, Richard stayed in one of his favorite hideaways, the guest cottage of Aaron Frosch in Quogue, Long Island, about seventy-five miles from New York City. From there he telephoned Elizabeth and was heard to say (according to gossip writer Rona Barrett), "Get your ass back here or you won't have an ass to sit on!"

Elizabeth promptly obeyed, and Richard met her at Kennedy Airport in a chauffeured limousine, already well into his day's ration of vodka. This was enough to set Elizabeth off, and by the time they reached Quogue, the point of explosion had been reached. "We both burst apart at the same moment," Richard told a friend. Hardly were they in Frosch's guesthouse than he ordered her to get out. The chauffeur drove a tearful Elizabeth in the same limousine back to New York, where she checked in at the Regency Hotel, the scene of their first happy married days.

John Springer issued a statement for her, confirming the separation. It was not a typical public-relations release, seeming heartfelt as it spoke of their having loved each other too much, of having "been in each other's pockets constantly." It ended with a message, presumably to the public at large, as though the separation was of paramount importance to everyone: "Pray for us."

Huge black headlines heralded the announcement. Reporters from the daily papers sped to Quogue. While Elizabeth was in the air headed for California, Richard entertained the press in the guesthouse, drinking a tumblerful of vodka and orange juice as he cheerfully discussed the breakup.

"It was bound to happen," he told the reporters. They were like two explosive sticks being clapped together until they exploded. Elizabeth was constantly worrying about her figure, her family, about the color of her teeth. "She expects me to drop everything to devote myself to these problems." He declared himself amused by the statement she had made to the press. "I find the situation wildly fascinating." And it was not a true separation; private and professional interests were keeping them apart for the time being.

But behind the alcoholic bravado, a frightened man was talking. The blowup with his wife was enough to cause him to go to New York and consult a doctor, after which he began a detoxification program. He still refused, however, to admit to himself, or to anyone else, that he was an alcoholic. Rather, he would explain, from time to time he was a drunk. For him there was a difference. Being a drunk was a matter of choice; for an alcoholic there was none.

He was to be in Rome in August of that year to costar in *The Voyage* with Sophia Loren and Marcello Mastroianni. Loren's husband, Carlo Ponti, was the producer, and Vittorio De Sica the director. About ten days after Elizabeth returned to California, Richard telephoned Sophia Loren in Rome and asked if he might arrive in Italy a month early and stay at the Ponti estate in Marino, near Rome. He explained that he wanted to avoid a hotel because of the press and the paparazzi. Graciously, Sophia offered him the use of their guesthouse.

In Los Angeles, meanwhile, Elizabeth had met a new friend, a result of the good offices of Peter Lawford, who was known for his ability at getting people together. Henry Wynberg, a friend of Lawford's, was one of the men-around-town in Beverly Hills often seen with unattached or temporarily unattached Hollywood stars. Born in Holland, he came to California in the early fifties, worked as a waiter, sold cars, and eventually developed his own business as a used-car wholesaler. Five years younger than Elizabeth, he was divorced from his actress wife, Carroll Russell, and had a son. His meeting with Elizabeth occasioned no comment—at the time.

Ten days after the separation, Richard set off for Rome, accompanied by a party that included Bob Wilson, Gaston, his bodyguard,

BURTON

a doctor, a nurse, and a secretary. Carlo Ponti and Sophia accommodated them all in the guesthouse of their estate. Richard attempted to adhere to the program his doctor set out for him. It included a special diet and a severely limited intake of wine. Sophia found him nervous and in need of reassurance.

There was time to kill for both of them, because De Sica was in ill health. Richard swam in the Pontis' pool and lunched with Sophia on the terrace of the villa. Once he had stopped drinking, she found him, as almost everyone else did, witty and vibrant. He did not leave the estate; for amusement he played Scrabble with Sophia, a game she was good at. She usually beat him—to her surprise, she learned Richard wasn't very good at spelling.

Aaron Frosch, in New York, soon announced that the separation was at an end. The cause of it had been Richard's drinking, he said, and now that he had stopped, Elizabeth would rejoin him in Rome. Richard was at the airport when Elizabeth stepped off the plane late in July. She was due to start soon on her new film, *The Driver's Seat,* and had booked a seven-room suite at the Grand Hotel. But first she drove with Richard to the Ponti villa. The avid reporters and photographers, and a crowd of onlookers, caught a glimpse of the two of them in the limousine, Richard's head on Elizabeth's shoulder and she with tears in her eyes.

The reconciliation had hardly begun before it was over. Without the alcohol to sustain him, Richard was bored and restless, and Elizabeth no longer fulfilled his needs. Sophia Loren, who saw them at lunch a few times at the villa, felt the marriage was doomed. Elizabeth, for one, wasn't certain she wanted to face again his radical changes of mood, the imminent possibility he would drink again. The moment when he began wasn't pinpointed, but Sophia saw him become aggressive and violent toward Elizabeth. Within four or five days of her arrival, she had retreated to the suite at the Grand Hotel. She was in such an emotional state that the start of filming had to be delayed for several hours.

The saddest day of her life until then, she told the producer of *The Driver's Seat,* was the day Mike Todd was killed. "Today is the second sad day in my life. I am desolate."

As for Richard, he was to tell a reporter, "If two people are absolutely sick of each other, or the sight of one another bores them, then they should get divorced or separated as soon as possible. Otherwise life becomes intolerable, waking up every morning and having breakfast with the same miserable face."

John Springer had gone to Rome to handle the press in connection with the reconciliation; he flew back to New York assuming the two were together again. Hardly was he back there when he received a phone call from Rome. Richard and Elizabeth had mutually decided to separate again.

Five days after Elizabeth had arrived in Rome, Henry Wynberg arrived there—coincidentally, he said. Coincidentally, too, he registered at the Grand Hotel. He later said that he happened to learn Elizabeth Taylor was in the same hotel when he read about the latest breakup in a morning newspaper. He telephoned her and made a date for drinks the same afternoon. From that moment on, Wynberg found himself in the public eye as the devoted escort of the world's most publicized woman. He was on the set with her during the filming of *The Driver's Seat;* they held hands for photographers. Gossip had it that Wynberg was one of the world's great lovers. It was reported that Richard made a remark to the effect that like the used cars Wynberg sold, it would fall off at just the right psychological moment.

In any case, Elizabeth had found the comfort she needed at just the right psychological moment.

After De Sica came through an operation, filming started on *The Voyage* and then stopped again. Marcello Mastroianni had gone on strike. Burton and Loren were being given major billing on the film, and he was relegated to a lower place. He had a bitter quarrel over it with Ponti, and flew to Paris. Richard took the opportunity to quietly fly to New York. Soon enough, reporters had ferreted out a reason. He was being seen with a young and lovely fashion designer, Barbara Dulien by name, having drinks at the Sherry-Netherland Hotel, and then in Quogue. It was even reported that he had made a quick trip with her to Los Angeles.

When Mastroianni was replaced, filming resumed on *The Voyage.* Richard, still vacillating about Elizabeth, telephoned her, suggesting they meet and talk it all over, but as he told Sophia—waking her in the middle of the night—"She means it. It's over. She's never coming back. I need help, Sophia." By her account, the practical Sophia suggested he take a sleeping pill.

He was not seen the following day. When Sophia entered the guesthouse the day after that, she was so shocked by the shambles she saw that she would not allow her maids to go in. Her private secretary arranged for the cleanup.

When filming of *The Voyage* moved to Sicily, Richard made the *Kalizma* his headquarters. His doctor and nurse had been dismissed, and he was drinking again. An American actress with a small part in the film found Richard pleasant to work with, but hardly able to stand erect after lunchtime. He was bothered with sciatica, and complained to a reporter that Sophia wasn't being very nice to him.

She had gotten up one morning at six for a scene that was to begin at seven-thirty, only to find a message that Richard would arrive at two P.M. When he arrived finally, he kissed her. She smiled with icy eyes. "God, she's pissed off," he muttered to a reporter.

Eventually, though, she said that a pleasant relationship had been established between them, and they were later to work together again. But "during the sad period when I knew him, he was a tragic figure, the way kings in Shakespeare, once grand, are broken upon the wheel of preordained tragedy."

Richard noted in his diary that Sophia treated him as though he were "a clown prince. So she should. I am both."

In November 1973, Elizabeth was in the hospital once more. This time she feared cancer. Although Wynberg was in attendance, it was Richard she now longed for. He received a telephone call from her while in Sicily. She was to be operated on. Could he come and be with her? At first he refused to fly all that way for one more of her operations. But he was worried nevertheless. Elizabeth's problem turned out to be a bleeding cyst, not cancer.

Sensing it was time to end the separation, Richard received permission from Ponti to fly to Los Angeles, if he could make the entire trip over a three-day weekend. After a long flight over the North Pole, he entered Elizabeth's hospital room, asked Wynberg to leave, told the nurses to bring an extra bed for him, and spent the night. Shortly after he returned to the film, Elizabeth rejoined him in Na-

BURTON

ples. And Richard, according to De Sica, finished the film in a much more sober state.

The Christmas holidays were spent by the two of them in Gstaad, and it was announced by John Chancellor on NBC that they were "reconciling permanently—as opposed to temporarily." But after the holidays and a presentation by Richard to Elizabeth of a thirty-eight-carat diamond, they were quarreling again. When they flew to Puerto Vallarta in January 1974, Richard was drinking more recklessly than ever.

Two months later, in the town of Oroville, in northern California, Richard began work on *The Klansman*, a film that mixed together the Ku Klux Klan, civil rights, a racial confrontation, and a rape case. Richard's role was the unlikely one of an aristocratic Southerner gone somewhat to seed, but a liberal at heart. He played it with a Southern accent and a limp. The limp was real, from sciatica and gout. His costar was Lee Marvin, also known as something of a drinker. The press began to gather, especially as word grew that Richard Burton was out of control. "If you want to come up here, okay," Paramount's unit publicist warned reporters. "If you want to interview a drunk and watch a drunk fall in the camellia bushes, come ahead." They came. Soon enough, Joyce Haber was reporting that the director, Terence Young, had to get most of his shots in the morning before his stars were "totally bombed."

Elizabeth arrived in Oroville in time to read a story in a San Francisco newspaper about Richard and an eighteen-year-old waitress he had met on the street in front of the local jail. He had invited her into his trailer, so the account said, and the next day had taken her to a jewelry shop and bought her a ring for $450. Then he bought another ring for an assistant in the store. Until then, the pretty waitress was famous only for the fact that she had been chosen as Miss Pepsi of Butte County. Now her picture appeared far and wide. True to form, she told reporters, "Mr. Burton and I are just good friends."

Richard had a hard time explaining that one away to Elizabeth, and she abruptly left for Los Angeles and a bungalow at the Beverly Hills Hotel. Now the curious came to Oroville like wolves gathering, and, unkindly, the film publicists seemed to encourage the influx of

BURTON

reporters. They came to see not a film in the making, but the spectacle of a famous and gifted man literally falling apart.

"His thin wrists branch out of a baggy shirt," Robert Kerwin wrote. "His loose brown trousers are an old man's trousers. The once robust and forceful face has a powdery pallor. The irises are bright blue, but the whites are deeply red, with only flecks of white. On his face is a dazed grin, as if he's been shocked awake under these heavy lights in the midst of surgery."

Willingly, with his ever-present glass brimming with vodka and ice, he answered their questions, mocking them as much as they implicitly mocked him. "Tell us about Dylan Thomas." He told them a fanciful story. "Tell us something about Wales." "Tell us about Sophia Loren." "Tell us about why Elizabeth left." The words of reply were often lovely and mad. And oddly poetic.

"There's something to death," he said, clutching his glass. "Something to death and something to truth, and we're after them all our beautiful lives on earth. Liquor helps. My father was a drinker, and I'm a drinker, and Lee Marvin's a drinker. The place I like best to be in the whole world is back in my village in Wales, down at the pub standing with the miners, drinking pints and telling stories. One drinks because life is big and it blinds you. It's grabbing at you from all directions all the time, and you have to tone it down. Poetry and drink are the greatest things on earth. Besides women. Would anyone like to hear some poetry?"

"He's committing physical and professional suicide," said a member of the production team.

"The man's suffering," Lee Marvin said. "Who knows what it is? He's fending off so many people that his mind is hardly his own anymore."

There were local girls, hoping to be made a pass at by the famous lover, and often enough he obliged. He was nice to them. One skinny girl of eighteen stayed with him all day on the location, as he carefully explained to her what was going on. She wore a white sweater, a black blouse, and overalls. She had "dumb eyes, pancaky skin, no breasts," wrote a reporter. After shooting broke for the day, he took her with him to the house he shared with four bodyguards.

He found another temporary companion in a thirty-three-year-old extra in the movie, a local woman with three children and a husband.

BURTON

Richard was due in Los Angeles to make an album recording of Saint-Exupéry's *The Little Prince*, and invited the woman to accompany him. Word came that his limousine was being followed by the angry husband in another car. Once they arrived in Los Angeles, the woman was promptly sent back to Oroville.

"When I saw how bad it was," Terence Young said, "I told everybody that we'd better just wind up the shooting. He was a terribly sick man. He was making a great effort, having to force his whole body to get the words out. I got a doctor down here, and he said, 'This man is dying. He'll be dead in three weeks.'"

In the film, on the last day of shooting, the character played by Richard died, and immediately after, Richard, still alive, was bundled into a plane and then taken to St. John's Hospital in Santa Monica, ostensibly for a bad case of influenza and a hand injured in his last scene. His longtime friend and adviser Valerie Douglas, then a publicist, loyally told the inquiring Joyce Haber that Richard had "influenzal tracheobronchitis." They were keeping him there because "they were afraid it would turn into pneumonia."

"Let's hope," wrote the sly Ms. Haber, "Richard's bronchitis dries up."

In the hospital, Richard was told that if he continued to drink, he might have no more than two weeks to live. To the doctors he said, "I'm amused you think I can be killed off that easily." But he took the drying-out treatment. He went there originally for ten days, but the process stretched out for six weeks. Elizabeth occasionally called, and he learned that she had begun divorce proceedings in Gstaad, Switzerland. The first few days of treatment he was allowed two or three glasses of wine a day. Then he was taken off spirits entirely.

He began to shake uncontrollably, so much so that he had to be fed intravenously. He slept poorly—not more than forty-five minutes at a time—and when he did he dreamed of his brother Ifor, who seemed alive and in the room with him. When he regained some strength and equilibrium he sent for his lawyer. "I wanted to make sure," he told David Lewin, "that the people I wanted looked after should I die would be looked after. The children, some twenty-eight or twenty-nine nieces and nephews, and I wanted to make sure that Elizabeth would be all right financially. All her money was tied up in assets like jewelry, and she doesn't like selling anything. I wanted to make sure she had enough in cash for anything she needed."

The doctors gave him bicycling exercises to improve his pulse rate. They had him take walks with the nurses and then to jog with them. "Running after them was a pleasure," he said. What he did not talk about was the blood transfusions he had been given to cleanse his system of alcohol.

There was a day when he emerged from the hospital for a walk, leaning on two bodyguards. A small, pretty young woman paused as she was about to enter the hospital.

"Richard?" she said, noticing that his face was pale and that his hands were shaking.

"Yes?" He looked at her, wondering who she was.

"It's Susan," she said. "Susan Strasberg."

By this time, she had come through an unfortunate marriage, and her daughter was in the hospital for corrective surgery. "Give us a kiss," Richard said. He hugged her, kissed her on both cheeks, and asked what she was doing here at the hospital.

Then they stood looking at each other, with little to say.

"It was lovely seeing you," Susan said before turning away.

Lewin, in conversation with Richard, asked him why he drank. Was it a form of self-destruction?

"I think it is a Celtic thing really," he answered. "Celts have this black cell which makes them go off and drink. If you add to that the problem of being an actor, then you have the makings of being a drunk. Acting is somehow shameful for a man to do. It isn't natural to put on makeup and wear costumes onstage and say someone else's lines. So you drink to overcome the shame. And perhaps most actors are latent homosexuals, and we cover it with drink." He was rationalizing about a problem that went very deep, that was all but unsolvable. He might just as well have agreed with a rather philosophical expert on poisons who theorized that the human cell contains within it an affinity, indeed a kind of love, for that which will destroy it.

In May he left the hospital, somewhat recuperated, for Puerto Vallarta. By this time Elizabeth was reunited with Henry Wynberg and having a gay time with him. They cruised in the *Kalizma* through the Mediterranean, and put in at the harbor of Monaco, where they were entertained at the palace by Princess Grace and Prince Rainier. Richard stayed alone in his house, attended by Bob Wilson and his wife. To friends and neighbors he appeared ill and depressed.

Prior to his hospitalization, he had agreed to portray Churchill in a television play called *The Gathering Storm*. The program was to be jointly produced by the BBC and Hallmark Cards. But now the director was unsure if Burton was well enough to perform. Unable to reach him, a group flew to Puerto Vallarta, where Richard assured them he would be able to film for them in England in August.

If he drank in Puerto Vallarta—and there were those who saw him visiting bars with one young girl or another—it was modestly. He went to Los Angeles for a few days, where he used the house of Valerie Douglas as a hideaway, then went to New York and Quogue, where Aaron Frosch arranged for his consent to the divorce Elizabeth was seeking. Instead of his appearance in the small Swiss courtroom, a medical certificate was produced stating that illness prevented him from appearing in person.

Elizabeth, on June 26, 1974, wore dark glasses as she told the judge that her life with Richard had become intolerable and that their differences were irreconcilable.

The next day, Richard sailed for Europe on the S.S. *France*. He told reporters that he had conquered his drinking and that he felt ten years younger. "Frankly," he said about Elizabeth, "she'll be better off without me. I intend to roam the globe searching for ravishing creatures."

PART
FOUR

20

The first ravishing creature located by Richard after his breakup was thirty-seven-year-old Princess Elizabeth of Yugoslavia, the daughter of exiled (after World War II) Prince Paul and Princess Olga. She was also distantly related to England's Prince Charles, and was married (her second time) to Neil Balfour, a banker who had run unsuccessfully for Parliament. Richard was already acquainted with her, as was Elizabeth Taylor. Their reacquaintance took place when Richard was asked to escort the princess and her daughter to tea at Lady Churchill's. Richard was getting to know members of the Churchill family as the time approached when he would portray the deceased British statesman for television.

But before he did that, the Hallmark company wanted Richard to take on a television remake of Noël Coward's *Brief Encounter*. He was at his home in Céligny, still recuperating from his alcoholic excesses of a few months before, when the call came through. The role of the married doctor who meets and falls in love with an equally married housewife at a suburban train station had been suggested to him a year or so earlier, but he had sensed that it would be difficult to equal or surpass the performance of Trevor Howard in the classic film.

The television version was originally scheduled for Robert Shaw

BURTON

and Sophia Loren, but Shaw was caught up in the delays in filming *Jaws* off Martha's Vineyard, and meanwhile filming had already started on *Brief Encounter*. Richard was dubious about replacing Shaw, but then, he said, "Sophia came on and in that gently imperious voice persuaded me."

Sophia was a good influence on him. She was tolerant and amusing with him during the few weeks they worked together, and as far as the drinking was concerned, he appeared to keep himself well under control. He would rise at dawn and ride his bicycle for a half-hour or so in the Hampshire countryside. His daughter Kate, on her summer vacation, came to visit him, and one Sunday he took her on a visit to Winchester Cathedral, made even more famous by the song. But he made sure to tell a reporter who encountered him in the church that he was indulging his daughter, and not any religious feeling. He remained firmly an agnostic, he said. Reporters attempted to make something out of the relationship with Sophia, but they were friends, and nothing more.

In a playful mood with one of the reporters, he dashed off a mock advertisement: "Intelligent, well-to-do actor, twice divorced, seeks nice lady aged between twenty-eight and thirty-eight to have baby with him." The offer, if the offspring turned out to be a boy, was twice that if a girl. And, had it been possible, he would have wanted to have a child with Elizabeth, preferably a son. Even though his words were humorous, it was clear that he was lonely. Having a woman near him and with him at all times was necessary to him. And the moment he met Princess Elizabeth again, he began pursuing her adamantly, with marriage in mind. She was a brightly intelligent and attractive woman, with three children of her own, two by her former marriage to an American, Howard Oxenberg. (Her eldest daughter, Catherine, eventually became well-known as a television actress.)

It took three weeks of proposals for her to yield, she told reporters, when their engagement was announced. "He kept on and on, and I said yes. It was as simple as that." But before marriage was possible her husband—from whom she was separated—had to be told and to agree to a divorce. Elizabeth read the news in a paper, and called both of them with her wishes for happiness.

BURTON

The engagement said more about Richard's state of mind, and his need for companionship and reassurance, than about any real romantic involvement. Viewed in the cold light of practicality, it was foolish to the point of zaniness. The princess must have been in a giddy frame of mind herself, for she agreed to take a small part in a film that he was to make later in Rome and in the south of France. And as Richard pointed out in his refreshingly immodest way to David Lewin, "I am very sexually attractive."

Portraying Churchill was both challenging and worrisome to Richard. That, combined with the euphoria of the new romance, made him occasionally depart from his program of abstinence. But it was not his playing of the role that caused comment so much as his public utterances and writings on the subject of the great world figure.

Noting his fascination with the man, and the reading he was doing about him, a Hallmark publicist suggested he write an article about Churchill. The New York *Times* issued a cordial invitation. Richard worked hard at the article. He had first regarded Churchill with a sense of awe, and speaking his words in the taping of the program for a month affected his own manner of speech. A waitress, he said, asked him if he would like a cup of coffee. He answered, "I cannot think of a more desirable and attractive proposition." To a reporter he said, referring to Churchill's liking for whiskey and brandy, "He would have provided mankind with an additional great benefit if he had left his liver for study and observation."

But it was in his article for the New York *Times* that he caused a real sensation. There had already been a considerable amount of revisionist theory about Churchill and his wartime actions, but Richard went a large step further.

"In the course of preparing myself to act the part of Winston Churchill," he wrote, "I realized afresh that I hate Churchill and all his kind. . . . How could he have ordered the enchanting and innocent city of Dresden razed to ruins?" He compared Churchill with such as Hitler, Stalin, Lenin, and even Tamerlane and Attila the Hun. He referred to Churchill's "idiot air marshals." But the most unkind cut of all he reserved for Churchill's way with words.

To speak "the bloody lines," he wrote, he became aware of Churchill's "use and misuse of the language he loved so much. His contortions of syntax were so acute that there were times when I thought I was going to go mad trying to figure out what the hell he meant."

The article appeared in the Sunday drama section of the *Times* a few days prior to the broadcast, and undoubtedly served to swell the audience. But the producers of the program hastened to disassociate themselves from their star's intemperate attack on the character he played. So did the Hallmark company, which usually presented programs so safe and sanitized and worthy that no one would ever think of boycotting its greeting cards. In England the shock was profound, and was felt throughout the press and into Parliament. One member stood up and valiantly stated that England would be far better off with more Churchills and fewer Burtons. Richard's head may have been symbolically bloodied, but remained unbowed.

In Rome with Princess Elizabeth by the time the fuss developed, he stood his ground. He aligned himself with his class in Wales, where, he said, Churchill was "a bogeyman who hated us, the mining class, motiveless."

Almost simultaneously, another Burton blast at Churchill appeared in *TV Guide*. This time some personality notes were included: "He drank steadily all day long with time off for sleep—champagne, whiskey, brandy—and lived for more than ninety years." (One wonders why Richard didn't feel more of an affinity with him.)

The film he was to do next was *Jackpot*, directed by Terence Young, who must have been assured that Richard had himself well in hand, after his experience with him in Oroville. Young's problem this time was with financing. *Jackpot* was the kind of film project put together on the terrace of the Carlton Hotel, where distributors from many countries were wont to gather during Cannes film festivals. So much advance financing from this one, so much from that one. But not all of the money materialized after filming began, and the work proceeded by fits and starts, mostly fits. Cast members departed, Robert Mitchum among them, when their pay didn't come through. Richard meanwhile seemed content to wait out the problems in his suite at the Negresco Hotel in Nice.

His princess came across a newspaper photo during a trip she made to London. In it, Richard was seen strolling arm in arm with a pretty young black woman who was identified as Jeanne Bell, a model. This, along with an occasional fall by Richard from abstinence, was enough to cause her to break the engagement.

Richard hastened to London in an attempt to repair the damage. Princess Elizabeth was staying at the Dorchester, and she kept him nervously waiting in the lounge until she allowed him to come to her suite. By that time, he was unsteady on his feet. The princess was kind, telling him that they would remain friends, and she advised him to stop drinking before he killed himself.

"I didn't realize," she said after the breakup, "that it takes more than a woman to make a man sober."

Richard must have realized this himself, for soon afterward he retreated to Céligny, where he went on a serious program to quit drinking. He had for assistance a Swiss doctor and the aforementioned Jeanne Bell. The program involved the use of sedatives and tranquilizers, along with proper diet and exercise.

Jeanne Bell's true name was Anna Morgan. Her major distinction was that she was the first black woman to appear in a *Playboy* magazine centerfold. Originally from Houston, she was a beauty-contest winner, then a model and actress. She met Richard when she was given a small part in *The Klansman,* and he was instrumental in getting her a part in *Jackpot.* "I said, 'You look nice, why don't you join me?' and she did."

While in Switzerland with him, Jeanne Bell described her role as a helpful companion, someone for Richard to talk to and listen to. During the period when he was adhering strictly to his new regimen she saw him drinking nothing but milk and mineral water. He took walks and read a great deal. And he was coming to the long-delayed realization that if he wasn't a confirmed alcoholic yet, he was well on the way. He would continue to avoid making that final admission, but any knowledgeable observer would have recognized him as virtually a classic case of the disease.

In January 1975, Elizabeth Taylor was in Leningrad and on location elsewhere in Russia, working in Cukor's film version of Maeterlinck's *The Blue Bird.* With her was Henry Wynberg, now her constant companion. There had been talk that they would marry, although both later denied they had seriously considered the step. In any case, unknown to Wynberg, Elizabeth telephoned Richard frequently in

Céligny. The pull between them still existed. Richard wanted to get together again, and Elizabeth, fully as anxious as he was, told him it would be possible only if he gave up drinking altogether. Arrangements were made between them to meet when she finished her film. On the final day of filming, Richard sent her a telegram asking her to meet him in Switzerland "to discuss business." With Wynberg still in the dark, she flew with him to Geneva.

To Richard's eyes, Elizabeth looked lovelier than in a long time. As illness-prone as ever while in Russia, she had gone through sieges of the flu and dysentery, and had dropped a considerable amount of poundage. Richard, reasonably free of alcohol toxicity, looked better too. The meeting took place in the office of Elizabeth's lawyer. The next day, impedimenta were disposed of, as though by royal fiat. Jeanne Bell left the house in Céligny, and Henry Wynberg took a plane to parts unknown. In New York, the slightly bewildered John Springer announced that his two famous clients were together again.

This happened in mid-August 1975. While living together again, both shilly-shallied about remarrying. Richard had more doubts about the wisdom of this than Elizabeth. But she was able to get not only her man but also her way. Two months after their reunion, they remarried—on a riverbank in northern Botswana! They had traveled, first to Israel, where they paid their respects to the Wailing Wall (Richard liked to claim that he had a Jewish great-grandparent), and then to Johannesburg for a celebrity tennis tournament for charity.

The marriage took place on Richard's fiftieth birthday, and the combination of the two events—as might have been expected—dumped him off the wagon.

Elizabeth managed to wake him enough to get him in the Land Rover that took them to Chobe, the site of the wedding, which was performed by a district commissioner from the Tswana tribe. Why Chobe, in Botswana? The commissioner explained it was because "they liked the place very much. They more or less fell in love with the area." He reported, too, that Richard and Elizabeth toasted each other with champagne, while two hippos gazed at them solemnly from the muddy water. Farther away a rhinoceros also looked their way.

For those curious about what the bride and groom wore for the occasion, the commissioner gave details. Elizabeth wore a green dress edged with lace and decorated with guinea-fowl feathers, while Richard wore a red shirt (ever the loyal Welshman) open at the neck, white slacks, red socks, and white shoes. Both rigorously avoided representatives of the press, which, once alerted, had no idea where they went to celebrate.

However, the next day they were in London, where Elizabeth threw a small party to celebrate both the marriage and Richard's birthday. It was noticed that Richard drank only mineral water and that he did not look well.

Richard later remarked about the wedding that it was "like a huge dream. I remember thinking: What am I doing here? Odd place to be married, in the bush, by an African gentleman. It was very curious. An extraordinary adventure, doomed from the start, of course."

The main purpose of the London visit was for Elizabeth to do some redubbing of her voice for *The Blue Bird,* one more in the series of flops that plagued her. Soon enough, she was in the hospital again with assorted complaints, but she emerged in time to leave for Gstaad with Richard for the Christmas holiday season. They weren't there long before Richard set eyes on another ravishing creature.

While Elizabeth lolled about the chalet, Richard went skiing, sometimes with Liza, and always accompanied by Brook Williams, who was now virtually his entire entourage and handled just about any matter that came up concerning Richard. An actor himself, he usually took a small part in Richard's films, and was as much a friend as an employee. Richard was waiting at the ski lift, and just as he got into his chair and was about to swing off, he caught sight of, as he put it, "this beautiful creature, about nine feet tall."

He asked Williams to find out who she was, since she appeared to be accompanied. Williams struck up a conversation with the man, and learned that the beautiful creature was Susan Hunt, the wife of James Hunt, a famous British racing driver. She had been a fashion model, and although Hunt appeared in Gstaad to celebrate New Year's Eve with her, they were in the process of a separation and divorce.

"Get her up to the house," Richard told Williams. So it was as the acquaintance of Brook Williams that she first came to the chalet, where, said Richard, "instinctively, Elizabeth recognized that Susan was something special. From the very beginning, she sensed a special adversary."

Richard was in one of his nervous periods. He had taken on the challenge of returning to Broadway. His agent was now Robert Lantz, based in New York, whose list of clients was one of the most prestigious in his field. *Equus,* Peter Shaffer's interesting play about a tormented psychiatrist attempting to treat a disturbed boy who blinded some horses, was scheduled for filming. While in London, Lantz had brought word to Richard that Sidney Lumet, the director, was seriously interested in him for the role of the psychiatrist, currently being played on the stage by Anthony Perkins.

With no film prospects in the offing, with *Jackpot* shelved, Richard had been considering trying the stage again. When Lantz suggested he replace Perkins in the play for a limited run, Richard read the play through several times until he convinced himself he could handle the role of Martin Dysart, the psychiatrist. He knew he was being tested (though he wouldn't admit this publicly) and that how he handled himself during his run in the play would determine whether he got the film role. The play producers were also demanding that he pass a thorough physical.

Elizabeth took a dim view of his returning to Broadway. "They'll be gunning for you," she told him. And when he left for New York in mid-January 1976, she remained in Gstaad to enjoy the winter social season there.

Elizabeth was well aware of Richard's fascination with Susan Hunt, nor did Richard bother to disguise it. When Richard stayed in Geneva for a few days before going on to New York, she was aware that Susan was there too. She wasted little time in picking out a candidate for her favors, Peter Darmanin, a thirty-seven-year-old advertising executive from Malta. By his account he met her in a Gstaad disco one evening, danced with her for an hour, and the next morning received a phone call from her. "I told her to come by for breakfast, and she did," he told Kitty Kelley, the author of *Elizabeth Taylor: The Last Star.* "We made love that first morning."

That affair lasted several weeks, until Darmanin was replaced with another run for Henry Wynberg. Reports of Elizabeth's friendship with Darmanin reached Richard in New York, where he was in the throes of rehearsal for his role in *Equus.* By this time he had company of his own—Susan Hunt. He had telephoned her in Switzerland and said, "Please come. I need you."

"When?" she asked.

"Now."

He recalled later, "She took the chance of a lifetime and came. How was she to know that with my reputation I wouldn't say, 'Allright, sweetheart, off'?"

The more he saw Susan, the more he was convinced that his separation from Elizabeth should remain permanent. He kept up the pretense, though, that his marriage was still in force. He was seen around New York with Susan, but any inquiring reporter was led to believe that she was Brook Williams' girlfriend.

A week before his opening in the play he telephoned Elizabeth and asked her to come to New York. She did, and stayed with him in the suite he had taken in the Lombardy, a quietly distinguished residential hotel in the East Fifties. In spite of the building's solid pre—World War II construction, the arguments between Richard and Elizabeth were clearly heard outside their suite. The shouting was loudest on February 22, a Sunday night. On Monday, Elizabeth left the hotel and flew to California.

Richard, instead of a mere separation, this time wanted a divorce, and wanted it quickly, so that he could marry Susan. "Why the hell," Elizabeth asked him, "did you have me come all the way here to tell me that?"

Richard had his reasons. He wanted the divorce settlement out of the way as fast as possible. Otherwise lawyers would have been traveling back and forth between Gstaad and New York. As usual, it was Aaron Frosch who worked out the details. Richard's monetary assets were in trusts, but there were the jewels, the houses, the artworks, and the yacht. Elizabeth got to keep the house in Mexico, the jewels, the artworks, and Richard's rights to the yacht. He was mainly concerned about his books, many of which were stored in the chalet in Gstaad. He kept a small Picasso that he had bought at auction in London some years before.

Financially, however, they remained tied together for several more years because of their mutual interests in corporations formed for tax-protection purposes. The details of who got or owed what were argued over by their lawyers, and eventually resolved.

Alexander Cohen, who had produced Richard's New York *Hamlet*, had asked Richard and Elizabeth to be hosts and presenters at the annual Tony Awards. Now he had to cancel not only Elizabeth's appearance but also a forty-fourth-birthday party he had planned for her in Greenwich Village later in the week. Richard, on emerging from the Plymouth Theater after his Monday-evening preview performance, told waiting reporters that the rumors of the new split were true, then went on to meet Susan Hunt and some friends at the Mont St. Michel restaurant. It was, in effect, a celebration. In the words of Valerie Douglas, his friend and aide in California, Richard's Elizabethan period was over.

21

Susan Hunt (formerly Miller) was tall, willowy, and pretty. Her father was a barrister and she had been educated in a convent. "She suggests visions of nuns and such," Richard said about her. She had been a model, had lived in Marbella, Spain, for a time, and felt easy in international society. She said little to the press, nothing about herself. Friends spoke of her as "nice" and "straight." At five-feet-ten, she was as tall as Richard, but in heels loomed over him. He said, "Without Susan, I think, without any exaggeration whatsoever, I might very easily be dead. When I played *Equus* it was the first time in my life I'd been on the stage without a drink, and I shook and shivered."

Soon enough she was installed in his twentieth-floor suite in the Lombardy. All was peaceful. Susan was in the audience instead of Elizabeth at his first-night performance. Still on his dressing-room mirror was Elizabeth's lipstick scrawl, "You are fantastic, love." He left it there, perhaps as a good-luck charm or a sentimental remembrance.

Before the critics were invited to that performance, Richard had taken over a Saturday matinee performance from Tony Perkins. He trembled as over the public-address system in the theater a voice announced, "At this performance the part of Martin Dysart will not be played by Anthony Perkins." Richard heard a loud groan of disappointment from the audience. The voice continued, "The part of Martin Dysart will be played by Richard Burton." At this, the entire house rose to its feet with a roar.

Out onstage to a standing ovation, Richard "tore off the first speech as though it were Noël Coward. I took eight minutes off the performance."

There was another standing ovation the following Tuesday, and they continued. Clive Barnes, of the New York *Times*, heard him "fluff three or four lines, but he somehow slid them into the tone of an aside, gaining a quick, feinting advantage even from a mistake. The voice of gold is formidable. . . . This is unabashedly a star performance." Barnes ended by saying, "He is the most promising middle-aged English-speaking actor of his time." Walter Kerr, in the same paper, called it "the best work of his career."

Outside the theater now, the crowds gathered. It was like old times. The reporters came, too, and Richard talked to them willingly and, for him, frankly.

"I was fairly sloshed for five years," he confessed to Mel Gussow of the *Times*. "I hit the bottle. I was up there with Jack Barrymore and Robert Newton. The ghosts of them were looking over my shoulder. I remember one movie, *The Klansman*, where I knew I was bad all the time and couldn't help it. It was a nightmare. Then I started to forget what happened the night before—the classic beginnings of alcoholism." He told Gussow he no longer drank except for an occasional glass of a very special Burgundy.

Members of Alcoholics Anonymous shivered when they read that. A month or so later he talked to writer Patricia Bosworth for the same paper and told her about the thorough physical examination he'd taken before doing the play. His main fear, he said, was that his lungs were gone because he smoked so many cigarettes (three packs or more a day). "But three doctors pronounced me physiologically thirty-five years old. I'm fifty, you know, but I don't feel it. I feel thirty-five."

When he appeared as he had promised at the Tony Awards, he was presented with a specially made medallion that said "Welcome Back to Broadway."

He did not stay for very long—the agreed-upon twelve weeks,

and an extension of two more weeks. During that time, he revealed, he was still fearful that he would crack, that he would down the drink "that takes you over the edge of being merely a social, hearty, laughing drinker into a morose and hung-over wretched creature who shakes and creeps and has nightmares, and it's always November, and it's raining." He leaned upon Susan for help. "Never once," he said, "did she hide the booze. There was a bottle of vodka and a bottle of gin right in the dressing room. All I had to do was open one and there it was."

Film offers began coming his way again. He had not been seen on the screen since *The Klansman,* and producers had been understandably cautious about approaching him. His appearance and success in *Equus* led to a firm offer to do the film for a half-million-dollar fee, and a larger offer to sandwich in *Exorcist II: The Heretic,* a sequel to the runaway success. Richard talked confidently about the end of his "slump," and how he felt it a duty to do more stage work, "an obligation to the business which has been very good to me." He was already talking with John Dexter, who had directed his *Equus* performance, to play Lear the following season, first at Britain's National Theater, then on Broadway. Alexander Cohen was eager to produce it. It was Susan, he said, "who has rejuvenated me with her enthusiasm and interest. Now I enjoy things I never did before."

But he could still suffer from his black moods. Marian Seldes, an actress in the play, once accompanied him in a limousine and heard him complain, "I'm bored . . . I'm bored." And if he stayed away from vodka, he could on occasion consume too much wine. He still maintained the fiction that he was not an alcoholic, merely someone on the verge and who had to be careful.

When Richard completed his run he flew with Susan to Haiti for what he thought would be his divorce. But he had neglected to get the necessary consent papers from Elizabeth. While there, they were entertained by President Duvalier, and they toured the island. They saw a house on a thirty-acre piece of property and he bought it as a hideaway for them. A month later, in early July, he returned to Haiti with Elizabeth's agreement, and the divorce went through. Susan, meanwhile, picked up her divorce in Arlington, Virginia, where no residence requirement was necessary. The marriage of Richard and

Susan took place in early August, also in Arlington, because there the blood tests took less than a day. After a five-minute ceremony—at which Richard was entirely sober—they flew back to New York and had dinner with ten invited guests at the Laurent, a good restaurant attached to the Lombardy Hotel.

Elizabeth was in Vienna by that time, working in the film version of *A Little Night Music*. When she heard about the marriage she sent the couple a congratulatory message, but commented, "I suppose when men reach a certain age they're afraid to grow up. It seems the older men get, the younger the new wife—so maybe I was just getting too old for him." If there was anything to the notion of the male menopause, she may not have been far from the truth.

But she was by no means being idle in the area of her own love life. Once she came out of a period of seclusion in California, she rejoined Henry Wynberg, and the two settled into a house she rented in the newly fashionable Truesdale section of Beverly Hills. When then Secretary of State Henry Kissinger came with his wife for a two-week vacation in Palm Springs and stayed with the Kirk Douglases, Elizabeth was invited there to a dinner party. Her escort was Wynberg. The acquaintance with Kissinger was influential in re-shaping her life. Kissinger was as much a celebrity collector as a celebrity himself. He saw to it that she was invited to a Kennedy Center charity gala and to a party afterward given by the Iranian ambassador, Ardeshir Zahedi.

This was in the pre-Khomeini days, and Washington, in addition to being a power center, was also a social center. Hosts and hostesses were competing for the available very important people. Roger Stevens, heading theater and opera programs at Kennedy Center, brought in the New York crowd of luminaries, and George Stevens Jr., son of the famed director, had located his American Film Institute in the Kennedy Center. He attracted to his fund-raising events many from the film field. The mix of political, film, theater, and music personalities was a heady one. Embassies attempted to outdo one another with parties and events. Zahedi was one of those at the center of the activity. He was handsome in his dark way, and spent the Shah's money freely. Dozens of his acquaintances looked forward each Christmas to his gifts, the least of which was a five-pound tin of Iranian caviar, the best and most expensive.

BURTON

Elizabeth found him enchanting, and it took two weeks before she was able to part from him. When she returned to California, it was with an awareness of Washington as a new field to conquer, and soon enough the time came to part from Wynberg. His male ego presumably offended, he ordered her out of her own house after a particularly virulent argument, and added to the insult by using the house, as well as her Rolls-Royce, for several more weeks.

Early in July, an invitation came to Elizabeth for a dinner party at the British embassy which Queen Elizabeth was giving for President Ford and the First Lady. It was unthinkable not to attend so august an affair, but she lacked a suitable companion. One was provided for her. He was John W. Warner, formerly a Secretary of the Navy under Nixon and at this time just finished with his assignment as administrator of the Bicentennial celebrations.

Romance blossomed between them quickly, as it usually did with the impetuous Elizabeth. He was a good-looking forty-nine-year-old bachelor, a conservative with political ambitions, and a lot of money. The latter had come to him through his marriage to and divorce from the daughter of the multimillionaire Paul Mellon. When Elizabeth went off to Vienna for her role in *A Little Night Music*, their affair was well advanced. And when word reached her of Richard's marriage, she immediately telephoned Warner and asked him to join her. He did. They were together from then on, and Elizabeth, through him, became a part of the glossier Washington scene.

While Elizabeth was waltzing around Vienna with Warner, Richard was in Hollywood with his new bride, Susan. His film, *Exorcist II*, was having delays, mostly occasioned by a script that lacked coherence. Richard loftily explained to Roderick Mann, a British journalist working for the Los Angeles *Times*, that he was doing this "horror film" because his daughters had loved the original *Exorcist* and had urged him to do the sequel.

He repeated his story of how Susan had saved him from going into the valley of death, described his chilling experience after his collapse in Oroville, and explained that he drank only occasionally now. Mann was surprised to see him down two vodka collinses before dinner and help himself to the very good red wine served with dinner. (From then on, any reporter who met him was made queasy if Richard drank anything with alcohol in it; they never knew which one of them might send him over the brink again.)

"Those who don't drink," Richard mused, staring into his wine-glass, "will never know the pleasure of the right wine in the right place at the right time." On another occasion, he would tell writer Jimmy Breslin that only the most interesting people drank—a saying with a certain amount of truth, but lacking a corollary that it was often the drinking that made them interesting up to a point.

Richard gave Mann a tip on drinking. His father, he said, "would come home and swallow a scoop of Vaseline before going to sleep. It works, too. In fact, when you know you're going to have to drink, try swallowing some first." After finishing dinner and the wine, he ordered another drink.

John Boorman, the director of *Exorcist II*, had made the successful *Deliverance* and had a good track record, but whatever his intentions were in this tale of a priest (Burton) attempting to guard Linda Blair from unfathomable forces of evil, they were never made manifest. Burton was among those puzzled. "I'm not sure what this is about," he said during the twenty-three weeks of filming. Susan could see disaster looming long before the critics got their claws into it. Richard did his best to justify the money he was getting, but she told him, "You must never do anything like this again, even to get a million dollars." But that, of course, had been the *raison d'être,* even though he kept claiming he had had to be persuaded to appear in it, this after the film had been called perhaps the worst large-budget film ever made. Even the director, Boorman, had to admit that "basically I made the wrong movie" and that theater managers, when they showed it, "were afraid of getting lynched."

"They must have shot ten different endings," Richard told Janet Maslin of the New York *Times.* "I'd become so beaten down by California sunshine and smog that I said, 'I'll do any ending.'" The one eventually used had him in a house on a bed with Linda Blair. "Suddenly the roof falls in," he said, "and the bed collapses and we slide into an abyss and I can't tell you what it was like."

With hardly a day between, after finishing *Exorcist II,* he hurried to Toronto, where Sidney Lumet was shooting *Equus* around him in the meantime. "His hair had been dyed a hideous shoe-polish black," Lumet recalled, "that turned orange when back-lit. Every suggested remedy seemed to risk even worse results. Finally Richard said hesitantly, "Maybe if I'm good enough, no one will notice the hair."

On familiar ground, and in the hands of a capable director, Richard gave one of his best performances, and by the time the film was finished he was already talking somewhat wistfully about his chances for an Academy Award. His next stop was London, where he narrated a radio history of the English royal succession, and played a lawyer with a curious gift in a science-fiction thriller, *The Medusa Touch*. The lawyer's mental powers were so advanced that he could make buildings topple, planes crash, and Westminster Abbey crumble. For four weeks of work he collected a half-million dollars. Susan was with him, and in what was becoming a familiar theme, he told again and again how she had saved him from near-death and how dependent he was on her.

He told David Lewin how lucky he was, because he had "deliberately, brutally sometimes, destroyed my own career with my own hands, and then been given the chance to come back. And on each occasion I have been saved by a woman. Although I like to be thought of as machismo, a tough, rugby-playing Welsh miner's son, there is a fundamental weakness in me. It has taken three fragile, beautiful, but strong-minded women to save me."

He was referring to Sybil, Elizabeth, and Susan.

"What Elizabeth could not save me from was the drink," he went on. "She had her own problems, so why should she look after me as well? She did look after me as best she could, but I was an invalid and needed total attention."

He was in a period of self-assessment, buoyed by the rejuvenating effect of the constant presence of a beautiful wife twenty-three years his junior.

"I don't think he knew," Lewin said afterward, "that Elizabeth needed him as much as he needed her. Married or not, it was always a useful game for her to play—that flamboyant, seemingly never-ending relationship—that kept her going, and the public intrigued, well into her middle age. A friend and I had this theory that Elizabeth alternated between strong and weak men and that Richard had been a strong one. Then, thinking it through, we realized we'd got it wrong—that Burton was the weak man."

BURTON

But now the irony was that with Richard's career seemingly on an upward trend, and Elizabeth's fading, she was the one who caught public attention as much as or more than ever. After an engagement to John Warner announced in October 1976, the marriage took place in December on a hilltop of Warner's thousand-acre Virginia farm. There had been a delay because, true to form, she had fallen off a horse and had to spend some time in a hospital.

From acting she turned her attention to politics—not all that radical a switch, in view of the television coverage she received wherever she went. Warner had his eye on a U.S. Senate seat, and the more the two appeared in public at various events and galas—of which Washington and the environs had more than enough to spare—the more her limelight reflected on him. She, at heart a liberal Democrat, switched her allegiance to the Republican party, and it was thought not beyond the bounds of possibility that Elizabeth might someday be the first lady of the land.

However, in the battle of the Virginia Republican primary in 1978, her charisma was not enough to carry Warner to victory. It took providence, in the form of a plane crash, to eliminate the victor and, subsequently, to give the nomination to Warner.

While Elizabeth was adjusting herself to the political life in Washington, Richard and Susan were in Africa for the location filming of *The Wild Geese*. They had been in New York briefly for Richard to discuss with producer Alexander Cohen and director Elia Kazan the plans for his doing *King Lear* on the New York stage the following summer (1978). He had with him a copy of *Lear*, and was taking the project seriously enough to work on the lines. He also brought with him the complete works of Dickens because, he said, "I asked myself what would be the most unlikely thing to read in the bush, so I thought I'd reread Dickens."

The company was based in Tshipise, a spa resort in the far north of South Africa. The prevailing architecture was a grouping of round African-style huts, in which most of the personnel stayed. Richard and Susan, however, stayed in a villa and had an air-conditioned trailer on set in which they could contend with the hundred-degree heat.

Even so, the filming was more than ordinarily strenuous, especially for a man about whom there had been some doubt as to whether he could handle the physical demands of the role. As Colonel Faulkner, he was the leader of a band of mercenaries sent to central Africa to rescue a deposed black president before he was murdered. With Burton in the enterprise were Richard Harris and Roger Moore. Before the film ended, hundreds of corpses were strewn around the veldt, and in one scene Burton had to jump into a moving plane. He refused to allow a double to do it. In the film, although slightly puffy around the eyes, he looked fit and acted his command role with authority. A straightforward action film, with some observations about racial conflict in Africa, it was the only film of Richard's in many years to do well at the box office.

Richard's next film was *Absolution*, from a screenplay by Anthony Shaffer, but there were problems in raising the financing. In the interim, Richard took Susan to Puerto Vallarta, where he bought a house farther up the mountain from where he had lived with Elizabeth. The town had grown into a full-fledged resort, and there were now direct flights there from Paris. In grateful recognition of Richard and Elizabeth, signs had been erected saying "Richard Point" and "Elizabeth Point." Another sign said: "The most beautiful place in the world, where one of the most famous couples found love." Susan was not pleased, and was already indicating weariness with questions that related to Richard's past with his former wife.

In March they were in Beverly Hills, living in a rented house, conferring with Kazan on the *Lear* he was to do, and waiting for the Academy Awards presentations. He had received his seventh nomination, although he was not too hopeful about winning, because, as he said, *Equus* had done only marginally at the box-office. Now the most nominated actor in film history, he lost out once more.

Although due in England for the filming of *Absolution*, he did not seem eager to get there, and instead concentrated with Susan on furnishing the new home in Puerto Vallarta. Those associated with him found him hard to contact. John Springer said, "After the marriage to Susan, I found it harder and harder to reach him. It was impossible to get him on the phone. Half the time I didn't know where he was. As his representative it was often urgent that I get in touch with him, and suddenly I couldn't. Those who worked with him—Robert Lantz, his agent; Aaron Frosch, his accountant—were having the same difficulty."

Lantz at last succeeded in getting him to England to fulfill his obligation on *Absolution*. Meanwhile, Richard, although continuing to talk about the importance to him of doing *Lear*—dear Susan had not yet seen him take on a Shakespearean role—was being increasingly difficult. Now he made it a condition that he perform the role only six times a week, the traditional number of performances being eight. Alexander Cohen balked at this. The production, he said, would cost $700,000 to mount, and it would be almost impossible to recoup that amount in the stipulated six-month run, with only six performances a week. The production was canceled.

With the free time available, Richard made another film, *Sergeant Steiner*, a World War II drama, with Robert Mitchum and Rod Steiger as his costars. "It was as though Richard was following the line of least resistance," Springer said. "To what degree Susan was influencing him is hard to know, but it did look as though she was weaning him away from the people with whom he had been associated. The one she became closest to was Valerie Douglas, who up to then had been a kind of gofer for Richard, and who she now trusted more and more with the details of his career. Richard blandly chose not to know what was happening."

In the spring of 1979, Richard's daughter Kate paid him a visit in Puerto Vallarta. She had spent a good many of her summer vacations with him, and, a girl of sunny disposition, had adjusted to his change of partners. Sybil had put nothing in the way of her relationship with her father. He was proud of her and of the education she was receiving. A bright girl who had her father's upper face, including similar eyes, and her mother's lower features, she had attended the United Nations School in New York and then gone on to Brown University, where she studied Russian with an eye to going into diplomacy or journalism, either one of which would please her father. But she also did some acting at Brown, and in her last year, instead of going on to postgraduate work, as she had planned, she suddenly decided she wanted to be an actress.

Richard had paid for her education and approved of her choice of school. She told him that Sybil was not against her taking acting training, and now she wanted his permission, too.

"Anything, anything but that!" Richard exclaimed. She was the first person, he pointed out, among his entire Welsh clan to go through college—he having spent only six months at Oxford. "Here you've gone to an Ivy League school, and what are you going to be? An actress!"

Richard still saw himself as deflected, more or less by accident, from a writing career. He read voraciously—"A book a day through-out his life," said Kate—and he had been hoping that Kate would inherit the same bent. He agreed, however, that if she were accepted for admission by a first-rate drama school, he would withdraw his objections. Kate applied to three, among them RADA (Royal Acad-emy of Dramatic Arts) and the Yale Drama School. She was accepted by all three. He urged her to go to RADA in London, but she told him she spoke American, not British, and she went to Yale for the three-year course instead.

The early summer of 1979 found Richard with Susan in Ireland making a low-budget costume picture, *Tristan and Isolde*. Susan had taken to advising him on his choice of films, and this one she came across, after he had neglected to read the script. Richard's role was King Mark of Cornwall. He had lines to say such as "The lady is not pleased with Cornwall. Nor, I think, with me." Isolde was being played by Kate Mulgrew, who had come out of a soap opera, *Ryan's Hope*, and then a few episodes of *Mrs. Columbo*. The producer, and writer of the screenplay, had also won her spurs with *Ryan's Hope*. The project was originally thought of as a TV movie, and ABC put up some of its financing as a feature. Richard would collect from the profits, if there were any.

"The movies he was doing at this point," Springer said, "were unreleasable, certainly in the United States. Unlike other important stars, who chose their projects with great care and often participated in their development, Richard simply went from one to another, as they came along."

"At that point in his life," Kate said, "my father needed to work. It was what kept him going, kept him on an even keel. He felt best when working."

BURTON

Later in the summer he was in Céligny. Two producers, Mike Merrick and Don Gregory, were interested in reviving *Camelot*, twenty years after its original production. They decided to take a chance on interesting Richard in his original role. Merrick asked Alan Jay Lerner to contact Richard and come with him for a meeting, which took place at lunch on the terrace of a Geneva hotel. Richard had driven up in a small red sports car.

"We sat and talked," Merrick recalled, "and Richard was humorous and charming. He asked some questions about changes that might be made because he was much older now, and about who might be in it with him, and who would direct the show. He talked about doing *King Lear* and how he felt the need to get his stage muscles revitalized. Then, at the end of our lunch, I said, 'I'm sure we would have a production if we had Richard Burton.' Upon which he said, 'I assure you, you have.' And that was it. We had his agreement. He got into his little red car and drove off."

His commitment to *Camelot* would be for a year, most of it on the road. The reason he had agreed to do it, he said, before the details were ironed out, was Susan's urging. She had happened to play the soundtrack from the original. "Why don't you do it again?" she said.

"I've *done* my musical," Richard told her.

Then, by his account, Alan Jay Lerner appeared out of the blue. "He can be very persuasive. I'm a very weak man, you see, and I simply can't say no."

Susan also pointed out to him how well Yul Brynner was doing with his long-running revival of *The King and I*. Ticket prices for musicals were skyrocketing, and on tour they played in large houses. There was not much self-sacrifice involved for Richard. He would be guaranteed fifty thousand dollars a week, which came to two and a half million for the year's run.

By this time, most of his former associates were gone. Weeded out were Ron Berkeley, his perennial makeup man, his agent, Robert Lantz, John Springer, Aaron Frosch, and even Brook Williams for a time. When Mike Merrick worked out the financial arrangements for Richard's services, he dealt only with Valerie Douglas and a contract lawyer. The only member of Richard's entourage who remained with him was Bob Wilson, the courtly gentleman who still acted as majordomo of his dressing room. "And then," said John Springer, "even he went."

"Everything," Merrick said, "every detail, had to be cleared through Valerie Douglas. She had become his agent as well as his personal manager. She was entirely devoted to him and protective of him. I believe the reason he stayed with her all those years, and put more and more trust in her, was that he had been aware that often, from time to time, the people around him were users and takers. Valerie was not one of those. She was direct and forthright, and she put everything right out on the table. Susan and she became very good friends. Susan was entirely devoted to Richard at that time, and she knew Valerie was too."

Mike added, "I can only provide a contrary image to the more prevalent one of the carouser and romancer and the drunkard. It's interesting how he chose and attracted to him such very nice women— I can't vouch for Elizabeth, because I never knew her—but there is no nicer, kinder human being than Sybil, and as far as their devotion to Richard went, Susan and Valerie were true blue. But it also has to be said that it had much to do with Richard's genuine niceness and human qualities."

John Springer put it another way: "Richard simply didn't want to deal with details, with the complexities of his career. So Susan and Valerie did it for him. I became annoyed with my being unable to find him, to not even know what city he was in. So finally I wrote a letter and gave it to Bob Wilson to personally deliver to him. In it I said I felt it was only fair to stop billing him my fee for services, and would be going on a hiatus as his representative until we could reestablish communication.

"A few weeks later came a wholesale clean-out of just about every-one who had ever had any connection with Richard or Elizabeth."

What angered Springer were indications that Susan felt that he was a bad influence on Richard, along with others of his associates. It was Marlene Dietrich who sent him a clipping from a German news-paper which said in effect that it was a priority of Susan's to get the "bad influences" out of Richard's life. Robert Lantz, his agent, was mentioned along with Springer, and both were identified as heavy drinkers. (This was not true of either.)

Springer said, "I'd imagine the only way in which this whole thing could be accounted for was that Susan didn't want those who had been involved with Elizabeth to now be involved with Richard. The exception was Valerie Douglas, who, until then, had been a sort of flunky—in the sense that if Richard and Elizabeth were going to the Coast, I'd call Valerie and ask her to make the arrangements, reservations, a car and driver to meet them, and that sort of thing. Richard was always appreciative of Valerie, and warm and friendly with her, but Elizabeth saw her more as someone who simply provided services for them and treated her as such. Whether this was reflected in Valerie's attitude toward her, there's no way to know. She and Susan became very close."

Susan may have appreciated Douglas's sarcastic remark about Richard's "Elizabethan era" having ended.

In any case, Springer said, "From then on, Valerie and Susan made all of Richard's decisions." A young publicity woman, Nancy Seltzer, was brought in to handle his press, and for a time there was a notable decrease in gossipy coverage of him, and Susan, although asked, refused all interviews.

Toward the end of 1979, Richard and Susan were in Toronto, where he was filming *Circle of Two,* the story of a sixty-year-old artist who meets a sixteen-year-old girl (Tatum O'Neal), develops a relationship with her, and finds new energy and inspiration. It was one more of the films that, if it landed anywhere, it would be on television.

"Susan has come in like a new broom," Richard told an interviewer. "I am strongly influenced by my wife." She was the one responsible for keeping him from drinking, for the healthful diet he was on, for tranforming the house in Céligny and doing interesting things with the interior of the new house in Puerto Vallarta. They would be going to Nigeria next for another film.

That film, and another to be made in India, failed to materialize, and instead the couple had a holiday in Kenya, where Susan had spent some of her childhood. Her father, a brigadier general in the British Army then, had been stationed there. Richard liked to say that Susan was upper-class British.

In spite of Susan's aversion to publicity, she fell prey to it. For the opening of the new *Camelot* in the O'Keefe Theater Center in To-

BURTON

ronto, the first week of June 1980, a handsome souvenir program had been printed. In a review of Richard's career, the booklet contained a picture of Elizabeth Taylor. This sent Susan into a fury.

"Susan Burton is insane concerning the subject of Elizabeth Taylor," the publicity manager of the theater told a reporter. "She said the photograph was an insult to her." Susan demanded that every one of the pictures in the ninety thousand copies of the program be removed. The publicity manager thought this would cause adverse publicity. She quoted Susan, "I don't give a shit. I want it out." Four employees of the theater stayed up all night cutting out pictures in time for the opening performance the following evening, and kept at it until the offending countenance was removed from all ninety thousand copies.

Susan received not only some attention from the press but also mixed reviews from people associated with the company. Jim Awe, who managed the tour for a time, said, "She's living with Taylor's ghost and trying to exorcise it. She pulls the strings. She's a tough cookie in a velvet glove."

Tina Vanderheyden of the O'Keefe Center staff admired her taste in clothes but remarked on her lavish spending. "Always designer originals," she said. Noted, too, was the fact that when the Burtons arrived at their hotel in Toronto, they had twenty-six suitcases with them. "Most of them Susan's," said Vanderheyden. It was Richard who saw to it that Susan was provided with a baby-grand piano wherever they traveled during the tour, and insisted on having it in his contract for the show. Susan played the piano well, and it was a favorite way for her to while away her free hours. Richard's was to read, as much as ten hours a day.

It was Susan who found for Richard the trunk that opened into a portable bookcase. It held one hundred books, and it went with Richard in his travels from then on. "Susan adored him," Mike Merrick said. She appointed herself his makeup person, after getting some tips on the craft from Ron Berkeley. Naturally, this too went into one reporter's description of her as "the iron maiden" who ran every aspect of Richard's life.

With Susan, Richard led a life that was almost the reverse of his flamboyant fifteen-year fling with Elizabeth. He eschewed bars and cocktail lounges as though they were places of evil—attractive to

him, yet deadly. While rehearsing *Camelot* in New York, prior to
the tour, he limited himself to a glass of wine a day. At the end of
a rehearsal day, he and Susan, with their dog, Lupe—they had found
it on a street in Puerto Vallarta and adopted it—would enter their
limousine and be taken to their suite at the Lombardy. Almost all
their evenings were spent quietly alone. He would read. Up early
in the morning, he would write in his diary, often recording, John
Springer remembers, the events of the day before, or going back
into his past experiences.

One close friend of Richard's, a director, believes that he was
taking Antabuse about this time. Antabuse is seldom recommended
as a treatment for alcoholism, and, when used, usually is taken by
a person who wants to stop alcohol intake entirely but can't bring
together all the psychological energies required. Colin Campbell,
who heads a Long Island council for alcoholics, states, "The medi-
cation is taken once each day and means that the person doesn't have
to rely on his willpower. If he drinks, he'll get sick. As an aid, it's
only for short periods of time."

The director who told me that Burton was taking Antabuse was
present at a dinner party given by Leonard Bernstein. Richard and
Susan were there. "It was an evening of crisis," he said. "Richard
did some drinking on Antabuse and got horribly ill. It was quite
awful and it made the evening very difficult. It was the one and only
time I met Susan, and my only impression of her was of a very sweet
girl in a dreadful situation, and looking white and strained."

Perhaps because of that incident, Richard became more and more
reclusive. He was happy to be back on the stage, in a somewhat
revised version of his old triumph. Alan Jay Lerner had rewritten
Camelot in line with the older King Arthur now played by Richard.
"He didn't have the energy of the first time," Lerner said, "and soon
enough we realized he was a sick man. Yet when he walked out on
the stage, someone described him as like a cold wind that slapped
you across the face. You knew that something enormous had arrived
on the stage. Richard was the kind of star for whom age doesn't
matter. The play had to be redirected because he couldn't move his
right arm, and though often in pain, he had a smile—like the sun
coming out over rain."

"For the rest of the cast," said Merrick, "he was a true father figure, generous and kind with his fellow actors, always wanting to see before the performance if everyone was all right."

From Toronto, *Camelot* moved on to an eight-week engagement at Lincoln Center's New York State Theater, where it was a sellout well before its arrival. This time around, *Camelot* received the critical raves it had not gotten before, and largely because of Richard. Frank Rich wrote in the New York *Times* that "Burton doesn't merely command the stage; he seems to own it by divine right."

Not long after the opening in New York, Richard made news in another way. Early in a performance, he began hesitating and fluffing lines. A murmur—"He's drunk"—ran through the audience. The stage manager saw that, drunk or not, Richard was ill and dropped the curtain. The lobby filled with hundreds of persons demanding their money back.

"He had been taking various medications," Lerner said, "and they gave him no tolerance for alcohol at all. Those of us with the show knew what had happened. He had had lunch that day with Richard Harris, and had had a couple of drinks, and it had just knocked him out. It was agreed between us that when asked—as we were—everyone would say he had a cold. Everyone knew—the stagehands, the orchestra members—and yet when the press came around, no one told the true story. They all had that high regard and protective feeling for him."

(One of the characteristics of Antabuse, or disulfiram, therapy is that the effects may persist for as much as a week after the last dose is taken. Richard, at lunch with Harris, may have thought he was safe from its effects.)

Not long after the incident, Richard made four successive appearances on Dick Cavett's talk show on the Public television network. The furrows on his face, the sunken cheeks, gave the lie to reports that he had had a facelift. Cavett, in introducing him, remarked that "On the rare occasion when he misses a performance, it is headline news around the world."

Richard revealed to an avid audience the charm and humor, the remarkable tale-telling ability, that those who knew him well had always known. He did delightful bits of business, taking off his shoes and revealing red argyle socks—this to illustrate for Cavett his habit of always wearing at least one article of red clothing. He mentioned that he was also wearing red underpants. He said it was probably a good idea to take his shoes off because when he watched talk shows he was always more conscious of the subject's shoes than the face.

In his final segment he grew more serious. The night he missed the performance, he said, he felt he was dying. What happened before the curtain came down was a blur to him. "I was taken home and put to bed by Susan, and then I woke about three in the morning. I said: 'Now tell me what happened,' because it was the ultimate in actors' nightmares.

"Alcoholism is a dreadful disease," he said. "My sympathy for American alcoholics is profound. They come up to me as being a representative of this dreadful disease and they tell me their stories. I can't say that I've beaten it. Jimmy Breslin, a dear friend of mine, wrote to me a few years ago when I was in trouble with drink. He said, 'Don't forget, you're always fighting. The other fellow is booze. You're evading, always evading, but one of these days, unless you're careful, he's going to nail you.' When you get through the day, you say: I've beaten the boxer. So, for the rest of your life you're stuck with that shadowy figure. There is every conceivable excuse to take a drink. I get a bad notice, I think I'll take a drink. A good notice, I'll take a drink."

He told of his feelings going onstage the following night. "I thought: How influenced are people by the press? I had been told the press exulted in the fact that I'd failed on Thursday night. When I made my entrance, I wasn't sure what was going to happen. I stepped out, and there was the most tremendous ovation. The stage manager told me it went on for something like three and a half minutes. I just stood there and could feel the audience supporting me, and the affection and the warmth. I gave possibly the best performance I've ever given. The entire evening flew on wings. It was one of the most extraordinary experiences I'd ever had in the theater."

Mike Merrick said that after the missed performance, "Richard called me the next day and said it would never happen again, and it didn't."

From New York the *Camelot* tour moved on to Chicago, to Dallas, Miami Beach, New Orleans, San Francisco, and Los Angeles. While in Miami, Richard had a reunion with Philip Burton, who had retired and was living in Key West. He stayed with Richard and Susan for a week, and was able to celebrate Richard's fifty-fifth birthday with him.

By the time the show reached San Francisco in February 1981, Richard was in severe pain from the condition that had been first diagnosed as bursitis of the shoulder and then rediagnosed as an impinged nerve in the cervical area. The pain was now so extreme that he had to hold a sword in his left hand rather than his right.

In Los Angeles, the advance sale was enormous. Mike Merrick remembered that a few days after the opening there, in March, "Susan Burton asked me if I had a personal physician. Richard was perspiring and nauseated. When I asked him if he was well enough to go on, he said, 'Of course.' How he got through that performance is beyond me. He kept going back to his dressing room between scenes and throwing up."

A few days later, Richard was in St. John's Hospital in Santa Monica, to be treated for what was said to be a viral condition, and to be tested for his neck condition. An operation known as a cervical laminectomy was advised. It was decided that *Camelot* would continue its run with a replacement, who turned out to be Richard Harris.

In April Richard had the operation at St. John's. A New York surgeon who specializes in neck and spine operations stated that he doubted such an operation would have been performed in New York City. In Los Angeles, he thought, less conservative surgeons could be found. Complications often occurred from the operation, he said, and in Richard's case they apparently did—a weakening of the neck muscles that would cause him continual pain.

During this period, the British actor John Hurt, of *Elephant Man* fame, encountered Richard. "For some reason," he said, "he wanted to meet me, I think on the chance that we might someday work together. Richard always liked to say that he saw very few films, including his own, but he had seen some of my work. A mutual friend brought us together for dinner, with his wife, Susan, there, and I remember thinking immediately that this was not a marriage made in heaven. He was moody, and quite hard on her."

Following the operation, in need of a long rest, Richard went with Susan to Céligny. In August, although it was not revealed at the time, he and Susan separated. A newspaper in Rome came out with a story purporting that Susan had found a new boyfriend and was demanding forty thousand dollars a month in alimony and the house in Puerto Vallarta.

In Hollywood, Valerie Douglas was asked about the rumor. "Preposterous!" she exclaimed.

But whatever the terms of the separation agreed on—and Susan did occupy the house in Puerto Vallarta from then on—the marriage was, in effect, over.

22

The announcement of Richard's separation from Susan was not made until February 1982, by which time he was in Europe portraying Wagner in a lengthy television series about the composer. Those who had worked with Richard in *Camelot,* when Susan was a constant presence, were surprised, even shocked to hear the news. Valerie Douglas and her publicity helpmate, Nancy Seltzer, had obviously been adept at throwing up a wall of silence around their famous client.

In October 1981 he had been in St. John's Hospital again for a new operation, and it had not been remarked on that he was without Susan. This operation was for a perforated ulcer, and the pain of that condition combined with the semiparalysis from his neck operation could hardly have made him pleasant to live with. Susan's mother, when asked about the breakup, maintained that it was his drinking that was the principal strain on the marriage.

In Puerto Vallarta rumors surfaced that Richard had been violent toward his wife, an indication in itself that he had begun to drink again. He had not worked since leaving *Camelot* in March, and he was hardly out of the hospital after his stomach operation when he accepted the arduous *Wagner* role, which would mean seven months spent in several European locations. To help him get through it, the head of physical therapy at St. John's Hospital took a sabbatical to travel with him. Following a full day of work on the film, Richard would undergo another hour of therapy each day.

It was not until the week after the announcement in February that Richard openly discussed the breakup. He told a reporter in London, "I'm a very difficult and dangerous man to live with, you know. It appears I instigated it, and she followed it through, and it was terrible. We were arguing and I said something like 'Bugger off,' and she did. You can put the blame on me." He added that she had become unhappy at not having a baby. "But I am too old. What would be the point of a fourteen-year-old child having a seventy-year-old father?" From Susan, however, came nary and never a word.

Elizabeth Taylor's marriage to John Warner had ended by that time too. *Her* announcement was made two months prior to Richard's. She told the writer Marie Brenner about that "terrible boredom I had in Virginia after John and I finished campaigning [for the U.S. Senate]. I was home all the time. I just sort of lay back at that point in my life and didn't do a thing. Then I began to watch the mindless boob tube. And I ate. I ate out of nerves, nerves, nerves, and got so fat. And then it became everybody's business."

She was a ripe target for Joan Rivers, who substituted frequently for Johnny Carson on the *Tonight Show*. Month after month Rivers made her the butt of "fat" jokes, claiming once that Elizabeth, who had admitted to a liking for junk food, had gotten stuck in the golden arch of a McDonald's. Warner's Senate press office had taken to handling her public relations, and they could hardly have done a worse job. Pictures of Elizabeth looking almost obscenely bloated appeared in the scandal-prone periodicals. Increasingly bored by the political scene, she went to Florida and worked and dieted off forty pounds. A meeting in Washington with a producer, Zev Bufman, led to a stage production of *The Little Foxes*, in which she took the role of the calculating Regina Giddens. To almost everyone's astonishment, she was acclaimed by the critics, and the show was a smash hit.

In February 1982 she and Bufman took the production to London's West End. Before the opening, Bufman arranged a lavish party to celebrate Elizabeth's fiftieth birthday on the night of the twenty-seventh.

BURTON

Richard, at the time, was filming in Pisa, one of the stops in a trek that duplicated Wagner's travels and abodes, others being Budapest, Venice, Munich, and Bayreuth. The cast was an impressive one, with Olivier, Gielgud, and Ralph Richardson in cameo roles, and Vanessa Redgrave and Marthe Keller in major ones. Without a helpful woman to lean on, Richard was helping himself to liberal gulps of wine, a fact noticed by reporters who scouted the production. His cigarette habit had grown worse—as many as four packs a day—and one reporter noticed that his hands shook as he lit up.

It was his eyes that lit up when he saw the beauteous Marthe Keller, but his pursuit of her amounted to no more than a friendly flirtation. A pretty young reporter revealed a brief fling she had with him. "He asked me," she said, "if I'd stay with him forever to protect him from other women. He explained that forever meant five years, because that was how long he gave himself to live."

A secretary with the production said that, indeed, there were those attached to the lengthy production who viewed him as a catch, and, as it happened, one caught him, or he caught her. But that was after he learned of the birthday party in London for Elizabeth. He was already scheduled to fly there on February 28, a Sunday, to appear as narrator at a benefit performance of *Under Milk Wood*. On Saturday morning he succeeded in reaching Elizabeth, who was staying in the Chelsea apartment of Norma Heyman, the wife of John Heyman. Could he attend her party? he asked her. The answer was yes. Could he be her escort? The answer, too, was yes. He chartered a jet and arrived in London just an hour before the party. The slimmed-down but still full-figured Elizabeth appeared wearing a glittering silver-and-lavender harem outfit, and off they went to Mayfair in his Daimler—their first reunion in five years.

And whatever wagon he was on, he went off, too. He and Elizabeth danced much of the night away, and when he took her home, the grown girls, Liza and Maria, asked him to come inside. He had not seen Maria for several years. The former cripple, an ugly duckling as a child, had grown into a tall beauty who modeled for fashion magazines. Richard learned that she had married only ten days before, and gave her his belated blessings.

"Where's my present?" Elizabeth had asked him. He had not had time to get one, but sent word to the theater that he wanted a drawing of Dylan Thomas that was being auctioned with other memorabilia of the author. Elizabeth was rehearsing on Sunday and was not in the audience at the Duke of York's Theater when Richard took the stage for his narration. But during a pause, Elizabeth, in her rehearsal clothes of blue jeans and a sweater, walked onto the stage. She curtsied to the audience, then said in Welsh, "I love you."

"Say it again, my petal," Richard replied. "Say it louder." There they were again, this long-running romantic twosome, back on the front pages. The London press speculated for days about whether they would marry again. But this was a sentimental reunion, and both now said they were resolved to remain free. After the performance, though, Richard took Elizabeth to a private dinner with the cast, and presented her with the Dylan Thomas drawing he had won at auction. But the occasion had its penalty for him. He switched to double vodkas from wine, and was ashen-faced and wobbly when he returned to Italy.

He was feeling stronger when, on a cold day on location, he asked the continuity girl, "Sally, what's my line?"

As he told it later, "I saw this little face in a balaclava helmet. The next day I noticed that she wore her hair differently. 'That looks very nice,' I told her, and the next day she wore it the same way. I was flattered. I thought: Perhaps she likes me."

Sally Hay was an attractive woman of thirty-four who had worked in various production capacities at the BBC since she was eighteen. Possessed of no more than a high-school education, daughter of the automotive correspondent of the Birmingham *Post,* Sally was bright and amusing, and known for her ability to achieve a sense of style on a tight budget. Never married, career-oriented, she had been seen around London on the arm of a well-known political journalist, as well as with other men friends.

Richard claimed that with Sally he was quite shy, and not the tempestuous seducer and lover of legend. "During the making of *Wagner,*" he said, "I gave a series of dinner parties, and I was always saying to people, 'Do you think Sally Hay will be able to come?' A friend of mine said, 'That's a super girl. Be careful with her.' "

Said Sally: "At first I was rather puzzled. I began to think I was imagining things. I thought: I must pull myself together. I was aware of someone watching me all the time, and I thought: It can't be

Richard Burton. But it was. Initially I was very apprehensive. I'd never thought I'd get married; nobody had ever asked me."

Richard proposed a living-together relationship first. "I don't want to make another mistake," he told her. "If after a year we're still happy, we'll get married."

At the end of June he and Sally went to London to see Elizabeth in *The Little Foxes* and take in the finals at Wimbledon. He took Elizabeth to dinner afterward at the White Elephant, a private restaurant frequented by theater people, and informed her of his serious intentions toward Sally. Elizabeth's reaction was reported to be chilly.

"I was very, very nervous indeed about meeting the beautiful Elizabeth Taylor," Sally said, "but I think she realized that. After about an hour, she took hold of my arm and said: 'It's okay.' " Unlike Susan, she did not try to exclude Elizabeth—whom she would refer to privately as E.T.—from their social life. A fine cook, Sally prepared excellent, beautifully served dinners for Richard's important friends, and Elizabeth was there frequently.

Meanwhile, London's gossipmongers managed to dig up Sally's father, now an alcoholic who had not worked in five years, was separated from his wife, and reduced to living in flophouses. No one could have been more sympathetic to his condition than Richard, who arranged treatment for him and a place to live.

In August there were rumors that Richard was seeking treatment for himself, for he was once more at St. John's Hospital. When he emerged after a week he stoutly denied the rumors, and Roderick Mann found him looking well. He had been in the hospital for more tests and therapy on his painful neck condition and deterioration of his spine. He was about to head for New York, where Kate, who had finished her postgraduate work at the Yale Drama School, was appearing in George C. Scott's Broadway revival of Noël Coward's *Present Laughter*.

Richard told Mann that Elizabeth had already seen her in the play and had gone to her dressing room afterward. "Kate, you're fabulous!" Elizabeth exclaimed. "I'm very proud of you. Now, where's the john?"

" 'Dad,' " Richard said Kate told him over the telephone, " 'she's crazy.' True, I told her, but enchanting."

Kate had met little difficulty in making her move into professional

BURTON

theater. At Yale she had appeared in two of the drama school's productions; the day before graduating, she had auditioned for Scott and gotten the part of Daphne Dillington, the madcap debutante. When Richard saw her in the play he was proud of her, but said little more than "You looked very pretty."

In a month he was back in Los Angeles again for talks with Elizabeth Taylor and Zev Bufman on reviving Noël Coward's *Private Lives.* In 1965 Coward had mentioned to Elizabeth that she and Richard would fit very nicely the parts of the two former marriage partners who are unable to live with or without each other. Richard now agreed to play Elyot to Elizabeth's Amanda, even though she would receive top billing. Because it would be her production, with Bufman, he was working for her in a sense. Salaries would be equal— an all-but-unheard-of seventy thousand dollars per week.

The two were together for a press announcement made at the Beverly Hills Hotel on September 23, 1982. The play, they said, would be put on the following spring. Headlines called it "The Liz and Dick Show."

Life was certainly interesting, Sally bubbled to a friend in a letter that somehow got into a London paper. There was a trip to Haiti, where she and Richard spent two weeks while he procured a divorce from Susan. With his two "sun" houses now occupied by former wives, they decided that Haiti would do as well, in a house on thirty acres overlooking the sea.

They next flew to London, where the BBC interviewed Richard for a program called *Portrait of a Superstar.* He was candid, openly admitting "I am an alcoholic." He still fell off the wagon occasionally, he said, and consumed "one or two bottles of vodka a day." On one of those two-bottle occasions it was said that Sally would not allow him back into their hotel suite.

Even so, Sally was enjoying her new status as companion and bride-to-be of the aging superstar. In another of her letters to her "friend," she wrote of the big packing job involved for an American stay of ten months on *Private Lives.* She supposed, though, that everything could be bought new on arrival.

In New York, Jimmy Breslin paid them a visit at their New York abode, the Lombardy Hotel. Over breakfast he talked with Richard about the drinking problem. "I suppose it has done terrific damage to me," Richard admitted to him, "but I wouldn't have missed any of it for the world. I have to think hard to name an interesting man who didn't drink."

Breslin accompanied him to the theater in which he was rehearsing *Private Lives*. In the car, Richard mused, "They drink a small glass of cold white wine these days. That's all you hear them order. A small cold glass of white wine. When did that start? I was seated in a restaurant the other night and I heard a man say, 'I'll have a vodka martini straight up.' I turned to the man and said to him, 'Well done, you're having a proper drink.' "

John Gielgud had had forebodings about Richard's stage venture with Elizabeth. "You aren't really going to do *Private Lives*, are you?" Richard had answered, "I expect Elizabeth will make me."

In Boston, where the play opened in April, the first night brought five curtain calls for Elizabeth and Richard, and the cast was in a mood of celebration when they went to Anthony's Pier 4 for Bufman's postperformance party. But the review by Kevin Kelly in the morning's Boston *Globe* sent Elizabeth into tears. "Clumping Through" was the headline. For Kelly, "Elizabeth Taylor was perfectly terrible—a caricature of a Coward heroine, inside a caricature of an actress, inside a caricature of Taylor." Richard came off only slightly better.

Faced with what to do, Elizabeth could hardly replace herself, so the director was replaced instead. Unaffected by reviews, the house sold out at steep prices for the seventeen days of the Boston run. The audience was not interested in how inelegantly spoken Coward's witty lines were, nor even that the stars were well beyond the age range for the roles, but in viewing life-size a reprise of the relationship that had so intrigued them through the years. In New York, at forty-five dollars per ticket, the houses were always full.

The claws were sharp in New York, too, although the reviews were slightly better written. John Simon could not resist being beastly. Of Taylor he said, "Her entire film career is clearly attributable to her former face, her former directors, and the cutting room." An overstatement, if there ever was one. And about Richard, "Though his voice is still that superbly muted funeral trumpet of a majestically dying swan, the rest of him seems pickled in a laboratory jar." Bravely, though, the pair carried on for seventy thousand a week.

BURTON

John Gielgud called it a fiasco. But audiences hugely enjoyed what had become less a play than a display of two spectacular personalities. Nonetheless, at curtain time, instead of ovations, there was a mass rush for the exits. Many in the audience called it an excruciating exhibition.

During one of the frequent cancellations due to a variety of Elizabeth Taylor complaints, Richard and Sally flew off quietly to Las Vegas, where they put up in the Frontier Hotel's thousand-dollar-a-day honeymoon suite, and on Sunday, July 3, 1983, were married. He declared it was his first marriage in which he remained entirely sober.

On their return to New York, Elizabeth threw them a little party in her dressing room and declared she was thrilled for them. She was supposed to be engaged at the time to Victor Luna, one in a series of consorts who surfaced from time to time.

The tour of *Private Lives* sputtered to an end in Los Angeles in October 1983, after too many cancellations of performances by Elizabeth, who was putting on weight again, and (by her own admission later) was hooked on such drugs as Percodan, and, between alcohol and various medications, was virtually in a stupor when she landed in a hospital for what was labeled a bowel obstruction. Richard was relieved about the show's closing, Sally told her friends, and had said he wouldn't make the mistake of working with Elizabeth again. They stayed on in Los Angeles for a time, putting up in Elizabeth's Bel Air mansion.

Scripts and proposals were still coming in to Richard, but he announced himself as semiretired and would not read them. He went with Sally to their new home in Haiti for the Christmas holidays, and then back to the villa in Céligny. There, several family members from Wales were invited for long visits. His sister Hilda, with him for two weeks during the Easter holidays, was encouraged by how well he looked. She was thrilled to be having lunch with Sophia Loren, to pay a visit with him to Roger Moore. "We had a fantastic time," she said.

In May he abruptly ended his semiretirement when an offer came to play the role of O'Brien in a British film version of George Orwell's *1984*. The film was already in production with John Hurt in the lead role of Winston, a rebel against the system who is physically and psychologically tortured by O'Brien. Paul Scofield had originally been cast as O'Brien, but had bowed out. Richard was taken with the script prepared by the young director, Michael Radford, and even more so by the chance to work with John Hurt, whom he admired.

His three weeks of location work took him to an abandoned RAF station in Wiltshire, although he and Sally were quartered in a pleasant country-house hotel. "It was a turning point in his life," John Hurt recalled. "He loved the script, Radford's approach, and the work. If he had a problem, it was with his memory. He found it difficult to keep the lines in his head, and would need several takes to get it right."

"He wasn't ill," Radford said, "but he was very frail. He didn't touch a drop and he went to bed early. He thought we were ridiculously young, and he liked the idea that somehow he was involved with the new wave of British filmmaking." Radford too noticed that "he seemed to have come to some sort of renewal of himself. He had a kind of elder-statesman air about him."

His daughter Kate, now active in her own career, was cast as the daughter of a rich senator in a multi-part television drama, *Ellis Island*, to be filmed mainly in London. The role of the senator was relatively modest, but the producer saw an opportunity to snag Richard for it. Kate, worried he would think she was trading on their relationship, called him to warn him an offer was coming. Nevertheless, he accepted it and two weeks after finishing his role in *1984*, he was performing on a soundstage with his daughter.

This was in July. He was rarely seen on the set without a Tab in one hand and a cigarette in the other. When not before the camera, he sat in a trailer and told some of his favorite stories. Kate had lunch with him in the trailer several times and he would say, "Have I told you this before, Kate?" Most of the time he had. Now twenty-six, Kate grew fond of Sally, her third stepmother. But everyone liked Sally, if only because Richard was so obviously happy with her. Yet Kate did not see as much of her father as she might have liked during the three weeks they acted together. She was trying to carve her own career rather than one based on being the daughter of Richard Burton. Even so, both were nervous during their first scene together.

"I came on like Sarah Bernhardt," she said.

Richard whispered to her, "Bring it down, Kate."

Seldom did he give her any advice, but during the time they worked together Kate had the feeling "that he was guiding me ever so gently."

During one difficult scene which Kate had to carry on her own, Richard watched from behind the camera. Dennis Browne, a network employee, was standing next to him. Richard turned to him at the finish of the scene and said, "I may be just a father, but don't you think she's awfully good?"

"He just lighted up with pride," Browne said.

Richard was still thinking of returning to the London stage, and he and Kate spoke of sometime being in a play together. Meanwhile he joked about having to play a smaller role than his daughter in *Ellis Island*. (His pay was considerably larger.) Kate continued on in it after Richard finished. He had accepted another film role, a sequel to *The Wild Geese*, after he passed the required physical examination.

Before leaving London, Richard had lunch with Alan Jay Lerner, who noticed that Richard had begun to stammer and stutter. "The best time I've every had was in *Camelot*," Richard told Lerner. "I really loved doing it with you."

Lerner thought they ought to get together on another show, and Richard agreed, "Yes, yes, I would love to do one."

Lerner, now residing in London, was on another of his marriages, this time to a lovely singer-actress. "We could do an album," he said, "you and my wife." The idea was to do some songs from *Camelot*, and selections from other Lerner shows. Richard, still denying that he had much of a singing voice, nevertheless was willing. Lerner promised to visit him in Céligny to discuss the idea further.

When John Hurt finished his work in *1984*, he went to Switzerland for location work on another film. While in Geneva, he drove out to Céligny the evening of August 3 to have dinner with Richard and Sally. Although he had worked with Richard for three weeks in an intense one-to-one acting relationship, it was only that evening that he felt he was getting closer to knowing and understanding him.

"He was more complicated than most people realized," Hurt said. "I have never met a more charismatic man, but he didn't know he had it, or where he got it. He was very perceptive, and at the same

BURTON

time shy about his perceptions, not liking to share them, on the grounds that they might not be understood."

During dinner the conversation turned to money, among other subjects. Richard mentioned that he had made thirty-six million dollars in films in straight fees. He and Sally and members of his family were adequately provided for, but where had it all gone? He seemed undisturbed about it. The next morning Hurt sat on the terrace with Richard. He had stayed overnight in the guest cottage because the roads were jammed from the Fête de Genève, which was in progress.

"Talking about money," Richard said, "you'd think someone could be half a billionaire with thirty-six million as starting capital, wouldn't you?"

"Wisely invested, I guess you'd be able to live on it," Hurt said.

There was a long pause. "I waited," Hurt said, "to see what the pause meant."

Richard finally said, "When you make that kind of money, better to be a buffoon and give it away than join another league."

"I think I know what he meant," Hurt said, recalling the Saturday morning conversation. "He was saying, 'Sure I could have become one of those supermillionaires. But I would have moved in a completely different circle—and it's not a circle an artist can comfortably move in.' The people were of a different ilk. At the same time, he inevitably led two different lives. He enjoyed immensely that he was capable of being in that kind of position, but he was reluctant to really involve himself with it.

"We sat talking for about three hours. He was in a reflective, almost philosophical mood. I realized that without the alcohol that brought out his flamboyance, he was sensitive and introverted. Now and then I sensed a touch of world-weariness, even of boredom, and yet of acceptance of what he had done and who others were."

Later, as Hurt was about to leave for Geneva, Richard leaned toward him and lowered his voice to say something that he did not want Sally, who was inside the house, to hear.

"*She* still fascinates, you know," he said.

"It became clear to me," Hurt said afterward, "that the love was a compulsion between them and was never gone."

He said good-bye, and Richard waved him off and went inside the house to pick up a book. He was reading William Blake.

the following morning he complained to Sally that he had an excruciating pain in his head. A doctor was called, then an ambulance. Rain was falling and thunder crashed as the ambulance sped to a nearby hospital. Richard was in a coma by then. He had suffered a massive cerebral hemorrhage. The case was hopeless. Transferred almost at once to the main cantonal hospital in Geneva, he died with Sally at his side.

23

Richard Burton's sudden death on August 5, 1984, was announced on front pages of newspapers throughout the Western world, and one problem that rose immediately for the closest members of his family was what to do about Elizabeth Taylor. Graham Jenkins took it upon himself to handle the matter. "I told her," he was quoted as saying, "that it was not right for her to come, there was too much fuss. It was inappropriate, pure and simple."

The ban extended to the service in Pontrhydyfen, too, but not to the memorial service in London at St. Martin's-in-the-Fields. By that time, Richard's death was becoming something of a public scandal. London's *Daily Express* claimed that Sally and Elizabeth had quarreled over the latter's attendance at the London service, and there were rumors that Susan Hunt was not wanted either.

Sally was quoted as saying, "There is one person who has tried to make capital out of every step this week. I finally told her to go away, to get lost." There were only guesses as to whom she might be referring. But by the day of the service, all was apparently forgiven. Susan slipped in unexpectedly, and Sally, as though determined to put to rest the rumors, invited both Elizabeth and Susan to lunch.

Sybil, however, was not present, and maintained her habitual silence. She was living quietly and happily with Jordan Christopher in California.

There was another fuss over the place of Richard's burial. His brothers and sisters wanted him reburied in Wales, saying he had always intended to be buried there and that he had even purchased his plot. Elizabeth had chosen one next to his. Was the Céligny burial chosen because Sally did not want Richard to rest in eternity beside Elizabeth? The real reason was more mundane. Richard was canny enough about money and inheritance taxes of the British variety to know that Britain's Inland Revenue Service would be greatly interested in his estate. With a status of Swiss "resident" he was not sufficiently protected; thus several years before, he had changed his status to "domiciled" in Switzerland. For tax purposes, assessment in the United Kingdom is based on where someone ultimately sees himself retired and being buried. When he domiciled himself in Switzerland, Richard at the same time bought his graveyard plot.

It took some time before an estimate of his wealth at the time of his death was made—in the area of five million pounds, or six million dollars. Sally Hay was said to have inherited the bulk of the estate. He had not been quite as improvident as he liked to intimate.

It was not long before London's Fleet Street, as Emlyn Williams prophesied at Richard's memorial, was "swarming with meticulously detailed judgments." Much of the judgment had to do with what was regarded as Richard's wasteful use of his talents. David Lewin flatly claimed that he had "sold out," that Elizabeth Taylor was in a sense the devil's handmaiden, and that Richard had not been able to resist the lure of the flesh and money pots. In Hollywood, the critic Arthur Knight took a similar tack. The press, for which Richard had provided so much titillating copy through the years, turned moral, even sanctimonious, as though hundreds of millions of people had been waiting impatiently to line up for tickets to see Richard in *Macbeth* and *King Lear*.

There were those angered by the attacks *in absentia*, John Hurt among them. "We must allow actors to be the people they are," he said. "And how many can you think of who are both great stage stars and great film stars? I mean those who can attract audiences to the box office of both? Richard was compared, to his detriment, to

BURTON

Laurence Olivier. But Larry was not a film star in the sense that Richard was."

Mike Nichols had another feeling about him. "This man who had so much," he wondered, "why did he need so much to be reassured? I think Richard was in love with ruin. His friend and hero, Dylan Thomas, was in love with ruin. And nothing is more romantic than waste. It had a great hold on him, I think, all the time he was not playing the great stage roles, as he knew he should have, and instead did the movies for money, becoming the biggest star in the world (through Elizabeth, really) and knowing it was a blind alley. He knew it—that stardom and money were blind alleys. But he was enthralled by the idea of large, romantic self-destruction."

Or was that aspect of his personality one of the real-life performances he gave, in which he played Richard Burton as it suited him at the time?

"My own feeling," Alan Jay Lerner said, "was that everything Richard did was a kind of drug, an escape from something, but I never knew from what. Liquor helped him escape, the audience helped him escape, the acting was an escape—but from what? Was there inside him some mandate, or goal, that he knew he could never attain? I know he had a devil of a time sleeping. Maybe the whole problem of Richard was some kind of chemical imbalance. It may not have been psychological at all. I was told something strange about the operation he had on his neck and back, that blood and alcohol had crystallized in his spinal column and were what was causing the pain. I knew how much he drank, but yet I never thought of him as a straight-out alcoholic."

A surgeon who specialized in back operations was queried about the spinal condition and said he had never heard of such a medical aberration. But Colin Campbell, a counselor and researcher on alcoholism, said that neck and spine problems were not uncommon among alcoholics.

For Campbell, Richard Burton represented a virtual model of an alcoholic's life pattern, even though spread out on a huge canvas. "We can literally chart the various steps," he said. "What we call the hereditary component was there, and the environmental factor. Drinking stands for maleness and masculinity. The more you can drink, and the better you appear to hold it, the more respect and approval you gain from your peers. The steps include an increase in tolerance of alcohol, then preoccupation with drinking, alibis, extravagance, aggression, the morning drinks, geographic escape, isolation, the first hospitalization, lapses in judgment, and so on. From the indications, I'd say that Burton was an alcoholic, unacknowledged, unadmitted, from his early twenties, and that by the time of his breakdown in the mid-seventies, he had reached an advanced stage of the disease. To me it would be unfair to view him in any other way than as a superior man with a severe handicap."

This view does at least help clarify the "problem" and the mystery of Richard Burton. He was introduced to drinking by his father at the age of twelve or so, and it became a means of buoying and sustaining his confidence, while physically and psychologically undermining him. If Elizabeth Taylor attracted and bemused him, she, a drinker herself, could understand his need, and share it with him. For a long time they had it cozy, the two of them, but inevitably the disease took its course, and each was too proud, then, to undertake the cure. With the glory, for Richard, was the accompanying shadow, the "boxer" he fought most of his life. He put up a brave front; he fought his battle with spirit, generosity, and humor; and he entertained his time and did much good work.

For his detractors, toward the end of his days, Richard left a message. Echoing Edith Piaf, he said, "I regret nothing."

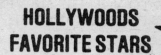

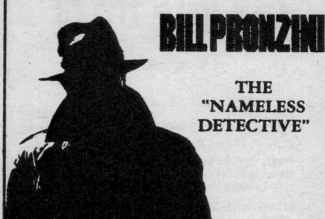

HERE IS YOUR CHANCE TO
ORDER SOME OF OUR BEST

HISTORICAL ROMANCES

BY SOME OF YOUR FAVORITE AUTHORS

____ **DARK WINDS** — Virginia Coffman
Their fiery passion unleashed a tempest of . . . DARK
WINDS   7701-0405-3/$3.95

____ **KISS OF GOLD** — Samantha Harte
First he taught her to live . . . then he taught her to love.
7701-0529-7/$3.50

____ **MISTRESS OF MOON HILL** — Jill Downie
From the ashes of her heart, he kindled a new flame.
7701-0424-X/$3.95

____ **SWEET WHISPERS** — Samantha Harte
She struggled with her dark past in the hope of a new love.
7701-0496-7/$3.50

____ **THE WIND & THE SEA** — Marsha Canham
Passion and intrigue on the high seas. 7701-0415-0/$3.95

Prices subject to change without notice

BOOKS BY MAIL

320 Steelcase Rd. E.
Markham, Ont., L3R 2M1

In the U.S. -
210 5th Ave., 7th Floor
New York, N.Y. 10010

Please send me the books I have checked above. I am enclos-
ing a total of $_____ (Please add 1.00 for one book and
50 cents for each additional book.) My cheque or money order
is enclosed. (No cash or C.O.D.'s please.)

Name _____

Address _____ Apt. _____

City _____

Prov./State _____ P.C./Zip _____

(HIS/ROM)

JOHN BALL
AUTHOR OF **IN THE HEAT OF THE NIGHT** INTRODUCING, **POLICE CHIEF JACK TALLON** IN THESE EXCITING, FAST-PACED MYSTERIES.

FREE!!
BOOKS BY MAIL
CATALOGUE

BOOKS BY MAIL will share with you our current bestselling books as well as hard to find specialty titles in areas that will match your interests. You will be updated on what's new in books at no cost to you. Just fill in the coupon below and discover the convenience of having books delivered to your home.

PLEASE ADD $1.00 TO COVER THE COST OF POSTAGE & HANDLING.